O. CROMWELLS HEAD TAVERN

kept by JOSHUA BRACKETT School Street BOSTON.

	£	s	d
Board		17	–
Lodging	.	2	6
Eating			
Wine			
Punch			
Porter			
Liquor	.	2	3
Horse-keeping 5 nights	.	12	6
Oats 6 pottle	.	3	

Cpt Howard – £1.17.3

Receiv'd pay J Brackett

TAVERNS OF THE AMERICAN REVOLUTION

TAVERNS OF THE AMERICAN REVOLUTION

ADRIAN COVERT

INSIGHT EDITIONS
San Rafael, California

THE
76
HOUSE

CONTENTS

FEATURED TAVERNS

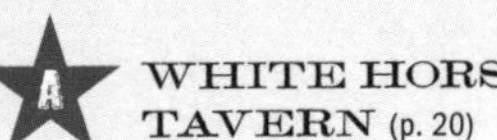

WHITE HORSE TAVERN (p. 20)

25 MARLBOROUGH STREET
NEWPORT, RHODE ISLAND

Est. 1673

Today operates as restaurant and taproom

LONGFELLOW'S WAYSIDE INN (p. 38)

72 WAYSIDE INN ROAD
SUDBURY, MASSACHUSETTS

Est. 1716 as Howe's Tavern

"If not in haste, do stop and taste."
—William Molineaux Jr., 1774

Today operates as a restaurant, taproom, gristmill, and inn

KING GEORGE II INN (p. 46)

102 RADCLIFFE STREET
BRISTOL, PENNSYLVANIA

Est. 1681 as Ferry House

Frequented by George and Martha Washington, John and Abigail Adams

Today operates as restaurant, bar, and inn offering medium- and long-term rentals

RALEIGH TAVERN (p. 58)

413 EAST DUKE OF GLOUCESTER STREET
WILLIAMSBURG, VIRGINIA

Est. 1717, rebuilt 1932

"Jollity, the offspring of wisdom and good living."
—Painted above the mantel
in the Raleigh's Apollo Room

Frequented by George Washington, Thomas Jefferson, Patrick Henry

Today operates as a bakery and museum

CITY TAVERN (p. 66)

188 SOUTH SECOND STREET
PHILADELPHIA, PENNSYLVANIA

Est. 1773, rebuilt 1976

"The most genteel tavern in America."
—John Adams, Diary, August 29, 1774

Today operates as a taproom and restaurant

WARREN TAVERN (p. 72)

2 PLEASANT STREET
CHARLESTOWN, MASSACHUSETTS

Est. 1780

Frequented by George Washington and Paul Revere

Today operates as a restaurant and bar

GRISWOLD INN (p. 76)

36 MAIN STREET
ESSEX, CONNECTICUT

Est. 1776

"My dear son Jared, take this my gun"
—John Francis Putnam, July 7, 1776

Today operates as inn, restaurant, bar, and wine bar

GREEN DRAGON (p. 78)

BAR OF SAME NAME OPERATES AT 11 MARSHALL STREET
BOSTON, MASSACHUSETTS

Est. 1701, destroyed 1828

"Headquarters of the Revolution"

COLONIAL INN (p. 81)

48 MONUMENT STREET
CONCORD, MASSACHUSETTS

Built 1716, est. 1889

Today operates as an inn, restaurant, and taproom

FRAUNCES TAVERN (p. 92)

54 PEARL STREET
NEW YORK, NEW YORK

Est. 1762 as the Queen's Head Tavern

Frequented by George Washington and John Adams

Today operates as a bar, restaurant, and museum

OLD '76 HOUSE (p. 96)

110 MAIN STREET
TAPPAN, NEW YORK

Est. 1755 as the Casparus Mabie House

Frequented by George Washington, Alexander Hamilton, marquis de Lafayette, British Major John André

Today operates as a bar and restaurant

BUCKMAN TAVERN (p. 107)

1 BEDFORD STREET
LEXINGTON, MASSACHUSETTS

Est. 1713 as Muzzy Tavern

Today operates as a museum

HARTWELL TAVERN (p. 108)

VIRGINIA ROAD
LINCOLN, MASSACHUSETTS

Est. 1756

Minute Man National Park

WRIGHT TAVERN (p. 111)

2 LEXINGTON ROAD
CONCORD, MASSACHUSETTS

Est. 1747

Today operates as church offices and an architectural office

MUNROE TAVERN (p. 114)

1332 MASSACHUSETTS AVENUE
LEXINGTON, MASSACHUSETTS

Est. 1735

Today operates as a museum

MILL STREET HOTEL & TAVERN (p. 116)

67 MILL STREET
MOUNT HOLLY, NEW JERSEY

Est. 1723 as the Three Tun Tavern

GENERAL WARREN INNE (p. 122)

9 OLD LANCASTER ROAD
MALVERN, PENNSYLVANIA

Est. 1745 as the Admiral Vernon Inne

Today operates as a restaurant, bar, and inn

PUBLICK HOUSE HISTORIC INN (p. 146)

277 MAIN STREET
STURBRIDGE, MASSACHUSETTS

Est. 1771 as Crafts Tavern

Today operates as an inn, restaurant, taproom, bar, and bakery

GADSBY'S TAVERN (p. 156)

138 NORTH ROYAL STREET
ALEXANDRIA, VIRGINIA

Est. 1785

Today operates as a restaurant, taproom, and museum

CAPTAIN DANIEL PACKER INNE (p. 166)

32 WATER STREET
MYSTIC, CONNECTICUT

Est. 1756

Today operates as a restaurant and bar

YE OLDE TAVERN (p. 167)

7 EAST MAIN STREET
WEST BROOKFIELD, MASSACHUSETTS

Est. 1760 as Hitchcock Tavern

Frequented by George Washington, John Adams, marquis de Lafayette

Today operates as a restaurant, bar, and inn

LAKE ONTARIO
Great Western Rail Road to Montreal
NEW YORK
VERMONT
NEW HAMPSHIRE
MAINE
MASSACHUSETTS
CONNECTICUT
RHODE ISLAND
PENNSYLVANIA
NEW JERSEY
MARYLAND
DELAWARE
VIRGINIA
NORTH CAROLINA
ATLANTIC OCEAN
Lewiston
Lockport
Buffalo
Dunkirk
Erie
Ithica
Albany
Troy
Saratoga
Ogdensburg
Portland
Blusburgh
Williamsport
Honesdale
Carbondale
Wilkesbarre
Whitehaven
Pottsville
Sunbury
Harrisburg
Hollidaysburg
Pittsburg
Lancaster
Philadelphia
Camden
Woodbury
New Castle
Paterson
Morris T.
Somerville
Brooklyn
Amboy
Bridgeport
New Haven
New London
Cumberland
Winchester
Potomac R.
Fredericksburg
Orange
Richmond
James R.
Petersburg
Norfolk
Portsmouth
Roanoke R.
Gaston
Weldon
Raleigh
Goldsboro
Fayetteville
Wilmington
Cheraw
Manchester
Delaware R.
Hudson R.
Connecticut R.

PREFACE

WHILE WRITING his short biography of Thomas Jefferson, the late Christopher Hitchens noticed a recurring theme in Jefferson's early career. The life of this consummate Virginian centered around his colony's most prominent institutions: the College of William & Mary, the House of Burgesses, and Williamsburg's Raleigh Tavern. While the prominence of both the college and the House of Burgesses was neatly confined to Jefferson's period of schooling and his term in the legislature, respectively, Hitchens found himself repeatedly revisiting the Raleigh Tavern to explain events leading to the development of both Jefferson the man and the idea of the United States of America. The Raleigh was the scene of Jefferson's first romantic rejection and the place where he and his colleagues drafted numerous resolutions that would ultimately lead to the Continental Congress and the Declaration of Independence. Taken by the tavern's prominence in Jefferson's story, Hitchens momentarily broke narrative to suggest that "a monograph should be written on the role of the tavern in the American Revolution."

I first read these words while tucked into one of the many dark nooks of San Francisco's Little Shamrock Irish Pub, established 1893. The Shamrock is located in the Sunset District, and is therefore eternally swallowed by a cold and bracing fog, making the bar's low wooden beams, brass taps, dart room, and board games the stuff of maximum comfort. Even before I decided to write this book, regular nights at the Shamrock had inspired me to spend more time enjoying the city's other early survivors, such as Vesuvio, Elixir, and The

Saloon—the last of Gold Rush vintage. But San Francisco has burned to the ground several times since its European settlement, and the oldest bars in the West are found nearer the Overland Trail. Nevada's oldest bar, the Genoa Bar & Saloon, established in 1853, is located at the eastern foot of the mighty Sierra Nevada Mountains, while California's oldest, the Iron Door Saloon, is just west of Yosemite, where the mountains begin their long slouch into the Central Valley and Pacific Ocean beyond.

Let there be no doubt: shooting whiskey where Mark Twain or Sam Brannan once stood is a badass experience, and one I plan on repeating throughout my life. But to take a pint from where George Washington hung traitors? Or where the redcoats tortured American patriots? Or where the first shot of the American Revolution was fired? Or where the Boston Tea Party was planned? Or where the first cocktail was mixed, Paine's *Common Sense* was read, and men were tarred and feathered? To drink at a surviving tavern of the American Revolution is to interact with history on an entirely different level. What better excuse for a road trip down the East Coast than in the pursuit of rum, beer, and history at America's oldest bars?

First and foremost, with this book I aspired to create a navigable catalogue of surviving Revolutionary taverns from which history nerds like me could plan their own tavern road trips. I chose the twenty-one taverns highlighted throughout this book primarily for their compelling stories, but also for my ability to stitch together visits to each within a two-week drive. For readers with more time and flexibility, I created what I believe is the most complete list of all surviving taverns from the Revolutionary era. No such index appears to have existed before, and the closest I found was a list of over a thousand old taverns and inns at the end of Elise Lathrop's *Early American Inns and Taverns*, first published in 1926. As invaluable as it was, Lathrop's list didn't indicate which taverns dated to the eighteenth century, or whether they still existed at the time she published her book, let alone today. As a result, I spent many hours digitizing and building off of the Lathrop list and researching approximate construction dates and clues to whether taverns still survived, and in what form. I sought to satisfy three major constraints for the taverns featured in this book:

PAGE 1 *Receipt from O. Cromwell's Head Tavern from 1768 noting purchase of liquor (likely rum) and five nights of bedding and oats for a horse.*

PAGE 2 *Drinking was among the most popular of colonial American pastimes. This oil on wood painting from around 1760, titled "Moses Marcy in a Landscape," shows Marcy enjoying his leisure time, wine glass in hand and with a full delft punch bowl on the table in front of him.*

PAGE 3 *Engraving of the Old Tun Tavern.*

PAGE 4 *Interior detail of the Old '76 House in Tappan, New York, est. c. 1755.*

PREVIOUS PAGES *"Declaration of Independence," by John Trumbull.*

FOLLOWING PAGES *Taproom at Longfellow's Wayside Inn.*

RIGHT *Interior detail of the Griswold Inn in Essex, Connecticut, est. 1776.*

the tavern had to be located in one of the original thirteen colonies, it had to have been built prior to 1800, and it had to have been used as a tavern at that time. The result, I hope, is the most complete list of surviving taverns of the American Revolution yet compiled and includes 171 surviving taverns: seventy-two restaurants or bars, forty-nine museums, thirty-six inns, twelve community buildings, and a smattering of offices and cafés. An additional 140 taverns, not listed in the index, live on as private residences.

I apologize at the outset for any surviving Revolutionary taverns whose stories I've inevitably missed or whose existence I've overlooked. Based on the Lathrop list alone, a reasonable estimate is that between one thousand and two thousand taverns existed in the colonies by 1776. Because they were often the only public building in town, it's easy to imagine thousands of locally relevant events occurring in taverns across the early United States, far outside my capacity to catalogue in this modest book. Compounding the challenge is that many taverns have undergone multiple name changes and renovations over the years, and current owners may be unaware of or unconcerned about their building's history. Several taverns I happened on by luck or word of mouth don't even have websites. To develop a manageable narrative, I tried to focus on the major military and political events occurring at taverns that still exist.

One item you'll notice I largely neglected was food. This was largely due to the fact that most surviving taverns serve similar

LONGFELLOW'S
Wayside
Inn
FOOD, DRINK
LODGING
MAN, WOMAN
and BEAST

fare—pot pies, soups, roast turkeys, beef Wellingtons, crab cakes: it's remarkably predictable, and almost always good. There's little in the way of culinary innovation, and honestly, that's exactly how it should be. Their drinks are slightly more varied. Some taverns, the White Horse (Rhode Island) and the Griswold (Connecticut), for example, have their own house beer, and most, like Longfellow's Wayside Inn, have a signature cocktail. I have included several drink recipes in the sidebars throughout the book. Another item I purposefully left out were ghost stories, which are more common than claims of "Washington slept here."

When I set out on this project, I conceived of the American Revolution as having lasted between the passage of the 1765 Stamp Act and the 1783 Treaty of Paris. This conception was destroyed almost immediately, when it became clear to me just how unsettled the political situation in the United States was following the war. History lacked examples of durable republican governments, and republican confederations of sovereign states were almost entirely unheard of. The young nation was beset by multiple armed rebellions, and ingratiating sycophants encouraged the leading military man, George Washington, to assume the role of monarch. Even after Washington declined a third term as president, the nation still had to familiarize itself with party politics. The 1800 defeat of John Adams at the hands of Thomas Jefferson marked the first peaceful transfer of power between American political factions and is sometimes referred to as the Revolution of 1800. With independence secured, rebellion squashed, and political tradition entrenched, this seemed the more appropriate close to the Revolution.

The best part of the surviving taverns of the American Revolution is that for them history hasn't stopped. These aren't museums, these are 250-year-old conversations about politics, culture, food, and life. Adams, Franklin, Jefferson, and Washington came and went, and here you are, standing in the same place, drinking (a much safer version of) the same drink. I am privileged to have visited the few I did and to have met the owners, staff, and customers who keep the conversation alive.

TIME LINE

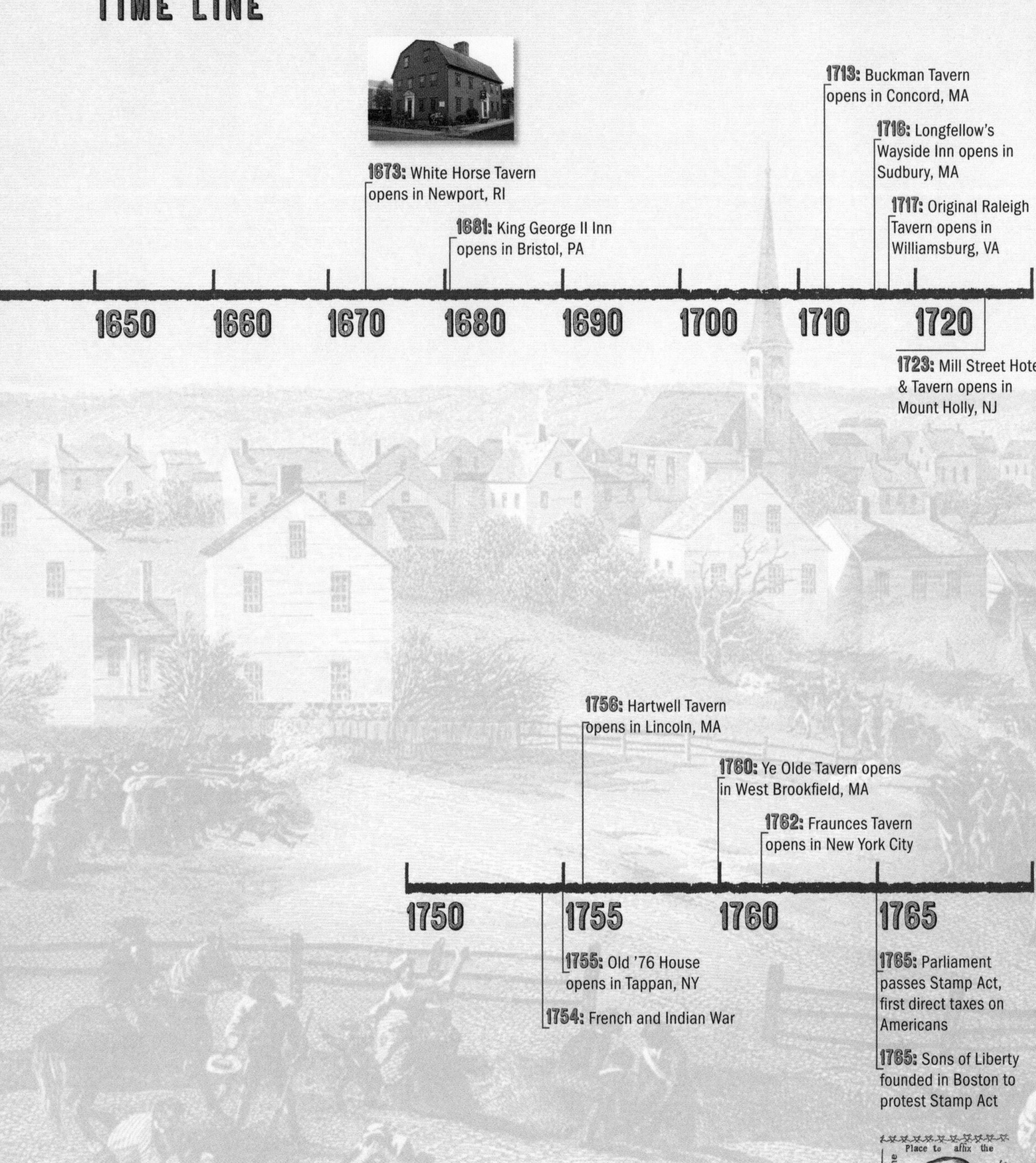

1673: White Horse Tavern opens in Newport, RI
1681: King George II Inn opens in Bristol, PA
1713: Buckman Tavern opens in Concord, MA
1716: Longfellow's Wayside Inn opens in Sudbury, MA
1717: Original Raleigh Tavern opens in Williamsburg, VA
1650
1660
1670
1680
1690
1700
1710
1720
1723: Mill Street Hotel & Tavern opens in Mount Holly, NJ
1756: Hartwell Tavern opens in Lincoln, MA
1760: Ye Olde Tavern opens in West Brookfield, MA
1762: Fraunces Tavern opens in New York City
1750
1755
1760
1765
1755: Old '76 House opens in Tappan, NY
1754: French and Indian War
1765: Parliament passes Stamp Act, first direct taxes on Americans
1765: Sons of Liberty founded in Boston to protest Stamp Act
Hereabours will be the Place to affix the STAMP

1735: Munroe Tavern opens in Lexington, MA

1745: General Warren Inne opens in Malvern, PA

1747: Wright Tavern opens in Concord, MA

1801: March 4, Thomas Jefferson sworn in as president; inaugural party held at Gadsby's Tavern

1730 1740 1750 1800 1810

Events between 1750 and 1810 appear on the red timeline below

1774: September 5, First Continental Congress

1775: April 19, Battles of Lexington and Concord

1775: November 10, U.S. Marine Corps created at Tun Tavern, Philadelphia

1776: July 4, Declaration of Independence

1776: Griswold Inn opens in Essex, CT

1785: Gadsby's Tavern opens in Alexandria, VA

1786: August, Shays' Rebellion

1787: Constitutional Convention

1770 1775 1780 1785 1790 1795 1800

1794: Whiskey Rebellion

1773: December 16, Boston Tea Party launched from Green Dragon Tavern

1773: December, City Tavern opens in Philadelphia, PA

1789: April 30, George Washington inaugurated as first president of the United States.

1783: December 4, George Washington bids farewell to his officers at Fraunces Tavern

1771: Publick House Inn opens in Sturbridge, MA

1781: October 19, Lord Cornwallis surrenders to Washington

1780: Warren Tavern opens in Charlestown, MA

1770: March 5, Boston Massacre

1780: September, British Major John André captured and executed as spy behind Old '76 House

1768: Four thousand British troops arrive in Boston to enforce tax collection

ABOVE *"Sea Captains Carousing in Surinam," by John Greenwood, c. 1752, depicts a tavern scene with notable Rhode Islanders Nicholas Cooke, Esek Hopkins, Stephen Hopkins, and Joseph Wanton (all at the table) drunk and being thoroughly doused with punch and vomit.*

CHAPTER 1

NURSERIES OF IDLENESS AND DEBAUCHERY

The tavern will compare favorably with the church. The church is the place where prayers and sermons are delivered, but the tavern is where they are to take effect, and if the former are good, the latter cannot be bad.

—HENRY DAVID THOREAU

On Thursday, May 29, 1760, John Adams put quill to paper and furnished his diary with the now-oft-quoted line that taverns had become "the Nurseries of our Legislators." At first blush, the sentiment appears surprisingly endearing for a man as famously irritable as Adams. We are fortunate that the Massachusetts Historical Society has provided the context, which must be quoted at some length for full impact. Referring to taverns as "Licensed Houses," Adams asserts:

> Few things I believe have deviated so far from the first Design of their Institution, are so fruitful of destructive Evils or so needful of a speedy Regulation, as Licensed Houses. The Accomodation of Strangers, and perhaps of Town Inhabitants on public occasions, are the only warrantable Intentions of a Tavern and the supply of the Neighbourhood with necessary Liquors, in small Quantities and at the cheapest Rates, are the only excusable Designs of a Retailer; and that these Purposes may be effected, it is necessary, that both should be selected from the most virtuous, and wealthy People who will accept the Trust, and so few of each should be erected, that the Profits may enable them to make the best Provision, at a moderate Price. But at the present Day, such Houses are become the eternal Haunt, of loose disorderly People of the same Town, which renders them offensive and unfit for the Entertainment of a Traveller of the least delicacy; and, it seems that Poverty, and distressed Circumstances are become the strongest Argument, to procure an Approbation . . . and for [these] assigned Reasons, such Multitudes have been lately licensed, that none can afford to make Provision, for any but the trifling, nasty vicious Crew, that most frequent them.

"Taverns will make many who may be induced by Phlip and Rum to Vote for any Man whatever . . ."
—John Adams

In other words, booze and hostels make for trouble, and the whole business should be restricted to gentlemen who can afford to properly operate taverns at a near loss rather than an enterprise for the "poor and distressed" whose mismanaged taverns promoted drunkenness. Adams's reasoning went beyond mere practicality and included moral, political, and classist dimensions:

> Young People are tempted to waste their Time and Money, and to acquire habits of Intemperance and Idleness that . . . reduce many of them to Beggary, and Vice, and lead some of them at last to Prisons and the Gallows. *But the worst Effect of all, and which ought to make every Man who has the least sense of his Priviledges tremble, these Houses are become in many Places the Nurseries of our Legislators;* An Artful Man, who has neither sense nor sentiment may by gaining a little sway among the Rabble of a Town, multiply Taverns and Dram Shops and thereby secure the Votes of Taverner and Retailer and of all, who will be induced and the Multiplication of Taverns will make many who may be induced by Phlip [flip, a mixed drink popular at the time, see page 91] and Rum to Vote for any Man whatever and for These I dare not presume to point out any Method, to suppress or Restrain these increasing Evils [italics added].[1]

Portrait of John Adams, engraved by James Smither, c. 1790.

It's a near-perfect summary of all that has since come to define John Adams: suspicious of democracy, terrified of the mob, and contemptuous of idleness and exploitation (Adams was a lifelong opponent of slavery).

But Adams's fear of social disorder wasn't just paranoia. "By the year 1760," writes American historian Howard Zinn, "there had been eighteen uprisings aimed at overthrowing colonial governments . . . six black rebellions, from South Carolina to New York, and forty riots of various origins."[2] Adams was thus both coolly prescient and significantly mistaken. He correctly understood that taverns and alcohol were destabilizing social forces, and he knew that corruption and greed exacerbated the problem. But while the aggressive and uncouth nature of tavern politics alarmed his patrician sensibilities, Adams didn't yet understand that the raucous energy of America's taverns would soon become the galvanizing force behind the Revolutionary struggle that would define his legacy.

Distrust of the tavern interest wasn't isolated to the cantankerous Adams, but broadly shared among America's other leading men. In 1808, Thomas Jefferson penned a letter to his grandson, then a young man newly arrived in Philadelphia, urging him to, "Look steadily to the pursuits which have carried you to Philadelphia, be very select in the society you attach yourself to, avoid taverns, drinkers, smokers, idlers, & dissipated persons generally; for it is with such that broils & contentions arise; and you will find your path more easy and tranquil."[3] (Jefferson's letter also makes a powerful case for political civility that today's politicians would do well to read.) In his declining years, Jefferson would complain to President James Monroe, "I had had great hopes that while in your present office you would break up the degrading practice of considering the President's house as a general tavern. . . . I learn the contrary with great regret."[4]

"I had had great hopes that while in your present office you would break up the degrading practice of considering the President's house as a general tavern. . . ."

—Thomas Jefferson to President James Monroe

Benjamin Franklin, America's bon vivant, nevertheless found few things more abhorrent than idleness and corruption, both of which found a natural home in taverns. In March 1764, he penned a blistering moral and economic critique of taverns with a bluntness that surpassed even that of Adams:

> It is notorious, the Number of Taverns, Ale-houses and Dram-shops, have encreased beyond all Measure or Necessity. That they are placed so near to each other, that they ruin one another; and Two Thirds of them are not merely useless, but are become a Pest to Society. There are very few of them that are able to provide the necessary Conveniences for entertaining Travellers, or accommodating the People either in Country or City; and this is entirely owing to that weak Policy in a former Assembly of making it the Interest of a Governor to encourage and promote Immorality and Vice among the People. Many Bills have been presented to the late Governors, to lessen the Number, and to regulate those *Nurseries of Idleness and Debauchery*, but without Success. From whence it seems evident, that so long as the Proprietaries are interested in our Ruin, ruined we must be: For no Deputy will dare to regulate this Mischief, because it will lessen the Revenue."[5, 6]

Portrait of Thomas Jefferson, engraved by John Chester Buttre after original by Gilbert Stewart, c. 1858.

White Horse Tavern

EST. 1673 ✻ TODAY OPERATES AS A RESTAURANT AND TAPROOM ✻ NEWPORT, RHODE ISLAND

The White Horse Tavern has the honored distinction of being the oldest tavern in the United States. The building was erected in 1652 as the home of Francis Brinley and was converted to a tavern in 1673 by new owner William Mayes Sr. While many surviving taverns today feature enough expansions and renovations to make you wonder what part of the structure is original, you don't have to ask with the White Horse. The stand-alone barnlike structure looks mostly as it would have since before the birth of George Washington. Throughout its incredible 343-year run (as of 2016), the White Horse is thought to have been out of commission only once, between 1954 and 1957.

In addition to its role as a tavern, the White Horse acted as the de facto Rhode Island capitol building, housing the Connecticut General Assembly, Criminal Court, and City Council. And with access to both a commodious harbor and government officials, Newport became a natural home to American privateers. Whenever Britain went to war with a rival imperial power, say France or the Netherlands, the Crown would hire American captains to attack enemy ships, and to the victors went the spoils. Privateering was so lucrative that some men continued looting ships even after the war was over—in other words, they became pirates. The famous pirate Captain Kidd was known to have anchored in Rhode Island, and the colony was so closely associated with piracy it was sometimes called "Rogue Island." One local pirate was William Mayes Jr., the son of the owner of the White Horse Tavern. Mayes Jr. is believed to have used his local popularity and family connections to evade British capture for years, eventually retiring from the trade to take over the White Horse when his father died in 1702. Mayes sold the White Horse to Walter Nichols in 1730, in whose family it remained throughout the Revolutionary War. Despite Newport's rugged history, its defenses were no match against British General Henry Clinton's 10,000 soldiers and fleet of ships. The Nicholses and other patriot families fled. Newport fell to the British without a fight, and the White Horse became a headquarters for Hessian mercenaries. Following the July 1780 liberation of Newport under French General Comte de Rochambeau, the Nicholses returned to Newport and added the tavern's signature gambrel roof.

ABOVE *The oldest of them all: The White Horse Tavern in Newport, Rhode Island, est. 1673.*

OPPOSITE BOTTOM *Tap for the White Horse Tavern's own Long Trail Limbo IPA .*

It was also after the French liberation that Washington visited Newport from March 6 to 13, 1781. Washington is known to have visited Rochambeau's headquarters at the Vernon House and to have worshipped at Trinity Church, both no more than three blocks from the tavern. Although there is no record of Washington visiting the White Horse, the tavern's standing as the largest meeting space in town makes it at least reasonably plausible that he might have paid a visit or that some of his entourage lodged there.

The White Horse was sold to the Preece family in 1895, who turned it into a boardinghouse. By 1954, it was falling into disrepair. The Preservation Society of Newport County acquired the building and had it restored and reopened as the White Horse Tavern in 1957. Over its 340 years, the White Horse has had only six owners.

Today the White Horse is a destination taproom and restaurant with everything expected in a historic tavern: low ceilings, low lights, its own beer, and a fireplace in every room. But the White Horse doesn't use its history as a crutch to draw tourists. The farm-to-table ethos of chef Richard Silvia delivers locally sourced goods, from duck scotch egg with house-made sriracha to beef Wellington with foie gras.

SOURCES

Joan Axlerod-Contrada, *A Primary Source History of the Colony of Rhode Island* (New York: Rosen Publishing Group, 2006), 26.

French E. Chadwick, "The Visit of General Washington to Newport in 1781," *Bulletin of the Newport Historical Society*, no. 6 (February 1913).

New England Historical Society, "The British Occupation of Newport" (n.d.).

Knowingly or not, Adams and Franklin were somewhat skirting the issue. After all, taverns didn't make men drunk; rum did. By the outbreak of the Revolution, America had developed its own triangular trade: American merchants sent cod to French West Indies sugar barons in exchange for cheap molasses, which was shipped back to New England and distilled into rum, before being sold in domestic taverns or traded abroad for English manufactures or African slaves. In 1770 alone, the colonies imported 4 million gallons of rum and distilled another 5 million gallons from imported molasses. Driven by cheap rum, per capita consumption of distilled spirits in America reached 3.7 gallons by 1776, compared to just 2.3 gallons in 2012.[7, 8] (The 1776 figure would today place America just behind Lithuania as

ABOVE *"A Midnight Modern Conversation," originally engraved by William Hogarth, c. 1732, depicts patrons in an eighteenth-century London drinking club gathering around a huge punch bowl in a state of extreme inebriation.*

the drunkest nation on earth.) Corrupt colonial officials were known to profit from tavern licensing fees, creating perverse incentives that saw the number of taverns explode, and drunkenness along with it. In short, taverns started becoming powerful, motley interests in their own right, an essential cog in the lucrative rum trade that Adams "dare not" confront.

The rising number of taverns also had the effect of exacerbating class distinctions. Beyond licentiousness and debauchery, Adams and Franklin had a practical objection to the spread of taverns: the colonial economy could not possibly produce enough food, drink, and other provisions to keep the explosion of new taverns properly supplied. As a result, only the wealthiest taverns were reliably stocked with

What Makes a Tavern?

SOURCE
Helene Smith, *Tavern Signs of America* (Greensburg, PA: McDonals/Swärd Publishing Company, 1989), 69.

AT THEIR MOST BASIC, American taverns were a combination of two British institutions: the inn (where one slept) and the pub (where one ate, drank, and socialized). Taverns were often a town's only public building and were sometimes used as banks, insurance offices, hardware stores, barbershops, hospitals, schools, garrisons, libraries, dance halls, brothels, playhouses, courts of law, and post offices. Due in part to this wide range of uses, Americans had many names for taverns, including *tippling house, public house, dram house, ale house, ordinary, grog shop, slog shop, pub, inn, wagon stand, exchange*, and *house of ill repute*. Taverns were gradually replaced by restaurants and hotels during the nineteenth century as America became increasingly wealthy, industrial, and urban. Most of America's founding taverns have long since been destroyed, though many still exist as private homes, museums, restaurants, bars, or inns. To see a list of surviving Revolutionary era taverns, see the "Index of Surviving Taverns" on page 174.

OPPOSITE *This engraving by John Keyse Sherwin, c. 1788, titled "Smithfield Sharpers of The Countryman Defrauded" depicts a London tavern scene.*

ABOVE *Engraving by William Ward with after work by George Morland, c. 1788, titled "Sportsman's Hall." While this is a depiction of an eighteenth-century English tavern, the simple furnishing and presence of a female innkeeper mirror décor and staff of many American taverns of the period.*

adequate supplies of food and drink for people and horses as required by law. Thus, taverns began to be characterized as either polished business establishments with elegant decor and genteel clientele or as cramped shanties with fleas and spoiled food. Evidence of colonial frustrations with country taverns still survive, such as this sarcastic account published in a local New York newspaper:

> TRAVELER: *Can you furnish provender for my horse?*
>
> LANDLADY: *No, we have none.*
>
> TRAVELER: *Can you furnish me with supper?*
>
> LANDLADY: *We have no bread, My husband started for the mill this morning and will return to-morrow.*
>
> TRAVELER: *Can you furnish me with a glass of whiskey?*
>
> LANDLADY: *We have none. My husband took his gallon bottle, and will bring some when he returns.*
>
> TRAVELER: *Madam can you tell me what you do keep of the entertainment of travelers?*
>
> LANDLADY: *We keep a tavern sir.*[9]

A traveler going from Bethlehem to Reading, both in Pennsylvania, in 1773 offered this unkind review of a country tavern:

> It was the dirtiest House, without exception in the Province. Every room swarming with Buggs. . . . If I did not pray all Night, I surely watched, as Sleep was entirely banished from my eyes; tho I enclosed myself in a Circle of Candle grease it did not save me from the devourations.[10]

Even the drinking culture began to diverge along economic lines. Whereas country taverns were often limited to beer, cider, and watered-down rum, wealthier city taverns boasted all these plus wine, madeira, and brandy, and their rum was mixed in large bowls with sugar and fruit into strong punch. One particularly mealy drink, an egg-beer-molasses-rum concoction known as flip, appears to have been popular across classes and may have been the forebearer of the modern eggnog cocktail (see sidebar page 91).

Perhaps the most fascinating aspect of colonial America's tavern debate was where the founding fathers placed the blame. On this, Adams wrote with particular force, arguing that the intemperate state of affairs was primarily the fault of mercantile greed and political ambition, not the poor life choices of individuals. In what could easily be read as a dress rehearsal for our own contemporary debates about personal versus collective responsibility regarding sugary foods, obesity, and self-control, Adams expressed both the caution of a politician and the moral clarity of a decent man:

> I should be called talkative indeed if I should attempt to develope the Causes of that strange Multiplication of such [public] Houses, that is lately grown up. But I fear, that some select Men are induced by a foolish Complaisance, and others by Design of Ambition to give their Approbation to too many Persons who are improper, and perhaps to too many that are proper for that Trust. I am afraid that some Justices may be induced by lucrative Motives, by mercantile Principles to augment the Manufactory of the Importation of Rum or Mollosus [molasses], without Attending to the other Consequences, which are plainly pernicious.[11]

The social order that Adams and Franklin feared was coming apart was one largely put in place one hundred years earlier by the

ABOVE *"The Attack Upon Odd Bobbs & Syllabubs: An American Scene During the War,"* c. 1780. *It wasn't uncommon for colonial Americans to drink their rum punch right from the bowl, as depicted in this tavern scene.*

Puritans. Like the founders, Puritans were conflicted about alcohol, cognizant of its potential for abuse though believing it contained powerful medicinal properties. Purtians regulated the sale of alcohol but also the political power of the alcohol interest, including taverns. In 1678, Maryland prohibited tavern keepers from serving on juries or holding elected office.[12] In York County, Maine (then Massachusetts), tavern keepers were allowed to sell liquor only to travelers and ill local residents, and to the former no more than a scant 1 gill (4 ounces) of liquor was allowed.[13] According to a 1692 Massachusetts law, taverns were "not intended for the Entertainment . . . of lewd or Idle people to spend or consume their money or time there."[14] In Pennsylvania, William Penn prohibited profanity, gambling, and toasts, and he instituted a dispiriting 8:00 p.m. last call.[15] This Puritan arc seems to have mostly avoided New York City, then the Dutch colony of New Amsterdam: regulation there focused less on drunkenness and more on outlawing "small foreign [English] measures" to ensure alcoholic beverages were served in properly generous Dutch vessels.[16]

OPPOSITE *Interior detail of the White Horse Tavern taproom.*

While taverns were placed under the heavy and jealous hand of Puritan law, average citizens could face expensive and corporeal punishment for imprudent behavior. In the *Annals of Philadelphia*, John Watson offers this:

> In the year 1705, men were fined 10 shillings for being found tippling in a tavern on [Sunday]. That same year there was made an act against fornication and adultery. For the latter, the parties received twenty-one lashes and hard labour for one year, or pay £50 fine, (the injured party had a right of divorce) and for a second offense seven years imprisonment. For fornication, twenty-one lashes or pay £10 fine each. At that time men were fined 12 pence for smoking in the streets![17]

America's Oldest Taverns

THE VAUNTED TITLE OF "AMERICA'S OLDEST TAVERN" is claimed by many, and judging the candidates isn't as straightforward as it may seem. After how many repairs, renovations, and expansions is a building no longer considered original? Must the business be continuously operating, or can it have served other purposes in the past? What documentation survives? Should we distinguish between taverns that today provide only sleeping accommodations, or must they also serve food and beverages? I interviewed tavern owners and consulted old engravings, town histories, and, where available, tavern licenses. Taking these questions into consideration and allowing for some flexibility in each, these are my best estimates for America's ten oldest operating taverns:

White Horse Tavern, Newport, Rhode Island (est. c. 1673)

King George II Inn, Bristol, Pennsylvania (est. c. 1681)

Dan'l Webster Inn, Sandwich Village, Massachusetts (est. c. 1692)

Longfellow's Wayside Inn, Sudbury, Massachusetts (est. c. 1716)

Mill Street Hotel & Tavern, Mount Holly, New Jersey (est. c. 1723)

Jessop's Tavern, New Castle, Delaware (est. c. 1724)

New Boston Inn, Sandisfield, Massachusetts (est. c. 1743)

Middleton Tavern, Annapolis, Maryland (est. c. 1750)

Pirates' House, Savannah, Georgia (est. c. 1753)

Old '76 House, Tappan, New York (est. c. 1755)

Puritan mores even found their way into such mainstream outlets as *Poor Richard's Almanack*, which took warnings against intemperance straight to its readers with this somber 1734 verse:

He that for sake of Drink neglects his Trade,
And spends each Night in Taverns till 'tis late,
And rises when the Sun is four hours high,
And ne'er regards his starving Family;
God in his Mercy may do much to save him,
But, woe to the poor Wife, whose Lot it is to have him.[18]

It's unclear how effective these laws and other social pressures were at dissuading individuals from abandoning their work and families for the tavern, but plenty of evidence suggests taverns continued being sanctuaries of social disorder. During tavern brawls, it was not uncommon for red-hot irons known as loggerheads (used to heat beverages) to be used as lethal weapons, leading to the phrase "to be at logger-heads."[19] Replete with rowdy mariners' taverns and brothels, the Philadelphia waterfront used to be referred to as "Helltown."[20] According to historian Kym Rice, "The pages of other tavern keepers' account books confirm innumerable instances of the breakage of glass, punch bowls, furniture, and even windows by customers."[21] In erudite Cambridge, Massachusetts, the Old Porter's Tavern had a view of the town square where hangings were common, lending popularity to the satirical verse:

Cambridge is a famous town,
Both for wit and knowledge,
Some they whip and some they hang,
And some they send to college.[22]

OPPOSITE *Engraving titled "Toby Fillpot," with period hand color by Robert Dighton, c. 1786.*

America's founding fathers inherited the puritanical distinction between alcohol use and abuse, but they also believed that moderate alcohol consumption was good for health. John Adams downed a tankard of cider every morning with breakfast, and Patrick Henry worked as a barkeep at Virginia's Raleigh Tavern.[23] As president, Thomas Jefferson sought to combat the whiskey scourge with cheap wine, writing, "No nation is drunken where wine is cheap; and none sober where the dearness of wine substitutes ardent spirits as the common beverage."[24] Washington developed his own beer recipe and famously launched his political career with a generous provision of 144 gallons of rum to Virginia voters for their thoughtful consideration of his (successful) candidacy for a seat in the House of Burgesses.[25] In his later career, Washington bade farewell to the 1787 Constitutional Convention with a booze-infused $15,400 blowout bash at City Tavern in Philadelphia,[26] and built what may have been the largest whiskey distillery in America at the time.[27] Benjamin Franklin even argued that "a little liquor" could help some men become "accomplished orators." Franklin could be poetic about

BELOW *Engraving by Thomas Howland Mumford depicting Philadelphia's London Coffee House as it looked during the Revolutionary War.*

GEORGE WASHINGTON MAY HAVE LOVED BEER, but as a young colonel in the Virginia Regiment, the American Cincinnatus could be a buzzkill. Washington complained that the local taverns were "a great nuisance to the soldiers" under his command, who were "incessantly drunk, and unfit for service." Sobriety may have made for good soldiery, but it made for ruinous politics. In 1755, the twenty-three-year-old Washington was handily defeated in his first campaign by an opponent who showered voters with drinks, a tactic known as "swilling the planters with bumbo." Washington learned his lesson, and in 1758 he pummeled voters with 144 gallons of rum, punch, hard cider, and beer for their thoughtful consideration of his (successful) candidacy.

SOURCES

Lisa Bramen, "Swilling the Planters with Bumbo: When Booze Bought Elections," *Smithsonian Magazine*, October 20, 2010.

George Washington to Robert Dinwiddie, September 23, 1756, in *The Writings of George Washington; Being His Correspondence, Addresses, Messages, and Other Papers, Official and Private*, ed. Jared Sparks (New York: Harpers, 1847), 188.

Colonial Cocktails

STONE FENCE

INGREDIENTS

2 oz. rum

10 oz. hard cider

Lemon twist

DIRECTIONS

Pour rum and hard cider into a pint glass over ice.

Stir.

Garnish with a lemon twist.

FOLLOWING THE OUTBREAK OF WAR at Lexington and Concord, Americans enlisted the help of the Green Mountain Boys, a small gang of ruffians in the northern hills of Connecticut led by Ethan Allen. Allen and his militia, along with Benedict Arnold, marched north and captured the British fort at Ticonderoga, sending its artillery back to the relief of occupied Boston. Before they marched, however, it's believed that Allen and the Boys gathered their wits and courage at Zadak Remington's Tavern, with the help of the Stone Fence, a strong rum and cider concoction.

SOURCE

David Wondrich, *Esquire*, November 6, 2007.

alcohol; he penned this ditty about Printer's (rum) Punch in a 1737 edition of *Poor Richard's Almanack*:

Boy, bring a bowl of China here
Fill it with water cool and clear;
Decanter with Jamaica ripe,
And spoon of silver, clean and bright,
Sugar twice-fin'd in pieces cut,
Knife, sive, and glass in order put,
Bring forth the fragrant fruit and then
We're happy till the clock strikes ten.[28]

In fact, Franklin's relationship to alcohol has perhaps made him the most misquoted man of all time (there is even a satirical holiday: Misquote Ben Franklin Day).[29] Many of "Franklin's" debunked colloquialisms strike a familiar, friendly, grandfatherly tone, such as, "In wine there is wisdom, in beer there is freedom, in water there is bacteria" (Franklin's death in 1790 preceded Louis Pasteur's development of germ theory by seventy years, making the remark improbable). One of the most popular misquotes, however, appears to be at least based on something Franklin did write. The much beloved Franklinism, "Beer is proof that god loves us and wants us to be happy," is believed to have originated in a 1779 letter to the French economist André Morellet as the slightly more poetic ode to the grape:

> Behold the rain which descends from heaven upon our vineyards, there it enters the roots of the vines, to be changed into wine, a constant proof that God loves us, and loves to see us happy.[30]

TAVERN WOMEN

It should come as little surprise that America's early tavern scenes were particularly male and almost entirely white—although there were exceptions. Women, widows in particular, were sometimes granted tavern licenses out of economic necessity to provide for their families. In fact, in some colonies, the first tavern licenses were restricted to "widows and decrepit men of good character."[31] It has been estimated that between 1620 and 1699, 71 percent of all female keepers of Massachusetts's country taverns were widows (25 percent in Boston).[32]

By the patriarchic standards of the colonial era, female tavern ownership was considered both sensible and problematic. Tavern keeping consisted primarily of domestic skills most colonial women would have learned as children, making them well suited to the profession. However, a blemished reputation could have ruinous social, economic, and legal consequences for colonial women, such that women tavern keepers had to go the extra mile to ensure their taverns were seen as havens for civility. In 1766, Anne Paterson placed an advertisement in the *Virginia Gazette* promising "a very genteel plentiful house"; Margett Moore promised Boston officials that her proposed tavern would serve only "country People of the better Sort."[33] In the 1670s, Boston resident Alice Thomas is believed to have become the first female tavern keeper in the colonies. Thomas was eventually arrested and convicted for " selling liquor without a license, profaning the Sabbath, receiving stolen goods, and promoting frequent secret and unseasonable entertainment in her house to Lewd Lascivious and Notorious persons of both sexes, giving them the opportunity to Commit Carnale Wickedness." She was whipped and jailed, though eventually released following a generous financial contribution to the civic treasury (the probable source of the funds didn't seem to matter to the magistrates).[34] In 1714 in New York City, the widow Mary Wakeum was indicted for serving blacks, servants, and criminals in her tavern and for allowing gambling and rampant drunkenness. According to historian Kym Rice, the grand jury labeled Wakeum "a Woman of Evil Life," insinuating that her tavern was a place of illicit sexual activity.[35]

ABOVE *"Female Patriotism, Mrs. Steel & General Greene," engraved by J. B. Hall after an original painting by Alonzo Chappel, c. 1856, shows South Carolina tavern proprietor Mrs. Steel offering to help General Greene.*

In 1713, a rare and refreshing break from Puritan hypocrisy seems to have come over Boston. Cotton Mather, scion of Puritan leader Increase Mather, set his sights on closing Boston's brothels and exposing their clientele, writing, "I am informed of several Houses in this Town, where there are young Women of a very debauched character." It's suspected that a number of Boston's leading men were among said houses' clientele and together worked to thwart Mather's plans.[36]

Longfellow's Wayside Inn

EST. 1716 AS HOWE'S TAVERN ✱ TODAY OPERATES AS A RESTAURANT, TAPROOM, GRISTMILL, AND INN ✱ SUDBURY, MASSACHUSETTS

On a rugged continent with little infrastructure, America's post roads were bustling commercial corridors along which taverns could do brisk business. It was on the Boston Post Road where, in 1716, David Howe expanded his house and opened an establishment known simply as Howe's Tavern, today Longfellow's Wayside Inn.

The Wayside Inn has some of the best-preserved records of any colonial tavern. In fact, the inn keeps an archivist to maintain its trove of original documents about both the tavern and the town of Sudbury. These include records on construction (a gambrel roof was added in 1750), prices (lodging was 4 pence, common dinner 12 pence, good dinner 20 pence in 1748), and past purchase orders (32 gallons of rum and 10 gallons of whiskey at 22 shillings per gallon on July 19, 1769). The alcohol order is even framed and on display. Howe's youngest son, Ezekiel, took over the property in 1748 and is believed to have renamed it the Red Horse Tavern.

ABOVE *Exterior detail of Longfellow's Wayside Inn.*

Ezekiel eventually became a lieutenant colonel in the Sudbury Militia. When word arrived in the early morning hours of April 19, 1775, that the British were marching on Concord, just a bit more than 6 miles away, Howe and his son, Ezekiel Jr., joined a company of Minutemen and set out at once. It is said that the Sudbury men were the first to arrive at the farm of Colonel James Barrett, which the British were raiding in search of contraband. Upon seeing the British there, Howe promised that "if any blood has been shed, not one of the rascals shall escape." Both Howe and his son would go on to attack the British in the guerrilla skirmishes that chased them back to Boston.

Howe Sr. remained in Sudbury during the war as a recruiter, while Howe Jr. remained on the front lines, fighting in the significant American victory at Saratoga that resulted in both the alliance with France and, two years later, Benedict Arnold's betrayal. Believing himself mortally wounded from the fight, Howe Jr. gave his pocket watch and sword to a fellow soldier to bring back to his family. He nevertheless survived, and today the watch and sword are on display at the tavern.

Both George Washington and the marquis de Lafayette are known to have passed the inn several times, although it's unclear whether they visited. William Molineaux Jr., a member of the Boston Committee of Safety, left no mystery of his visit. In June 1774, he used

"If not in haste, do stop and taste."

—WILLIAM MOLINEAUX JR., 1774

his diamond ring to etch a message into the tavern's window, which hung undisturbed until the 1870s, and is on display today:

What do you think?
Here is good drink.
Perhaps you may not know it.
If not in haste, do stop and taste.
You merry folks will show it.

This was not the last time the tavern was associated with verse. In 1861, the tavern, still known as the Red Horse, hosted its most famous guest, the writer and poet Henry Wadsworth Longfellow. Longfellow was so taken by the inn's history and dilapidated charm that he used it as the inspiration for *Tales of a Wayside Inn* (1862), the famous book of poems that includes "Paul Revere's Ride." Before long, people came from around the country to visit "Longfellow's Wayside Inn." The owners knew a clever idea when they saw it and renamed the tavern, which has stood the test of time.

The tavern was purchased by Henry Ford in 1923 and restored it to its current glory. Today the taproom is low and dark and from the ceiling hang steel mugs; the bartender specializes in mixing the Coow Woow (pronounced coo woo), America's first cocktail (see sidebar on page 43). Upstairs are several living history rooms preserved with period furniture, and the restaurant contains four dining rooms. Elsewhere on the property are a chapel and functioning gristmill.

The fire-light, shedding over all
The splendor of its ruddy glow,
Filled the whole parlor large and low;
It gleamed on wainscot and on wall,
It touched with more than wonted grace
Fair Princess Mary's pictured face; . . .

The scroll reads, "By the name of Howe."
And over this, no longer bright,
Though glimmering with a latent light,
Was hung the sword his grandsire bore
In the rebellious days of yore,
Down there at Concord in the fight.

—Prelude; *Tales of a Wayside Inn*

TOP *Interior detail of Longfellow's Wayside Inn taproom.*

GEOGRAPHY AS DESTINY

One wonders why taverns, prone as they were to corruption, vice, and violence and cursed by America's leading men, were tolerated in the first place. Here the inescapable role of geography must be considered, in particular, the isolation of American life and the huge distances between both the colonies and Europe and between the colonies themselves. Roads were often little more than Native American foot trails, making overland travel slow, bumpy, and unpleasant. Trips beyond 10 miles typically required staying the night,[37] and officials at the time estimated that overland delivery of a letter from New York to Charleston, today a 12-hour drive, could take ten weeks.[38] What lay west of the Mississippi River and north of the San Francisco Bay were still mysteries, and travel to Europe was a grueling months-long odyssey. Lacking major industry, the American economy was land rich and cash poor. Hotels didn't exist, and a typical tavern was equipped with only between six and eight beds, into which up to sixteen men could be packed.[39] As a result, tradesmen, circuit judges, and other traveling people relied on taverns to provide food, drink, and sleeping accommodations for themselves and their horses.

Taverns were of such importance that Massachusetts and Connecticut required every town to maintain at least one.

Right away we're confronted with a telling symptom of an object's prevalence in society: its prevalence in language. In addition to *tavern*, colonial Americans also used the names *tippling house, public house, dram house, ale house, ordinary, grog shop, slog shop, pub, inn, wagon stand, exchange,* and *house of ill repute.* A majority of the terms used—*tippling, dram, ale, grog, slog*—refer to drinking, drunkenness, or a type of drink, and *ordinary* refers to a complete meal offered at a fixed price. *Inn* and *wagon stands* were commonly understood references to sleep and travel, *exchanges* were taverns that provided financial services, and *house of ill repute* was a not-so-subtle reference to the world's oldest profession.

This linguistic richness could itself be a result of eighteenth-century America's vastness and isolation. At their most basic, American taverns were combinations of two English institutions, the inn and the public house. However, on the American frontier, taverns were typically the only public building within a day's travel. As a result, in addition to bar, restaurant, and hostel, American

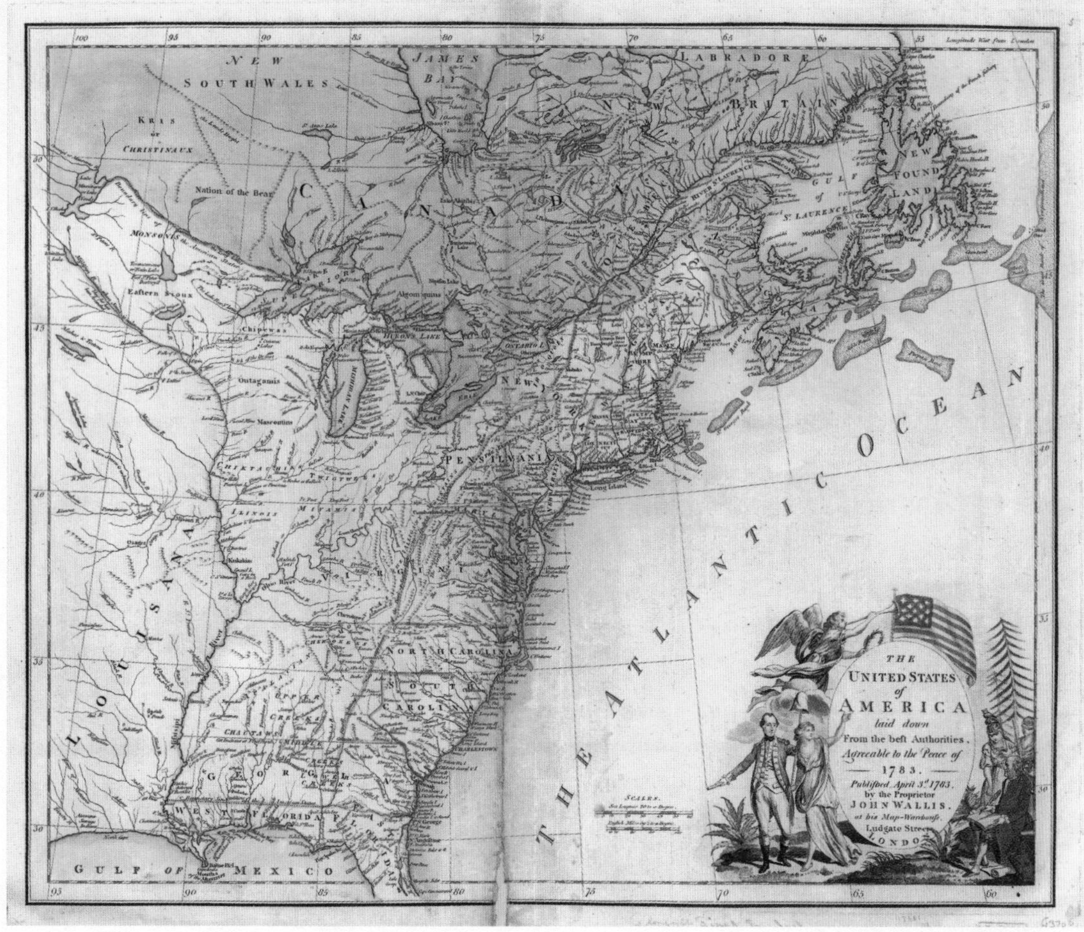

ABOVE *Period map by John Wallis, titled "The United States of America laid down from the best authorities, agreeable to the Peace of 1783."*

taverns were also used as banks, insurance offices, hardware stores, barber shops, hospitals, schools, garrisons, libraries, dance halls, brothels, theaters, courts of law, and post offices.[40] Taverns were of such importance that Massachusetts and Connecticut required every town to maintain at least one.[41] The plan for the settlement of Maine in 1683 included instructions that "an Ordinary is to be Sett up at every Island or fishing place by an approved man of that place."[42] An example of how significant institutions are reflected in language, and perhaps the greatest measure of the tavern's importance to the struggle for independence, was how many future battles were named after them: including the battles of Spencer's Tavern, Torrence's Tavern, Paoli's Tavern, and Vanbibber's Tavern.[43]

Some of these ordinaries became vital trading posts and meeting and resting places for stagecoach drivers hauling goods and supplies. Common colonial goods were ale, bacon, rope, beans, beef, butter, carriage mountings, castor oil, cheese, clocks, cider, corn, feathers, flaxseed, flour, firearms, furniture, furs, glassware, hats, lard, lead, leather, lime, millstone, oats, onions, peach brandy, pork, porter, potatoes, skins, shot, soap, spanish moss, staves, sugar, tobacco, twine, vinegar, wheat, whiskey, and window glass.[44] In some cases, taverns along busy country intersections gave rise to entire towns, often the name of the tavern becoming the town's own. The Pennsylvania towns of Unicorn and Red Lion are thought to have been named after taverns.[45] As a physical space, public life in the twenty-first century has no equivalent.

ABOVE *Signboard for Philadelphia's A Man Full of Trouble tavern. The building serves as apartments today.*

SIGNS OF THE TIMES

Perhaps the most famous features of early American taverns are their names and signboards. Whereas the symbols and signs of other industries tended to be standardized—a hand and shears for tailors, a pestle and mortar for pharmacists, a pipe for tobacco sellers, a hand and pen for schools, and a hand and hammer for blacksmiths[46]—tavern signs are almost psychedelic by comparison. The sign of the Man Full of Trouble Tavern, Philadelphia's only surviving pre-Revolutionary tavern building (now apartments), depicted a man with a monkey, a magpie, and a wife, which, according to a popular rhyme, "is the true emblem of strife."[47] The Pinch-em-Slyly Tavern was destroyed by fire in 1827, but its name lives on as Pinch-em-Slyly Road in Stony Point, Virginia. Other odd names are the Death of the Fox, Hen and Chickens, Shooting the Deserter, and the Three Broiled Chickens. Even contemporaries found undeniable charm in tavern names. The *British Apollo*, a London magazine, printed the following in 1710:

I'm amused at the signs,
As I pass through the town,
To see the odd mixture—
A Magpye and Crown;
The Whale and the Crow,
The Razor and Hen;
The Leg and Seven Stars,
The Axe and the Bottle;
The Tun and the Lute;
The Eagle and Child;
The Shovel and Boot.[48]

Colonial Cocktails

THE COOW WOOW

INGREDIENTS

2.5 oz. white rum

1.5 oz. ginger brandy

DIRECTIONS

Pour rum and brandy into a cocktail shaker with ice.

Shake well.

Strain into a chilled martini glass.

CLAIMED TO BE AMERICA'S OLDEST COCKTAIL, the first Coow Woow (pronounced *coo-woo*) was supposedly shaken in 1664—which is plausible, as the drink's two ingredients were among the more common types of liquor during the early colonial era. However, the original iteration, mentioned in a 1684 letter from the future archbishop of Canterbury, Thomas Tenison, was dismissed as a poor man's drink of "molasses and ginger." One imagines a fiery gasoline cultured with throat-cutting impurities. Somewhere down the line, bartenders tamed the dragon, and it is today the toast of the Longfellow's Wayside Inn.

The vivid pictorial tradition of early tavern signs is said to have been born in preliterate, multilingual Europe. One story involving an Englishman in Calais, France, explains why. Searching for the Silver Lion Inn and unable to speak a word of French, the Englishman is said to have growled at strangers with a silver dollar in his mouth until a sharp local got the drift and showed him the way.[49] Despite relatively high literacy rates in the American colonies by 1776, taverns still largely adopted pictorial signboards.

While many tavern signs used only pictures, some also incorporated rhyme and even political satire. Helene Smith's excellent history of eighteenth- and nineteenth-century tavern signs recounts the following examples:

I William McDermott lives here,
I sells good porter, ale and beer,
I've made my sign a little wider
to let you know I sell good cider.[50]
Rove not from pole to pole, but stop in here,
Where naught exceeds the shaving but the beer.

On one side, an early King's Post sign read:

Before this hill you do go up
Stop in and drink a cheerful cup.

And on its reverse:

You're down the hill and all danger's past,
Stop and drink a cheerful glass.[51]

The Four Alls Tavern featured this sign:

1. King—I govern ALL

2. General—I fight for ALL

3. Minister—I pray of ALL

4. Laborer—I pay for ALL[52]

The political sting of a similarly themed Four Alls tavern on London's Rosemary Lane was eventually replaced by the censor-friendly "Four *Awls*"—a carpentry tool.[53]

American taverns were particularly unconcerned about political or social improprieties. Nevertheless, the sign of the Quiet Woman, a Philadelphia tavern, that depicted a headless woman was so unpopular

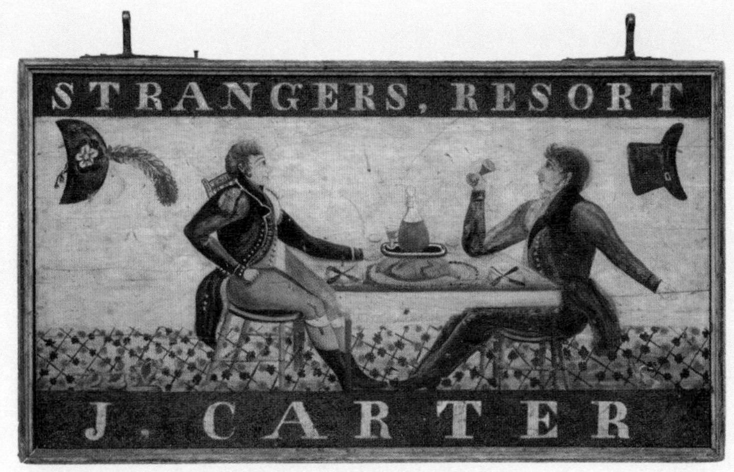

OPPOSITE *Signboard for Bull Run tavern, Shirley, Massachusetts.*

THIS PAGE *A selection of surviving colonial tavern signboards, including Carter's Inn (top left) and Crowfut's Inn (top right).*

the owner was eventually forced to replace it. For reasons unknown, a Woodstown, New Jersey, tavern was once called Nigger's Glory. Tavern signs could even be deadly. According to Smith, the sign from the Hancock Inn in Boston was so large that it killed an unfortunate passerby as a windstorm brought it down.[54]

Some tavern names were common throughout the colonies. No official census exists, although we know America had at least five taverns named White Horse, Blue Anchor, and Blue Bell (blue was associated with freedom). There were at least six Rising Sun taverns, seven named after Benjamin Franklin, seven Bull's Heads, and eight Indian Queens. There were at least nine Red Lions and nine Green Trees, as well as ten Cross Keys and eleven Eagle Taverns. After 1776, many King George Taverns became George Washingtons, of which there were at least sixteen. The most popular tavern name appears to have been Black Horse, of which there were at least eighteen known. The number three also commonly appears in tavern names, including the Three Crown Tavern, the Three Jolly Sailors, Three Keys, and Three Mountain.[55] A "Tun" was an ancient 252 gallons cask for wine or beer, and taverns sometimes incorporated the word into their name to boast of their liquor stocks—thus the "Tun Tavern" or the even more impressive "Three Tun Tavern."[56] (The U.S. Marine Corps was founded in Philadelphia's Tun Tavern in 1776.)

King George II Inn

EST. 1681 AS FERRY HOUSE ✻ TODAY OPERATES AS RESTAURANT, BAR, AND INN OFFERING MEDIUM- AND LONG-TERM RENTALS ✻ FREQUENTED BY GEORGE AND MARTHA WASHINGTON, JOHN AND ABIGAIL ADAMS ✻ BRISTOL, PENNSYLVANIA

First opened in 1681, the King George II Inn predates the colony of Pennsylvania and is one of the oldest continuously operating inns in the United States. The inn was built by Samuel Cliff, who is said to have received a 262-acre land grant from the provincial governor of New York on the condition that he build a ferry across the Delaware River connecting the towns of Bristol and Burlington. Ferries were common in early America and their operators poled, rowed, or pulled travelers across rivers by ropes affixed to both shores.

As was common practice in the colonies, a tavern was opened on one end of the ferry to allow passengers to either rest up or wait out poor weather before or after their crossing. The no-frills Cliff named his ferry tavern the Ferry House, which is believed to have occupied the space of the current bar and adjacent dining room. A young George Washington is believed to have stayed at the tavern en route to Connecticut for a military commission, and Martha Washington is thought to have lived for a time in today's room 1. Below the bar today survives another fascinating quirk: an early jail room kept in the cellar that still has the original bars over the old window.

ABOVE *Detail of boarded prison window in basement of King George II Inn.*

Charles Besonett purchased the tavern in 1765, renamed it the King George II Inn, and had it repaired and expanded to its present appearance following a devastating fire. The tavern's new name didn't last long. American patriots eventually opened musket fire on the hated image of King George that graced the inn's sign, forcing Besonett to rename the inn Fountain House.

The inn was part of George Washington's famous attack on the Hessians on Christmas night, 1776. As Washington crossed the Delaware River near McConkey's Tavern north of Trenton, officer John Cadwalader was to cross at the King George II Inn 20 miles downstream and converge on Trenton from the south. Poor weather and heavy ice flows prevented Cadwalader's crossing, and Washington was left without reinforcements. Luckily for Washington, Trenton's defenses were already weakened by a diversion of Hessian troops to Mount Holly, New Jersey (see Mill Street Hotel & Tavern, page 116), and his surprise victory became one of the most celebrated of the Revolution. Years later, President John Adams and First Lady Abigail Adams are believed to have dined at the King George II Inn while en route to Philadelphia.

The inn was known as Ye Old Delaware House for most of the nineteenth and early twentieth centuries, before finally returning to the name of the King George II Inn in the 1950s. While the restaurant and bar have closed at times during its 325-year history, the building has continuously provided guest rooms for medium- and long-term stays. In this last respect, the King George II Inn functions as one of America's most authentic surviving colonial taverns. Today the inn's bar and restaurant have been fully restored to a neighborhood tavern, including an added back patio overlooking the Delaware River.

SOURCES

John Adams, "Letter to Abigail Adams, 4 May 1797," Adams Family Papers, Massachusetts Historical Society.

Marie Murphy Duess, *Colonial Inns and Taverns of Bucks County* (Charleston, SC: History Press, 2007).

Americans Drank All Day

HANGOVERS MAY BE BAD, but cholera and dysentery are worse. Due to unsafe sources of drinking water, Americans developed a social tolerance for day-long consumption of low to moderately alcoholic beverages like spruce beer, cider, and watered-down rum (known as "grog"). It has been estimated that the annual per capita consumption of distilled spirits in America reached 3.7 gallons by 1776, which today would rank it behind only Lithuania as the drunkest nation on earth (Americans consumed 2.3 gallons per capita in 2012). In an observation that still bears a ring of truth today, Thomas Jefferson believed "drunkenness is much more common in all the American States than in France, but it is less common there than in England."

SOURCES

"From Thomas Jefferson to Brissot de Warville," 16 August 1786, in *The Papers of Thomas Jefferson*, vol. 10: *22 June–31 December 1786*, ed. Julian P. Boyd (Princeton, NJ: Princeton University Press, 1954), 261–63.

"Non-Medical Determinants of Health: Alcohol Consumption," OECD. Stat, retrieved August 6, 2015.

Kym Rice, *Early American Taverns: For the Entertainment of Friends and Strangers* (Chicago: Regnery Gateway, 1983), 94.

LAST CALL

By the 1760s, American society was dotted with the colorful names of new taverns and their experimental alcoholic concoctions. Growing alcoholism sparked a controversial political debate involving issues of class, morality, economics, and political power as old Puritan strictures gave way to new economic and social realities. Tavern culture began to dominate American political culture, stoking fears among some founding fathers of social and political breakdown that would remain the great bogeyman of post-independence politics.

ABOVE *"Peter Manmigault and his Friends" by George Roupell, 1757–1760.*

OPPOSITE *"The Contrast," by an unknown artist with after work by Robert Dighton, c. 1780. Travelers came to expect close questioning from their landlords, both to establish their character (and allegiances) and to gather information.*

ERTY TREE
STAMP
ACT
Tea

CHAPTER 2

TAXATION WITHOUT REPRESENTATION

The events of 1754 marked a turning point for British-American relations when imperial rivals Britain and France went to war over competing claims to the Ohio River Valley, leading American colonists to rally at taverns in opposition to the French. The eventual British-American victory in the French and Indian War (1754–1763) removed the French threat, though not before plunging the British treasury deeply into debt. Parliament attempted to improve its finances by taxing the supposedly grateful American colonists, setting a pattern of British overreach followed by American rebellion. Colonial legislatures, once dominated by provincial interests, began holding secret meetings at nearby taverns and finding common cause in opposition to the Crown's policies. While the list of American grievances with Great Britain grew leading up to 1776, it was a dispute involving the rum trade that set in motion the long march to independence.

Though devoid of precious metals, the Caribbean islands offered riches of another type: sugarcane. Labor intensive and hugely useful, sugarcane's by-product, molasses, could be used for making everything from jam and rum to refined sugar. Europe's imperial powers seized Cuba, Barbados, and Hispaniola between 1493 and 1625, and by the eighteenth century, virtually the entire Caribbean archipelago was producing sugarcane under European rule and with African slave labor. Undercut by cheaper competition from other imperial powers, British sugar barons employed an old trick to keep the competition in check: the trade barrier. In 1733, the British Parliament passed the Molasses Act, which levied a 6 pence and 9 pence duty on all molasses and rum, respectively, imported into the American colonies from outside the empire.[1]

OPPOSITE *"The Bostonians Paying the Excise-Man, or Tarring and Feathering," England, 1774, an engraving with period color by Philip Dawe, depicts a British customs official in Boston being tarred and feathered with the Boston Tea Party in progress in the background.*

Without enforcement, the Molasses Act arrived like a dead letter, and colonists instead professionalized the business of smuggling cheap molasses from the French-owned Caribbean islands to fuel New England's rum stills. According to Massachusetts lawyer and rhetorician James Otis, originator of the refrain "no taxation without representation," Molasses Act duties raised only £259 in 1735 when they should have raised about £25,000.[2] So long as the American economy was small and Britain was at peace with its European competitors, and with evasion of custom duties common practice throughout the empire, disregard for the molasses tax was generally tolerated and seen as what we might today call a victimless crime.

War between Britain and France changed that dynamic. In the twenty years between 1730 and 1750, the population of Britain's thirteen American colonies nearly doubled to 1.2 million.[3] This rapid expansion began transforming the colonies from frontier curiosities—the refuge of European adventurers and banished religious factions—into valuable cogs in Britain's triangular transatlantic trade network. It also resulted in a clamoring for new farmlands and the westward expansion of colonial boundaries, especially into the fertile Ohio River Valley. But the American colonists were boxed in by Spanish Florida to the south, French Appalachia to the west, and French Canada to the north. Territorial skirmishes, some involving the young Virginian Colonel George Washington, broke out along the disputed border, ultimately helping push France, England, and other European powers into what became the Seven Years' War, known in America as the French and Indian War.

Without enforcement, the Molasses Act arrived like a dead letter, and colonists instead professionalized the business of smuggling cheap molasses from the French-owned Caribbean islands to fuel New England's rum stills.

The French and Indian War pitted the French and their Indian allies against the combined forces of Britain, American colonists, and their own Indian allies. The war found America's business interests conflicted. American colonists saw the French as a military threat and an economic rival, particularly regarding western expansion and control of the lucrative Native American fur trade. At the war's outset, representatives from the seven northernmost colonies (Connecticut, Maryland, Massachusetts, New Hampshire, New York, Pennsylvania, and Rhode Island) convened the Albany Congress in New York to discuss colonial defenses. Representing Pennsylvania, Benjamin Franklin

ABOVE *"Join, or Die." illustration by Benjamin Franklin from* The Pennsylvania Gazette, *May 9, 1754, encouraged political unity between the colonies.*

proposed the creation of a primordial central government, headed by a "governor-general to be appointed by the crown, with a power . . . to lay and levy general taxes, and raise troops for the common defence, and to annoy the enemy."[4] On behalf of what became known as the Albany Plan of Union, which ultimately failed, Franklin printed the famous "Join, or Die" political cartoon, widely considered the first image to promote unity among the American colonies.

Both the life-or-death stakes depicted in the propaganda and the Albany Congress's existence itself suggest the French threat was taken seriously. American taverns served as recruiting stations to fight the French and their Indian allies. One advertisement from 1759 called for recruits to assemble at Boston's Sign of the Bear Tavern:

> All able-bodied fit Men that have an Inclination to serve his Majesty King George the Second, in the First Independent

> Company of Rangers, now in the Province of Nova Scotia commanded by Joseph Gorham, Esq.; shall, on enlisting receive good Pay and Clothing, a large Bounty, with a Crown to drink the King's Health. And by repairing to the Sign of the Bear in King-Street, Boston, and to Mr. Cornelious Crocker, Innholder in Barnstable, may hear the particular Encouragement, and many Advantages accruing to a Soldier, in the Course of the Duty of that Company, too long to insert here; and further may depend on being discharged at the expiration of the Time entertain'd for, and to have every other Encouragement punctually compli'd with.[5]

For America's rum makers, however, France was a valuable business partner. American distillers and French sugar barons had already established a symbiotic relationship: the French relied on New England cod to feed their slaves, and Americans relied on cheap French molasses to produce rum. American rum wasn't the best, but it was the cheapest, and Americans traded whatever rum they didn't drink for both English goods and African slaves, developing their own triangular trade between Africa and French Hispaniola. Americans continued trading for French molasses throughout the war and were treated to safe passage from the French navy.[6]

Britain would eventually emerge victorious from the war, with full control of North America east of the Mississippi, £140 million in debt,[7] and a class of sugar barons fuming at the quasi-traitorous Franco-American molasses trade. Saddled with debt and determined to both tax and hold its new American possessions, Britain decided to install thousands of permanent troops in North America.

It is here where Parliament shows a dash of cunning. On April 5, 1764, Parliament passed the Sugar Act, halving the Molasses Act duties though greatly increasing enforcement. Some Americans saw through the ruse. Writing to botanist and friend Peter Collinson in England, Benjamin Franklin doubted the act's wisdom, arguing it would hurt overall trade: "What we get above a Subsistence, we lay out with you for your Manufactures. Therefore what you get from us

LEFT *"Exterior of a Distillery, on Weatherell's Estate," from William Clark's Ten Views in the Island of Antigua, shows slaves working a rum distillery in the Caribbean.*

Drinking Habits of the Founding Fathers

AMERICAN COLONISTS BELIEVED moderate alcohol consumption was good for your health. John Adams began each day with a mug of hard cider, George Washington developed his own beer recipe, and Thomas Jefferson was America's most obnoxious wine snob. During his presidency, Jefferson took on the powerful whiskey industry by lowering duties on imported wines to better compete with American whiskey, writing, "No nation is drunken where wine is cheap; and none sober, where the dearness of wine substitutes ardent spirits as the common beverage." Ben Franklin, meanwhile, argued that a "little Liquor" could help a man "become [an] accomplished orator."

SOURCE

Sharon V. Salinger, *Taverns and Drinking in Early America* (Baltimore: John Hopkins University Press, 2004).

in Taxes you must lose in Trade. . . . Does no body see, that if you confine us in America to your own Sugar Islands for that Commodity, it must raise the Price of it upon you in England?"[8] To Franklin's neoliberal argument, Samuel Adams added this prophetic slippery slope: "But what still heightens our apprehensions is that these unexpected proceedings may be preparatory to new taxations upon us; for if our trade may be taxed, why not our lands? Why not the produce of our lands and everything we process or make use of?"[9] Of the permanent troops, many colonists suspected Britain was merely dumping its unwanted military and civilian bureaucrats, and their salaries, on the American economy. Now that the French threat was removed, how else to explain it? Following these objections, Parliament eventually lowered the tax to 1 pence per gallon on all imported molasses (not just French). The smuggling infrastructure, however, was already in place, and many colonists continued ignoring the duties. It has been estimated that between 1765 and 1770, 33 percent of all molasses imported into the colonies was smuggled duty free, resulting in £11,200 worth of lost revenues to the British government.[10]

OPPOSITE *"Philadelphia Tavern Scene" by an unknown artist shows four men seated at a tavern enjoying a smoke and a jug of what is likely rum.*

RIGHT *Portrait of Samuel Adams.*

Raleigh Tavern

EST. 1717, REBUILT 1932 ✻ TODAY OPERATES AS A BAKERY AND MUSEUM ✻ FREQUENTED BY GEORGE WASHINGTON, THOMAS JEFFERSON, PATRICK HENRY ✻ WILLIAMSBURG, VIRGINIA

"Jollity, the offspring of wisdom and good living."

—FROM THE MANTEL OF RALEIGH TAVERN

The Raleigh Tavern was built around 1717 by Dr. Archibald Blair, whose storehouse and apothecary still stand nearby in Colonial Williamsburg. Blair rented the Raleigh to a succession of tavern keepers, eventually settling on the somewhat locally famous Harry Wetherburn. A Coochland County deed from the era states that Thomas Jefferson's father, Peter Jefferson, purchased two hundred acres for the bargain price of Wetherburn's "biggest bowl of arrack punch."

The tavern was named after Sir Walter Raleigh, who had attempted England's first permanent settlement in Virginia—the doomed Roanoke colony—and whose leaden bust stood above the doorway. As the main gathering place for civic, social, and entertainment in Williamsburg, the Raleigh was a café, restaurant, hostel, dance hall, and bar. Much of the Raleigh's political action occurred in the famed Apollo Room, over whose mantle was painted in gilt, "Hilaritas Sapientiae et Bonae Vitae Proles" (Jollity, the offspring of wisdom and good living). The steps of the Raleigh were once used to sell slaves.

The Raleigh is historic for three key events and interesting for several lesser ones. George Washington and other patriots from Virginia's House of Burgesses met at the Raleigh in 1769 to form the Virginia Non-Importation Association (a boycott of British goods) in response to Parliament's despised Townshend Acts. As the crisis with Great Britain worsened, the burgesses met at the Raleigh in March 1773 and reached two critical resolutions penned by Jefferson himself: an understanding that opposition to British effrontery was common cause to all colonies and that the colonial legislatures should establish a formal line of communication with one another through

TOP *Sketch of the Raleigh Tavern's Apollo Room.*

INSET *Bust of Sir Walter Raleigh, which sits above the front door of the Raleigh Tavern* "committees of correspondence." So important were the committees that Jefferson and several founders would later bicker over who had the idea first.

The third major incident to involve the Raleigh occurred during the winter of 1774. In response to Boston's recent Tea Party, Britain passed the Intolerable Acts, which closed the Port of Boston, eliminated self-governance and the right of assembly in Massachusetts, provided for the quartering of British soldiers in colonists' homes, and made explicit British expatriation rights for trials. When news of the Intolerable Acts reached Virginia, the outraged burgesses proclaimed June 1, the date the Boston blockade would take effect, as "a day of fasting, humiliation, and prayer." Virginia Governor Dunmore dissolved the house, and the members adjourned to the Raleigh, pledging another boycott of all trade with Britain and calling on the Committees of Correspondence to put forward delegates for what would become the Continental Congress.

Virginia's capital was moved to Richmond for military reasons during the Revolutionary War, and the role of the Raleigh Tavern in the war declined. According to a Richmond newspaper, the Raleigh "willfully burnt down" on December 11, 1859, only a few months after hosting a banquet for President John Tyler. Today's Raleigh Tavern Museum and Bakery was faithfully rebuilt in 1932 on the original foundation, informed by sketches and written descriptions. While the Raleigh no longer serves ale, madeira, or punch, the Historic Williamsburg Colonial District where it is located is host to several replica taverns that are still pouring.

SOURCES

Colonial Williamsburg Foundation, "Raleigh Tavern," http://www.history.org/almanack/places/hb/hbral.cfm.

Lawrence A. Kocher and Howard Dearstyne, "Arcihabald Blair'd Storehouse (NB) Architectural Report, Block 18-1 Building 6A Lot 46" (Williamsburg, VA: Colonial Williamsburg Foundation Library 1990).

"Letter from Joseph Shelton Watson to David Watson." *Virginia Magazine of History and Biography*. December 31, 1921, 162–64.

Jared Sparks, *The Writings of George Washington: Life of Washington* (Boston: American Stationers Company, 1837), 123.

The TIMES are Dreadful Doleful Dismal Dolorous, and DOLLAR-LESS.

An Emblem of the Effects of the STAMP

O! the fatal Stamp

Adieu, Adieu to the LIBERTY of the PRESS.

Thurſday, October 31. 1765 — NUMB. 1195

THE PENNSYLVANIA JOURNAL; AND WEEKLY ADVERTISER.

EXPIRING: In Hopes of a Reſurrection to LIFE again.

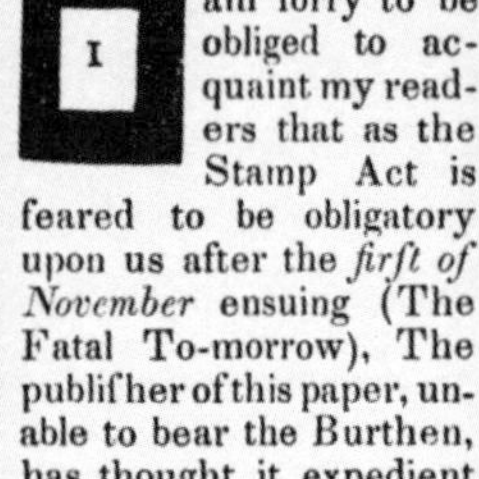

I am ſorry to be obliged to acquaint my readers that as the Stamp Act is feared to be obligatory upon us after the *firſt of November* ensuing (The Fatal To-morrow), The publiſher of this paper, unable to bear the Burthen, has thought it expedient to ſtop awhile, in order to deliberate, whether any methods can be found to elude the chains forged for us, and eſcape the inſupportable ſlavery, which it is hoped, from the laſt repreſentation now made againſt that act, may be effected. Mean while I muſt earneſtly Requeſt every individual of my Subſcribers, many of whom have been long behind Hand, that they would immediately diſcharge their reſpective Arrears, that I may be able, not only to ſupport myſelf during the Interval, but be better prepared to proceed again with this Paper whenever an opening for that purpoſe appears, which I hope will be ſoon.

WILLIAM BRADFORD.

The Molasses Act debate ultimately proved most colonists were willing to accept British regulation of trade, provided the burden was small and if the revenues went to colonial defense. Sam Adams, however, was right: Parliament lowered the molasses tax partly because it had other taxes up its sleeve. On February 27, 1765, Charles Townshend, chancellor of the exchequer, rose before the House of Commons and introduced the Stamp Act. Whereas the Sugar Act raised modest sums for a reasonable purpose through a tax on avoidable imported luxuries (such as rum), the Stamp Act imposed much higher and much more visible duties on everyday goods such as legal documents, newspapers, marriage licenses, and playing cards (nearly all of which were sold in taverns). In a woeful misreading of the situation, Townsend explained to Parliament: "And now will these Americans, children planted by our care, nourished up by our indulgence until they are grown to a degree of strength and opulence, and protected by our arms, will they grudge to contribute their mite to relieve us from the heavy weight of that burden which we lie under?"[11]

TOP *Masthead for* The Pennsylvania Journal and Weekly Advertiser *with a skull and crossbones representation of the official stamp required by the Stamp Act of 1765.*

ABOVE *Facsimile of revenue stamp.*

OPPOSITE BOTTOM *Drawing showing a Stamp Act official attacked by angry citizens.*

Colonel Isaac Barré, who had served alongside American colonists at the Battle of Quebec during the Seven Years' War, warned his colleagues in Parliament of the impending overreach. In his point-by-point rebuttal to Townshend, Barré also coined a phrase that would stick to American patriots throughout the conflict ahead:

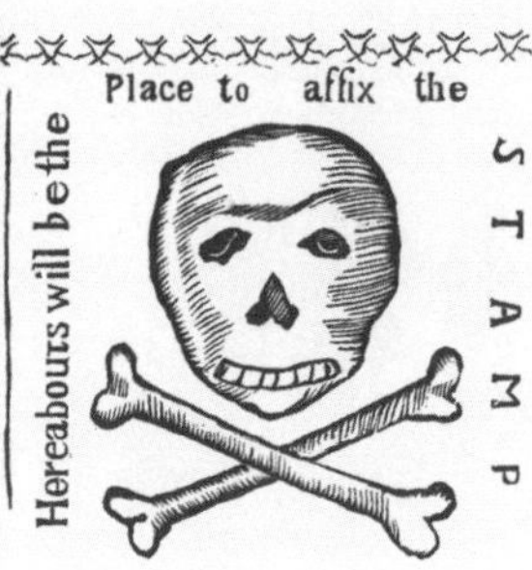

> They planted by your care? No! Your oppression planted them in America. They fled from your tyranny to the uncultivated, inhospitable country. . . . Yet, actuated by principles of true English liberty, they met all hardships with pleasure, compared with those they suffered in their own country. . . . Nourished up by your indulgence! They grew by your neglect of them. As soon as you began to care about them, that care was exercised in sending persons to rule them in one department and another . . . men whose behavior on many occasions has caused the blood of those Sons of Liberty to recoil within them. . . . Protected by your arms? They have nobly taken up arms in your defense. . . . I claim to know more of America than most of you, having seen and been conversant in that country. The people, I believe, are as truly loyal as any subjects the king has; but they are a people jealous of their liberties, and who will vindicate them to the last drop of their blood if they should ever be violated.[12]

Parliament passed the Stamp Act by a margin of 294 to 42, and King George III signed it into law on March 22, 1765.

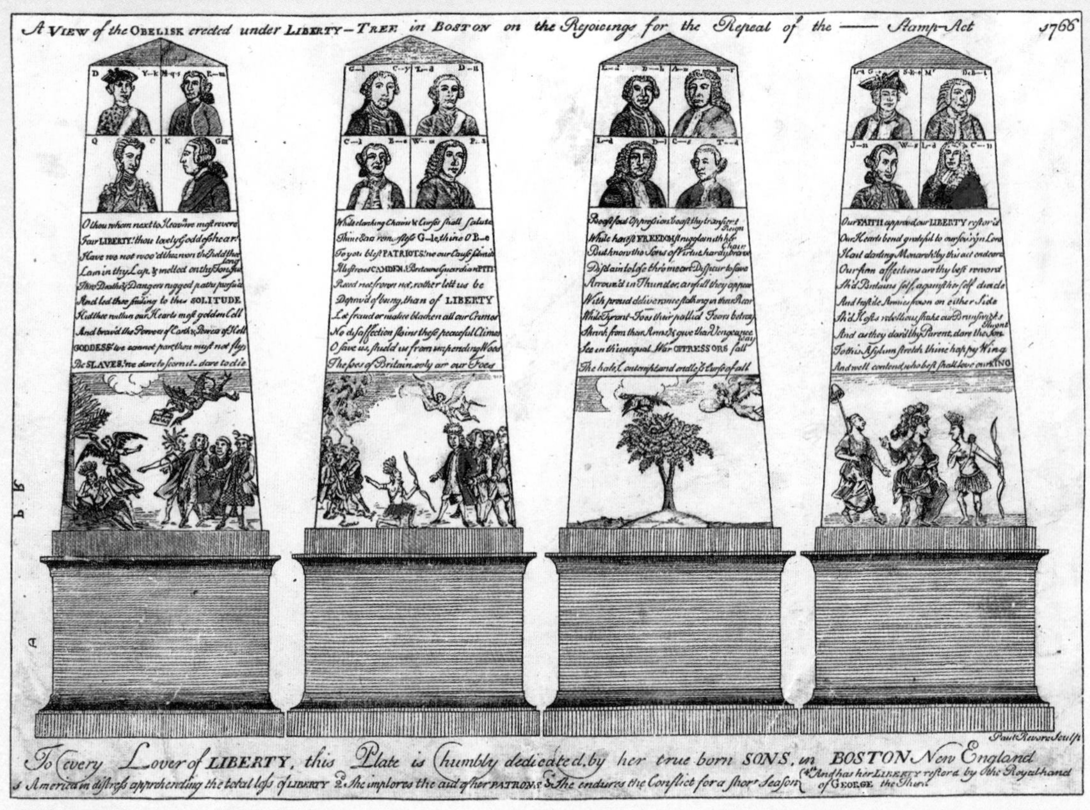

ABOVE *"A view of the obelisk erected under Liberty-tree in Boston on the rejoicings for the repeal of the Stamp Act 1766," by Paul Revere, Boston, 1766, is a schematic rendering of the illuminated obelisk erected on Boston Common in celebration of the repeal of the Stamp Act.*

OPPOSITE TOP *Broadside encouraging action by the Sons of Liberty.*

OPPOSITE BOTTOM *George Washington's freemason punch bowl on display at the Mount Vernon Museum.*

SONS OF LIBERTY

News of the Stamp Act unleashed a wave of shock, outrage, and mob violence. A Boston mob hung an effigy of stamp collector Andrew Oliver over an elm tree, ransacked his office, looted his house, and had his effigy beheaded and torched. Oliver resigned his post the following day at the base of the same tree, designated the Liberty Tree, and mob violence swept the other colonies.[13] Riots were reported in port cities from Savannah to Newport to Portsmouth.[14] Patriot leader Samuel Adams railed that the Stamp Act reduced colonists to "the miserable state of tributary Slaves,"[15] while Joseph Warren wrote to his friend in London that "the whole continent is inflamed."[16] A European visitor in America recounted being stunned by the open expression of political dissent in American taverns, writing, "Dined in a tavern in a Large Company, the Conversation Continually on the Stamp Dutys. I was really surprised to here the people talk so freely, this is common in all the country, and much more so the Northward."[17]

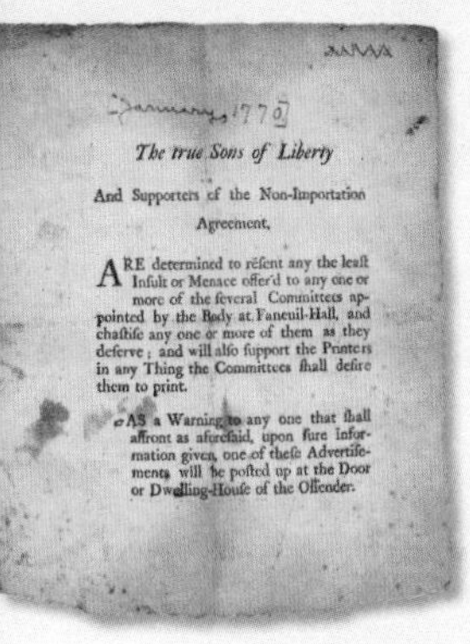

January 1770

The true Sons of Liberty

And Supporters of the Non-Importation Agreement,

ARE determined to resent any the least Insult or Menace offer'd to any one or more of the several Committees appointed by the Body at Faneuil-Hall, and chastise any one or more of them as they deserve; and will also support the Printers in any Thing the Committees shall desire them to print.

AS a Warning to any one that shall affront as aforesaid, upon sure Information given, one of these Advertisements will be posted up at the Door or Dwelling-House of the Offender.

American mobs, like their European counterparts, were sometimes capable of pitiless brutality, and one 1765 trend-setting incident in Norfolk, Virginia, set the standard for mob violence throughout the war. Captain William Smith, who had been suspected of ratting out local smugglers to the authorities, was captured by an angry mob and, as he later recounted,

> tho' they could find no evidence against me, they bound my hands and tied me behind a Cart . . . dawbed my body and face all over with tar and afterwards threw feathers upon me; they then put me upon a Ducking Stool and threw rotten eggs and stones at me [then] threw me headlong over the wharf, where I was in imminent danger of being drowned, had not a boat taken me up when I was just sinking, being able to swim no longer.[18]

The hatred burned so hot that even the mayor joined the mob against Smith.

Though rarely lethal, tarring and feathering was sometimes merely the humiliating first course. A Charleston, South Carolina,

Raise Your Bowl

SURE, POUNDING BOOZY tropical drinks from a shared bowl sounds like a sweaty headache, but that's how the Founding Fathers rolled. Before whiskey took over the scene in the nineteenth century, rum was the real spirit of '76. Imported from the Caribbean or distilled in America from Caribbean molasses, taverns mixed rum, sugar, water, and chopped fruit into large punch bowls, and patrons dipped their own personal drinking vessel into it. George Washington's unsurprisingly tough punch bowl (completely covered with freemason symbols) is on display at the Mount Vernon Museum.

mob tarred and feathered the loyalist Christian minister John Roberts, then hanged him from a hastily built gallows before torching both his body and the gibbet.[19] According to one estimate, by March 1770, colonists had tarred and feathered at least thirteen individuals—eight in Massachusetts, two in New York, one in Virginia, one in Pennsylvania, and one in Connecticut—all of them either customs officials or suspected informants.[20]

As brutal as the mob could be, many historians consider America's Revolutionary mob relatively disciplined. According to historian Lloyd Rudolph, "In America, the mob stopped when it had attained what it set out to do" and was "never swept into an irrational destruction of lives and property" later seen in Revolutionary France.[21] Indeed, mob violence essentially stopped whenever Parliament repealed the act under protest. This conservatism likely had several causes. First, the relative social equality enjoyed by eighteenth-century white Americans enabled political and economic interests to partially transcend class distinctions. Second, unlike their French counterparts, American Revolutionaries weren't surrounded by hostile great powers and were thus spared the hysteria that fueled the French Terror. In short, rich, poor, and working-class Americans were more likely to indentify with one another. The result was that the American Revolution never devoured its own children.

Meanwhile in Boston, opposition to the Stamp Act unified the mob under a cabal of elite tradesmen known as the Loyal Nine. Having met in secret, little is known of the group—except for the crucial fact that in August 1765, they took for themselves the name given by Colonel Barré: Sons of Liberty. Under the leadership of Samuel Adams, John Hancock, and Joseph Warren, the Sons soon began holding their meetings in the basement of Boston's Green Dragon Tavern on Union Street, among the most fabled Revolutionary taverns of them all. The tavern was owned by the St. Andrew's Lodge of Freemasons and soon became the headquarters of several secret societies. Like many other taverns from the era, the name is believed to have derived from both a famous London tavern and British heraldry, in this case the earls of Pembroke and the arms of the House of Tudor.[22] Less romantic theories suggest the name was the inevitable result of a copper dragon

Under the leadership of Samuel Adams, John Hancock, and Joseph Warren, the Sons soon began holding their meetings in the basement of Boston's Green Dragon Tavern on Union Street, among the most fabled Revolutionary taverns of them all.

OPPOSITE *"A New method of Macarony making as practised at Boston," by an unknown artist, London, 1774, shows two American revolutionaries tarring and feathering the tax collector.*

45
45

City Tavern

EST. 1773, REBUILT 1976 ✱ TODAY OPERATES AS A TAPROOM AND RESTAURANT ✱ PHILADELPHIA, PENNSYLVANIA

As home to America's first hospital, public library, university, philosophical society, and stock exchange, the Philadelphia of Benjamin Franklin was the commercial and intellectual capital of the American colonies. These strengths, plus the city's good fortune of being located midway between Boston and Williamsburg, also made Philadelphia the political center of the American Revolution. Of the many ingredients that went into creating the Philadelphia Renaissance of 1776, one of the most important was the opening of the City Tavern.

Many of America's earliest taverns were little more than shambled dens in cramped homes. However, by 1773 Philadelphia's growing wealth and prestige demanded accommodations more becoming of the city's financial power, and so the local business elite pooled resources to build what John Adams would marvel as "the most genteel tavern in America."

ABOVE *Interior detail of Philadelphia's City Tavern.*

Investors took great care to market the City Tavern as the place for knowledge, business, and entertainment. Proprietor Daniel Smith took out advertisements that described the tavern as having been built "at very great expense . . . perfectly in the style of a London tavern" and was "properly supplied with English and American papers and magazines." Following independence, the tavern was billed as "the most convenient and elegant structure of its Kind in America," offering cuisine "served up in a stile, if not superior, at least equal, to any in the United States of America."

Located near Independence Hall, the meeting place of the Continental Congress, the City Tavern probably hosted more founding fathers than any other tavern at the time. Members of Congress wrote about the tavern's role in their everyday work life, such as one account from Congressman Samuel Read in a letter to his wife: "We sit in Congress generally till half-past three o'clock, and once till five o'clock, and then I dine at City Tavern, where a few of us have established a table for each day in the week, save Saturday, when there is a general dinner."

In addition to business lunches and working dinners, the City Tavern hosted some of the most extraordinary banquets of the era. Philadelphia's elite held a celebratory bash for five hundred guests at the City Tavern at the close of the First Continental Congress in October 1774, with toasts "accompanied by music and great guns." During the British occupation of Philadelphia between fall 1777 and June 1778, control of the tavern fell into the hands of British colonels, who expanded its use to include gambling (British troops also boorishly renamed the nearby Indian King Tavern the British Tavern).

The real party, however, was held in 1787. The Constitutional Convention had just come to a close, and Philadelphia wouldn't let Washington return to Mount Vernon without bidding him a proper farewell. On September 14, the city sent the Father of the Nation home in style. In a celebration sponsored by the First Troop Philadelphia City Cavalry, Washington and fifty-four other gentlemen consumed seven bowls of rum punch, eight bottles of cider, thirty-four bottles of beer, fifty-four bottles of madeira, and sixty bottles of French bordeaux. In today's dollars, the total amount is estimated to have run $15,400.

Though impressive for its time, the City Tavern was still a glorified tavern and was eventually eclipsed by the spacious accommodations and complete services offered by nineteenth-century hotels. Despite its rich history, the tavern fell into disrepair and eventually burned to the ground in 1854. In 1973, the National Parks Service commissioned an exact replica of the City Tavern to be built near Independence Hall in time to celebrate America's bicentennial. Today, the City Tavern specializes in colonial-inspired drinking and dining and is routinely ranked as one of Philadelphia's must-see restaurants.

SOURCES

John W. Jackson, *With the British Army in Philadelphia* (San Rafael, CA: Presidio Press, 1979), 211–14.

Gordon Lloyd, "The Constitutional Convention," Teaching American History.org.

Kym Rice, *Early American Taverns: For the Entertainment of Friends and Strangers* (Chicago: Regnery Gateway, *1983*, 38, 78, 79, 93.

John F. Watson, *The Annals of Philadelphia* (Philadelphia: J. M. Stoddart & Co., 1881), 401.

sign having turned green by the weather.[23] For its role in housing the Sons of Liberty and the planning of the Boston Tea Party, Daniel Webster later christened the Green Dragon the "Headquarters of the Revolution."[24] The original tavern was destroyed in 1854, though another tavern calling itself the Green Dragon exists today on Marshall Street in Boston's North End.

ABOVE *"Green Dragon Tavern: Where we met to Plan the Consignment of a few Shiploads of Tea, Dec 16, 1773," by John Johnston, Boston, 1773. The Green Dragon Tavern served as an important meeting place for those planning the Boston Tea Party.*

Boston wasn't alone in its opposition to the Stamp Act. On Halloween day 1765, New York merchants organized an unprecedented economic boycott of all trade with Great Britain "unless the Stamp Act shall be repealed."[25] In the Virginia House of Burgesses, Patrick Henry took the floor and introduced the Stamp Act Resolves as students from the College of William and Mary, including the twenty-two-year-old Thomas Jefferson, gathered around the lobby door to listen to the debates.[26] Henry's resolutions formed the foundation of America's official response and contained two critical points: that Americans were "entitled to all Liberties, Privileges and Immunities" enjoyed by English citizens and that the right to tax the colonies derived only from the consent of the colonists themselves (helpfully pointing out that this right had "never been forfeited" to either the Parliament or the king).[27] Jefferson later recalled Patrick Henry's Stamp Act Resolves as "the dawn of the revolution."[28]

Not content with resolutions from the individual colonies, Massachusetts called for a Stamp Act Congress to determine a united response. On October 19, 1765, this assembly, which gathered in New York City between October 7 and 25, adopted resolutions largely influenced by Henry's Virginia Resolves. To that already seditious list, the Congress added this provocative trinity:

> III. That it is inseparably essential to the freedom of a people, and the undoubted right of Englishmen, that no taxes be imposed on them, but with their own consent, given personally, or by their representatives.
>
> IV. That the people of these colonies are not, and from their local circumstances cannot be, represented in the House of Commons in Great-Britain.
>
> V. That the only representatives of the people of these colonies, are persons chosen therein by themselves, and that no taxes ever have been, or can be constitutionally imposed on them, but by their respective legislatures.[29]

"They are of various Characters and opinions, but it's to be feared in general, that the Spirit of Democracy, is strong among them."

— British General Thomas Gage

The impudence! To this de facto declaration of independence, Britain was boxed in, and the path to peaceful resolution greatly narrowed. British Secretary of State Henry Conway warned, "If we enforce the Stamp Act . . . we shall have a war in America."[30] After hosting the Massachusetts delegation to the Stamp Act Congress for dinner, British General Thomas Gage wrote, "They are of various Characters and opinions, but it's to be feared in general, that the Spirit of Democracy, is strong among them."

The Stamp Act affair proved disastrous for British credibility among American colonists. By the time the act was to take effect, every last stamp distributor had resigned his post under pressure from

Colonial Cocktails

SYLLABUB

"IT IS USUAL AT A LARGE ENTERTAINMENT," wrote Abigail Adams from London in 1785, "to bring the solid food in the first course. The second consists of lighter diet, kickshaws, trifles, whip syllabub." The syllabub is used to top the second course, and is a summery and sweet white wine concoction.

INGREDIENTS

5 oz. floral white wine (I use Viognier)

2 oz. heavy whipping cream

1 tsp. maple syrup

¼ tsp. lemon juice

2 egg whites

½ tsp. sugar

Shaved nutmeg

DIRECTIONS

Combine wine, cream, syrup, and lemon juice into mixing glass. Stir and pour into a rocks glass.

In a separate bowl, combine the two egg whites with a pinch of sugar and beat until frothy.

Spoon froth over cocktail, and garnish with shaved nutmeg.

SOURCES

"Abigail Adams to Lucy Cranch, 27 August 1785," in *The Adams Papers, Adams Family Correspondence,* vol. 6: *December 1784–December 1785*, ed. Richard Alan Ryerson (Cambridge, MA: Harvard University Press, 1993), 312–14.

Corin Hirsch, "Five Colonial-Era Drinks You Should Know," *Serious Eats*, August 9, 2014.

a mob. Stunned, Parliament voted to repeal. However, Britain was determined to shift *some* tax burden onto the colonists and called on America's representative in London, Benjamin Franklin, to explain his countrymen's position on taxes and provide advice on how a tax acceptable to the colonies could be constructed. To explain colonial resistance to the Stamp Act, Franklin concocted an argument that tried to distinguish between internal and external taxation. Franklin reasoned that external taxes (on imported goods) were calculated into an item's retail price and therefore easier to disguise, whereas internal taxes (collected at the point of sale) were provocative and humiliating.[31] Townshend called Franklin's argument "perfect nonsense." In the end, however, he was willing to indulge Americans' irrational preference

BELOW *Proof sheet of one-penny stamps, 1765.*

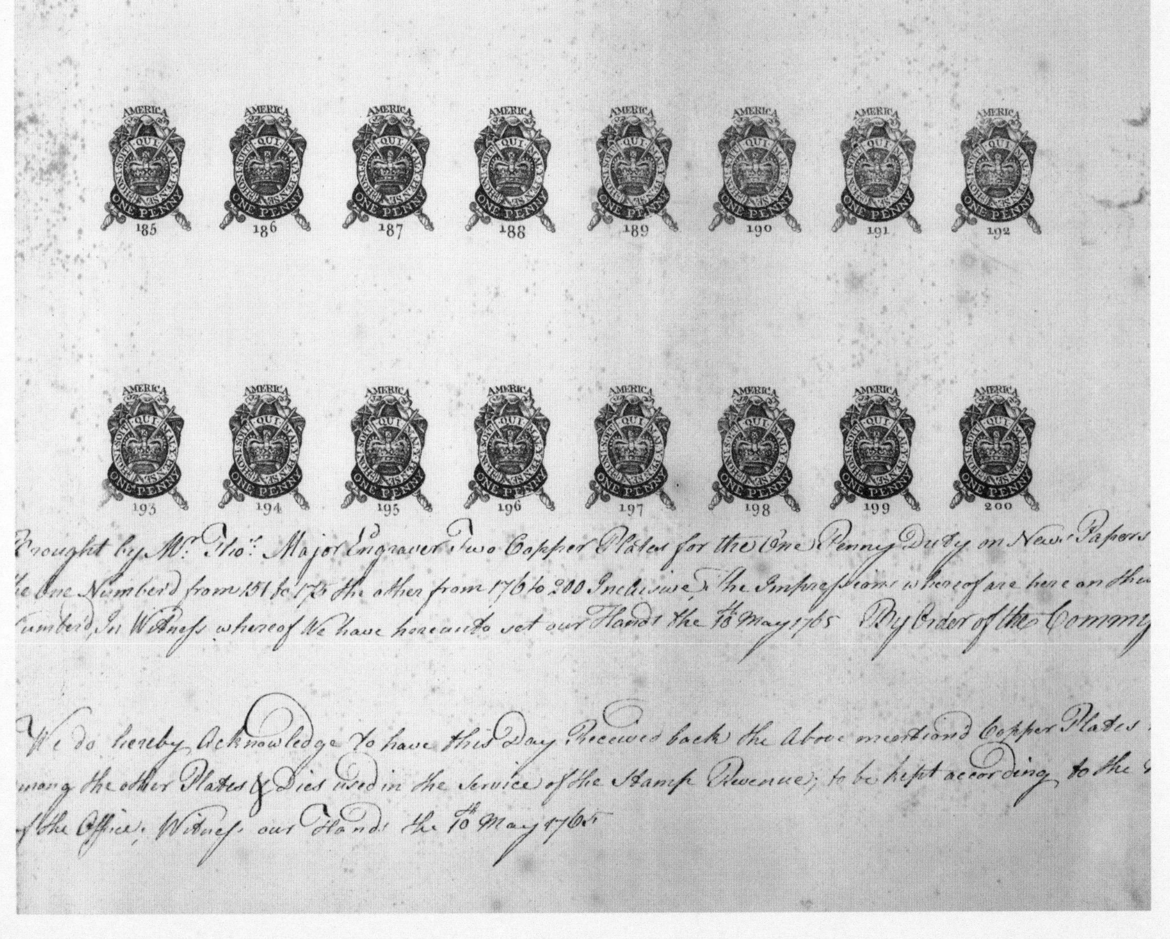
rought by Mr. Thos. Major Engraver two Copper Plates for the One Penny Duty on News Papers
e One Numberd from 151 to 175 the other from 176 to 200 Inclusive, the Impressions whereof are here on the
umberd, In Witness whereof We have hereunto set our Hands the 10th May 1765 By Order of the Commi

We do hereby Acknowledge to have this Day Received back the Above mentiond Copper Plates
mong the other Plates & Dies used in the Service of the Stamp Revenue; to be kept according to the
f the Office; Witness our Hands the 10th May 1765

Warren Tavern

EST. 1780 ✱ TODAY OPERATES AS A RESTAURANT AND BAR ✱ FREQUENTED BY GEORGE WASHINGTON AND PAUL REVERE ✱ CHARLESTOWN, MASSACHUSETTS

In the days following the Battles of Lexington and Concord, as many as twenty thousand militiamen from across New England poured into Massachusetts to keep the British trapped in Boston. Part of the American strategy was to secure the highest ground overlooking Boston Harbor: Breed's Hill and Bunker Hill above Charlestown. On June 17, 1775, British troops crossed the Charles River from Boston to Charlestown to attack the American-held high ground, resulting in the Battle of Bunker Hill. British forces under William Howe achieved a pyrrhic victory, suffering more than a thousand casualties—more than twice that of the Americans. The Americans, however, lost both General Joseph Warren and the city of Charlestown, which the British torched. In 1780, five years after Charlestown was destroyed, residents there opened a new tavern in Warren's honor.

A native of Massachusetts, the Harvard-educated physician Joseph Warren joined Boston's St. Andrews Lodge of Freemasons in 1761, which met at the Green Dragon Tavern. Warren eventually became the lodge's grandmaster, enmeshing himself with such radicals as John Hancock, Sam Adams, and Paul Revere. Using the pseudonym "A True Patriot," Warren's ferocious pen, combined with his stirring oratory, soon established him as one of the brightest leaders of the American cause. It was Warren's speech during the 1775 anniversary commemoration of the Boston Massacre that provoked British regulars. In a clear case of political retaliation, outraged British soldiers arrested "A simple Country man" for attempting to conduct illegal trade with a British soldier, then had him tarred, feathered, and paraded through town with the words "AMERICAN liberty, or a specimen of democracy" hung from a sign around his neck, further outraging Bostonians and strengthening their opinion against the British.

At this point in the crisis with Britain, Warren's blend of political and military leadership made him perhaps the best-known patriot in the country. He drafted the Suffolk Resolves, the official position adopted by the Continental Congress in response to Parliament's Coercive Acts. As the de facto head of the Boston insurgency, Warren sent Paul Revere on his famous midnight ride to Lexington and, unlike other political leaders, picked up his musket and joined the fighting. In Lexington and Concord, he fought alongside militia in attacking the British flank and was nearly shot dead by a British musket ball, which knocked a hairpin from

"Don't shoot until you see the whites of their eyes."

—GENERAL ISRAEL PUTNAM OR COLONEL WILLIAM PRESCOTT, 1775

his wig. Although named a general by the Massachusetts Provincial Assembly, Warren volunteered to fight alongside regular infantrymen on the front lines of Bunker Hill, where he was killed instantly by a bullet through the head.

The Warren Tavern is today believed to be both the oldest tavern in Massachusetts and the oldest surviving structure in Charlestown. It was originally constructed as a tavern and has served at times as a men's club, Masonic lodge, and other businesses. The building had fallen into disrepair by the 1970s, when records from the local Masonic lodge proved George Washington and Paul Revere had dined at the tavern making it a historic landmark. The tavern was acquired by new owners, and an extensive restoration effort was soon under way. Today, the Warren Tavern's full bar and classic pub fare have cultivated a strong local niche, while its low-beamed ceilings and uneven original floorboards, where Washington once stood, captivate history buffs.

ABOVE *The Warren Tavern fell into extreme disrepair until documents associating the tavern with Washington sparked its restoration in the 1970s.*

SOURCES

Samuel Adams, "Letter to a Southern Friend," in *The Writings of Samuel Adams*, ed. Alonzo Cushing, vol. 3 (New York: Putnam, 1907), 200.

George Bancroft, *History of the United States from the Discovery of the American Continent* (Boston: Little, Brown, 1858), 256.

by limiting whatever taxes came next to those "external" taxes based on the fact that Franklin assured Parliament his American brethren would pay these without issue. Parliament followed suit by passing the Townshend Acts in 1767, which established a series of trade regulations and external taxes on the colonies, just as Franklin recommended.

Franklin's bad advice ultimately led to another round of outrage and escalation. When the colonies learned of the Townshend Acts, they erupted again. In addition to the standard protest on taxed goods (in this case, imported glass, lead, paint, and tea), the Townshend Acts granted the British East India Company a monopoly of the tea trade. Here Britain made another fatal error: rather than co-opt America's powerful smugglers, the Townshend Acts gave trade preference to America's loyalist merchants. Worst of all, the acts attacked colonial self-government by requiring civil servants to be paid by the revenues from the new taxes rather than colonial legislatures (thus making them accountable to Britain). Finally, the Townshend Acts were passed with a concurrent lowering of British taxes, making the appearance of a burden shift unmistakable. Far from the acceptable measures Franklin had promised, the Townshend Acts were a near-perfect recipe for offending the American colonies even more. That the taxes were to be levied at the Custom House rather than at the point of sale mattered to almost nobody.

Following the Townshend Act crackdown, collections officer Joseph Harrison and his men boarded John Hancock's sloop *Liberty* looking for contraband. They found more than two hundred barrels of undeclared oil and tar, which Hancock's attorney, John Adams, claimed were merely being stored on the ship because the local warehouses were full. Harrison anticipated mob violence and had Hancock's ship towed into the harbor and beyond the grasp of the Sons of Liberty pending investigation. Without Hancock's ship to liberate, the mob instead beat Harrison and his men, attacked his home, and dragged his pleasure boat (which he neglected to tow into harbor) onto the Boston Common and set it on fire.[32]

Southern opposition to the Townshend Acts was led from the Raleigh Tavern in Williamsburg, Virginia, then one of the best-known taverns in the colonies. The Raleigh was built around 1717 by

Dr. Archibald Blair, brother of the Reverend James Blair, founding commissary of the College of William and Mary (Blair's storehouse and apothecary still stands in Colonial Williamsburg).[33, 34] Blair rented the Raleigh to a succession of tavern keepers, eventually settling on the somewhat locally famous Harry Wetherburn. A Coochland County deed from the era states that Thomas Jefferson's father, Peter Jefferson, purchased 200 acres for the bargain price of Wetherburn's "biggest bowl" of punch.[35] The tavern was named for Sir Walter Raleigh, who had attempted England's first permanent settlement of Virginia—the doomed Roanoke colony—and whose leaden bust stood above the doorway.[36] As the main civic, social, and entertainment venue of Williamsburg, the Raleigh acted as a café, restaurant, hostel, dance hall, and bar. Much of the Raleigh's action occurred in the famed Apollo Room, over whose mantle were the words, painted in gilt, "Hilaritas Sapientiae et Bonae Vitae Proles (Jollity, the offspring of wisdom and good living).[37]

On May 2, 1769, Virginia's royal governor, Norborne Botetourt, dissolved the House of Burgesses for adopting resolutions in opposition to the Townshend Acts. Undeterred, the delegates, included among them George Washington and Thomas Jefferson, retired to the Apollo

Washington's Bitches

GEORGE WASHINGTON loved dogs, and it's believed that he owned at least one dog in each of the seven groups of breeds today recognized by the American Kennel Society. An avid foxhunter, Washington is even credited with creating his own breed, the American foxhound, by crossing his own American hounds with French staghounds gifted to him by the marquis de Lafayette. Of these hounds, three were named after common drinking expressions: Tipsey, Tippler, and Drunkard. But did these expressions mean the same thing then as today? Better consult Ben Franklin's Drinkers Dictionary (page 172).

LEFT *"Brissots Interview with Gen. Washington," engraving by Owens after Kirk, 1797.*

SOURCE
Mary Thompson, "George Washington and Animals, Domestic and Exotic," December 5, 2012.

Griswold Inn

EST. 1776 ✵ TODAY OPERATES AS AN INN, RESTAURANT, BAR, AND WINE BAR ✵ ESSEX, CONNECTICUT

On January 31, 1776, the Connecticut General Assembly contracted Uriah Hayden of Saybrook (today's Essex), Connecticut, to build what would become one of largest American warships of the Revolution, the *Oliver Cromwell*. The massive construction project created an influx of new tradesmen and carpenters into the shipbuilding town. For Sala Griswold, who had recently opened a tavern near the docks, business was booming. Thus was born the Griswold Inn, one of—if not *the*—oldest continuously operating inn in the United States.

"The Gris," as it's affectionately known by local residents, is actually several colonial-era buildings quilted together over the centuries. The main structure from 1776 is thought to be the first three-story frame structure built in Connecticut, and today it provides space for the hotel lobby and some of the dining rooms. The largest dining area is the Covered Bridge Dining Room, so named because it's an actual covered bridge brought in from New Hampshire in the 1800s. The heart of the Gris, both architecturally and in spirit, is undeniably its taproom, whose story begins even earlier. The taproom was built in 1738 as Connecticut's first schoolhouse and in 1801 was rolled down Main Street by a team of oxen and attached to the main structure. The taproom's well-preserved cylindrical ceiling is coated in its original clamshell-horsehair plaster. In fact, the Griswold's overall excellent condition and continuous operation can be at least partially attributed to the fact that it has changed ownership only five times in its 240-year history.

The maritime history, creaky floorboards, and horsehair-clamshell ceiling would be enough to establish any tavern's historical credentials. But the Gris goes beyond that in several noteworthy ways. First, it boasts a museum-scale collection of maritime artwork that completely covers the Covered Bridge Dining Room, ceiling and all. Second, the Gris hosts an impressive collection of firearms from the fifteenth through eighteenth centuries, including muskets from the Revolutionary era, which have fallen into the Gris's hands over the years. It's here where the history housed in the Gris provokes a chill. In a stroke of extraordinarily good fortune, one of the Griswold's Revolutionary muskets contained a secret note folded into the barrel. Unfurled, it reads:

"My dear son Jared, I send you this my gun."

—JOHN FRANCIS PUTNAM, JULY 7, 1776

My dear son Jared,
I send you this my gun,
Do not handle it in fun,
But with it make ye British run,
Join ye ranks of ye Washington,
And when our independence is won,
We will take a drink of good old rum.
—John Francis Putnam, July 7, 1776

A father is thus handing his weapon to his son, two days after the Declaration of Independence was adopted, to fight for American liberty with the promise of a future victory toast. The note is on display in the Gris's dining room, along with a £45 purchase order signed by Governor Trumbull for guns to arm the *Oliver Cromwell*.

Essex's importance as a shipbuilding town continued even after the Revolution, providing the Griswold with yet another brush with history. During the War of 1812, British Captain Richard Coote of the HMS *Borer* sailed into Essex unopposed, torched nearly every ship in the harbor, and allegedly marched into the Griswold and hauled off its stock of rum. The raid on Essex was one of the worst economic disasters suffered by the United States during the war, leading to the financial ruin of several of Essex's leading shipbuilding families.

The Gris served as a temperance hotel during the late 1800s, though liquor eventually came back. Today the Gris is often packed with locals, and the addition of a new wine bar stocked with choice varietals from both the New and Old Worlds has renewed the inn's appeal.

ABOVE *The Gris keeps a holiday tree in the taproom year round.*

SOURCE

Jerry Roberts, "The British Raid on Essex," ConnecticutHistory.org, retrieved October 22, 2015 from http://connecticuthistory.org/the-british-raid-on-essex/.

Green Dragon

EST. 1701, DESTROYED 1828 ✱ BOSTON, MASSACHUSETTS

Of all the taverns lost to history, perhaps none is more legendary than Boston's Green Dragon Tavern. Built around 1701, the Dragon was purchased by St. Andrew's Lodge of Freemasons in 1764. A patron in the Green Dragon's taproom might have bumped into the maltster Samuel Adams, the smuggler John Hancock, or the physician and orator Joseph Warren. The Green Dragon was the birthplace of the Sons of Liberty and both the launching point and after-party for the Boston Tea Party, for which Daniel Webster granted the Dragon the distinguished title of unofficial "Headquarters of the Revolution."

Colonial period sketch of the Green Dragon.

The origins of the tavern's colorful name is a something of a debate, with the standards for the earl of Pembroke, West Saxons, and the Tudors all given as potential inspirations. A more pragmatic explanation credits the copper dragon, corroded and green, that hung above the door. As recounted by Smith, a contemporary of the tavern once wrote of the "fabled dragon in hammered metal above the door. . . . Crouched on its iron crane, its fearful red tongue licking the air before and its curled tail lashing out behind, the dragon sign was the wonder of the boys of the neighborhood." The original Green Dragon Tavern was located on Union Street west of Hanover Street in Boston's North End until its demolition in 1828. Today, a newer tavern of the same name is located at 11 Marshall Street, about one block from the original location.

"Headquarters of the Revolution."

—DANIEL WEBSTER

After dumping British tea into Boston harbor, American patriots reassembled at the Green Dragon Tavern where they toasted victory and sang the Rally Mohawks song:

Rally, Mohawks—bring out your axes!
And tell King George we'll pay
no taxes on his foreign tea!
His threats are vain—and vain to think
To force our girls and wives to drink
His vile Bohea!
Then rally boys, and hasten on
To meet our Chiefs at the Green Dragon.
Our Warren's there, and bold Revere,
With hands to do and words to cheer
For Liberty and Laws!
Our country's Braves and firm defenders
Shall ne'er be left by true North-Enders,
Fighting Freedom's cause!
Then rally boys and hasten on
to meet our Chiefs at the Green Dragon.

room and formed a boycott on all trade with Great Britain until the acts were repealed.[38] These "nonimportation agreements" (the word *boycott* hadn't yet been coined), were replicated in other major American cities and killed two objectives with one stone: exerting economic pressure on Britain and spurring the development of American industry.

Faced with increasing mob violence and lacking any better ideas, British Lord Hillsborough, colonial secretary of state, decided to send in the troops. On October 1, 1768, four thousand British regulars sailed into Boston Harbor to restore order. As is almost always the case, the presence of a foreign military was more provocative than pacifying. Bostonians resented and harassed the occupiers, and the troops came to hate the people they were supposed to protect. The situation was primed to explode.

After eighteen months of mutual harassment, the wheels finally came off. On the morning of March 5, 1770, the front page of the *Boston Gazette* led with a searing polemic against Lord Hillsborough. Not bothering to contain its sarcasm, the author, writing under the pen name Americanus, asked

> whether your Lordship ever seriously intend that a Revenue should be *really* collected in America? I would fain have charity enough to think, you did not; or you could never has selected such a swarm of despicable, abject, miserable, ignorant, low *rabble* to execute this your Lordship's very *arduous* and *novel* undertaking![39]

Newspapers and pamphlets were often read aloud in taverns, providing both news and entertainment to the patrons. It is suspected by some that Crispus Attucks was in such a tavern the morning of March 5, 1770, and could have overheard this account and other anti-British stories (the paper also included a story questioning the legality of the *Liberty* affair).[40] What is known for certain is that Attucks, a free sailor of mixed African and Wampanoag descent, joined a crowd of several dozen men and boys outside the Royal Exchange Tavern[41] on King Street later that night. From there they heard the apprentice Edward Gerrish hurl an insult at British Private Hugh White, who was standing sentry at the Custom House. In response, White delivered a blow to the boy's head with the butt of his musket. Soon after, White

FOLLOWING PAGE
"The bloody massacre perpetrated in King Street Boston on March 5th 1770 by a party of the 29th Regt," by Paul Revere, Boston, 1770. Print shows British troops firing on a group of citizens on a street in Boston, Massachusetts, in what came to be known as the Boston Massacre.

found himself confronted by an angry mob several dozen strong. First came snowballs, then rocks, sticks, oyster shells, and clubs. White called for reinforcements.

Standing in front of his men, Captain Thomas Preston ordered the crowd, now numbering in the hundreds, to disperse. The order

Colonial Inn

BUILT 1716, EST. 1889 ✱ TODAY OPERATES AS AN INN, RESTAURANT, AND TAPROOM ✱ CONCORD, MASSACHUSETTS

Interior detail of one of the Colonial Inn's several taprooms.

While the Colonial Inn saw some of the most gruesome action of the Revolutionary War, it was not a tavern at that time. On the morning of April 19, 1775, British troops arrived in Concord following an overnight march from Boston and began searching the town for suspected militia supplies. Concord's local physician, Dr. Timothy Minot Jr., lived and practiced medicine at his home on Monument Street about a half-mile from North Bridge. As British soldiers set to torch whatever military supplies they could find, Massachusetts militiamen from the surrounding area began convening opposite the bridge, which was under British guard. As the ranks of militiamen swelled to over four hundred, they confronted the ninety or so British regulars at North Bridge with colonial Major John Buttrick's famous line, "Fire, for God's sake, fellow soldiers, fire!" The Massachusetts militia sent the British regulars back to Boston and their own wounded to Dr. Minot, whose home became a battlefield hospital. One of his bedrooms, today room 24 in the Colonial Inn, was used as an operating room, and room 27 served as the morgue. Minot's house and two adjacent buildings were converted to an inn in 1889, and today the inn provides colonial era-inspired dining, lodging, and two distinct taprooms.

was ignored. The shouting mob warned Preston that if his men fired into the crowd, he'd pay for it with his life. Inevitably, Private Hugh Montgomery was struck by a piece of ice and in his fall discharged his musket, provoking several other soldiers to fire into the crowd in confusion. Attucks and two other men were killed instantly, two others would later die of their wounds, and the panicked crowd fled in horror.[42] Paul Revere's engraving of the Boston Massacre, included in the next issue of the *Gazette*, was reprinted throughout the colonies, provoking yet more outrage. Faced with declining trade, rampant smuggling, low revenues, and now blood, Parliament decided the Townshend Acts, like the Molasses Act and Stamp Act before it, were unenforceable and not worth the expense. Parliament largely repealed the acts on April 12, 1770, saving face by leaving intact the tax on imported tea.

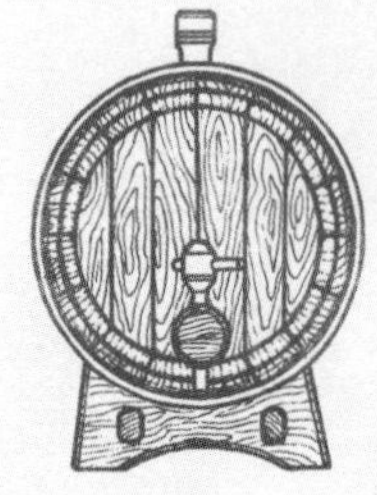

Lindsey hurriedly sailed into Pawtuxet and alerted the patrons of Sabin's Tavern of the Gaspee's *vulnerable position.*

Tensions again rose during the summer of 1772. The Crown considered Rhode Island, along with Massachusetts and Connecticut, to be centers of American smuggling and therefore targets for customs enforcement. British Lieutenant William Dudingston of the HMS *Gaspee* was patrolling Narragansett Bay on June 9. Dudingston's hall-monitor mentality (he stopped and held all vessels indiscriminately, even when loaded with perishable goods) made him many enemies, and on that morning Captain Benjamin Lindsey of the *Hannah* decided to flee Dudingston rather than submit to a lengthy inspection. Dudingston gave chase and carelessly ran the *Gaspee* aground in shallow water. Lindsey hurriedly sailed into Pawtuxet and alerted the patrons of Sabin's Tavern of the *Gaspee*'s vulnerable position. Sniffing revenge, a crew led by tavern keeper Joseph Bucklin sailed out to the *Gaspee*, shot Dudingston, and burned the ship where it stood.[43]

By spring 1773, Parliament was claiming the right to expatriate both British soldiers and American civilians accused of crimes on American soil to Great Britain to stand trial. This proved too much for Jefferson, who was joined by Patrick Henry and several others for a secret meeting at the Raleigh Tavern to discuss Virginia's response. It was at the Raleigh Tavern where the Virginia patriots reached two critical resolutions: an understanding that opposition to British effrontery was common cause to all colonies and that the colonial legislatures should establish a formal line of communication with one another. Jefferson himself wrote the resolutions, which were promptly passed by the House of Burgesses, which was in turn promptly dissolved by Royal Governor Dunmore. As Jefferson recalled in his autobiography, "But the committee met the next day, prepared a circular letter to the Speakers of the other colonies, inclosing to each a copy of the resolutions and . . . forward[ed] them by express" to the other colonial legislatures.[44] Thus were born the Committees of Correspondence: groups of selectmen from each colonial legislature tasked with maintaining open lines of communication between the colonies so that they could coordinate action against the British. So important were the Committees of Correspondence that Jefferson and several founders would later bicker over who had the idea first.[45]

BELOW *Sketch of Raleigh Tavern.*

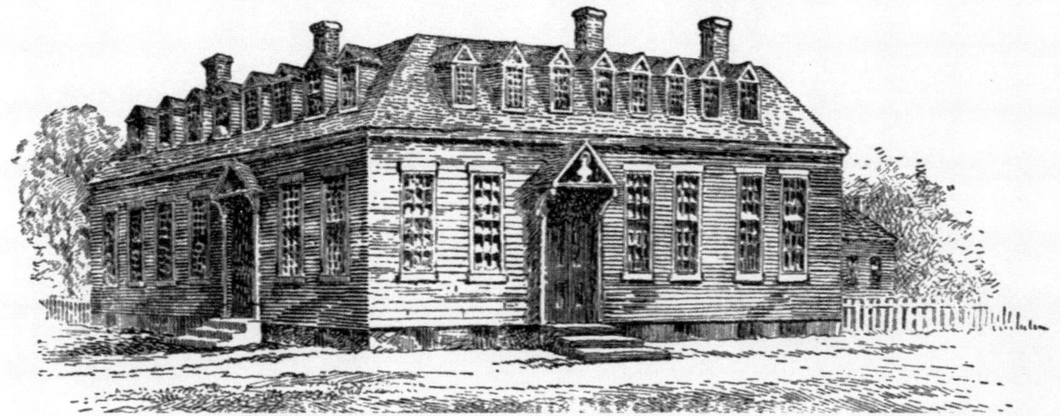

LAST CALL

Beginning with the enforcement of the 1764 Sugar Act, a cycle of taxation, protest, and repeal radicalized tavern politics and critically undermined British-American relations. The Townshend Acts further inflamed American opinion, leading the colonial legislatures to consider a united front in negotiations with Great Britain. The Boston Massacre in 1770 emboldened radicals, and local chapters of the Sons of Liberty began organizing in taverns throughout the country. Parliament repealed each of the Townshend taxes save for those on tea, and in doing so unwittingly set into motion the next round of escalation, and ultimately, war.

CHAPTER 3

THE DIE IS CAST

By 1773, American and British positions on the issue of taxation had become irreconcilable. After yielding to American opposition to most of the Stamp and Townshend duties, Parliament decided to hold the line on the tea tax. Overnight, tea became recognized as the most potent symbol of British oppression, leading to the Boston Tea Party in May and Britain's heavy-handed response. With Britain and America suddenly on the path to war, taverns became recruiting stations, battle headquarters, and critical hubs for information and propaganda. When war finally broke out, several tavern keepers rose to prominence as military leaders in their own right, and financial and economic instability after the war ensured that taverns continued to play an outsized role in American politics.

Unable to sufficiently tax the American colonies, Britain's ongoing debt crisis demanded resolution. Making matters worse, one of Britain's largest economic institutions, the East India Company, was suddenly facing bankruptcy. Business had been wracked by a famine in India and the ongoing smuggling of cheap Dutch tea into the American colonies. On May 10, 1773, Parliament intervened with a plan they believed would benefit everybody. By deflating the price of East India Tea as much as possible, Parliament could provide American consumers with cheap tea and enable the East India Company to cash out its surplus. Presented with what they considered an obvious solution, Parliament passed the Tea Act on May 10, 1773.

LEFT *"The repeal, or the funeral procession of Miss Americ-Stamp," by an unknown artist, England, c. 1766. Engraving shows a group of men in a mock funeral procession on the banks of the Thames River lamenting the death of the Stamp Act.*

When news of the Tea Act reached America that September, it provoked an entirely different interpretation. Patriots argued that Parliament was using its power of monopoly to undercut American merchants and use the temporarily low tea prices to trick colonists into tacitly legitimizing the hated tea tax. The tax on tea, now the only duty left from the otherwise repealed Townshend Acts, became the focus of American political dissent and the emblem of the most famous protest in American history.

Unaware of the unrest in the American colonies, seven ships left England for Boston, New York, Charleston, and Philadelphia[1]

BELOW *"A view of Charles-Town, the capital of South Carolina," by Thoman Leitch, London, 1776. Print shows a distant view of Charleston, South Carolina, with a British ship in the foreground.*

between October and November 1773, carrying 600,000 pounds of cheap East India Company Tea. On October 16, and with the tea well on its way, an estimated eight thousand people, the largest crowd ever assembled in the American colonies at that point, gathered in the Philadelphia State House yard to determine that city's response. The crowd resolved the tea should be turned back and formed a "Committee for Tarring and Feathering," complete with a chairman, and issued a letter to Captain Ayres of the tea-bearing ship *Polly* describing the fate awaiting him should he land. The letter began, "As you are perhaps a Stranger to these parts we have concluded to advise you of the present Situation of Affairs in Philadelphia." It went on to inform the captain that his ship had been "sent out on a diabolical Service" and was full of "combustible Matter," and that unless he wanted to see his ship "set afire, a Halter around your neck—ten gallons of liquid Tar decanted on your head—with Feathers of a dozen wild Geese laid over," he'd better turn around—fast.[2] Ayres heeded the advice and returned for England, as did the captain of the ship *Nancy* in New York. The Charleston Sons of Liberty seized the tea aboard the *London* and let it rot in the Exchange Building's basement.

ABOVE *"The alternative of Williams-burg," by Philip Dawe, c. 1775, shows a Virginian loyalist being forced to sign a document, possibly issued by the Williamsburg Convention, by a club-wielding mob.*

Inspired by Philadelphia and anxiously awaiting the arrival of tea ships in their own harbor, the Boston Sons of Liberty formed their own Committee for Tarring and Feathering, notifying residents:

> You may depend, that those odious Miscreants and detestable Tools to Ministry and Governor, the TEA CONSIGNEES, (those Traitors to their Country, Butchers, who have done, and are doing every Thing to Murder and destroy all that shall stand in the Way of their private Interest,) are determined to come and reside again in the Town of Boston. I therefore give you this early Notice, that you may hold yourselves in Readiness, on the shortest Notice, to give them such a Reception, as such vile Ingrates deserve.[3]

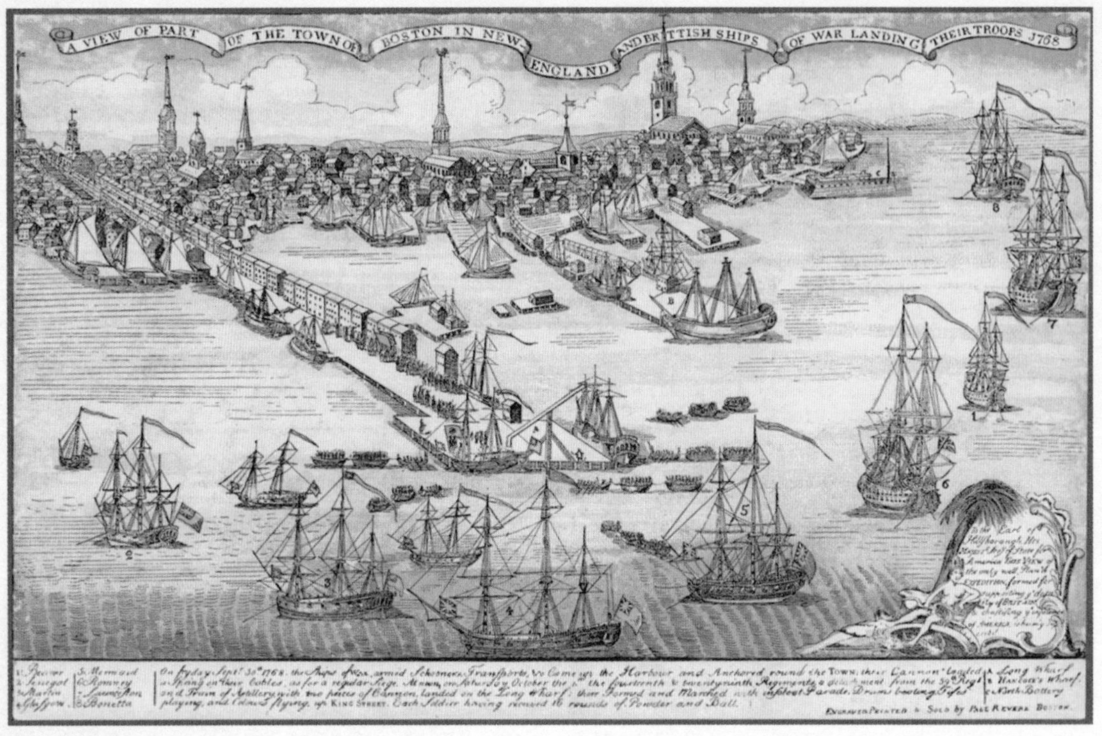

BOSTON TEA PARTY

Unlike Philadelphia, Boston was under the occupation of thousands of British regulars. On November 28 the ship *Dartmouth* arrived in Boston, followed shortly after by the *Eleanor* and the *Beaver*, loaded down with 342 chests of tea. Although the Sons of Liberty were unable to prevent the ships from docking, they could prevent the tea from being unloaded. British law required that customs duties be paid on all cargo within twenty days of arriving in port; otherwise the ship and its cargo would be seized by customs officials and sold at auction (resulting in the tea making it to market). The Sons of Liberty petitioned Massachusetts Governor Thomas Hutchinson to order the ships back to England. Hutchinson, however, was equally determined to see the tea land. Without action, the tea would make it to market in days. On December 13, an estimated six thousand residents swarmed Faneuil Hall for a town meeting to discuss how to resolve the crisis. At the midnight hour, the Sons of Liberty attempted to convince the captain of the *Dartmouth* himself to petition that he

ABOVE *"The town of Boston in New England and British ships of war landing their troops! 1768," by Paul Revere, Boston, 1770.*

OPPOSITE *"The destruction of tea at Boston Harbor," by Sarony & Major, New York, c. 1846. Lithograph depicts the Boston Tea Party in 1773.*

be allowed to disembark for England with his tea. Hutchinson and the customs officials refused.

December 16 came, and with it the time for a decision. And so, having exhausted all legal means, the Boston Sons of Liberty convened in a tavern and made a decision that would change American history. The taproom of the Green Dragon Tavern was already something of a legend by this point and had served for years as the primary meeting place for Paul Revere, Sam Adams, John Hancock, Joseph Warren, and the St. Andrews Order of Freemasons. Within the dark, musky confines of the Green Dragon, fifty men (who participated is still somewhat of a mystery) left the tavern disguised as Mohawk Indians, forced their way aboard the ships, and within four hours had dumped the entire cargo of tea, worth between $1 million and $2 million in today's dollars, into Boston's harbor. When they were finished, the Sons marched back to the Green Dragon, immortalizing its role in the Boston Tea Party in the "Rally Mohawks" song:

Rally, Mohawks—bring out your axes!
And tell King George we'll pay no taxes on his foreign tea!
His threats are vain—and vain to think
To force our girls and wives to drink His vile Bohea! [a Chinese black tea sold by
the East India Company]
Then rally boys, and hasten on
To meet our Chiefs at the Green Dragon.
Our Warren's there, and bold Revere,
With hands to do and words to cheer For Liberty and Laws!
Our country's Braves and firm defenders
Shall ne'er be left by true North-Enders, Fighting Freedom's cause!
Then rally boys and hasten on to meet our Chiefs at the Green Dragon.

The events in Philadelphia and Boston provoked copycat protests throughout the colonies. In Annapolis, the Sons of Liberty surrounded the home of merchant Anthony Stewart, owner of the brigantine *Peggy Stewart*, which was anchored at port and loaded with tea. Threatened with tar and feathering, Stewart eventually bowed to pressure from the Sons of Liberty and burned not only the tea but his entire ship in the harbor.[4] Small stocks of tea were found and burned in front of taverns in Northborough and Shrewsbury, both in Massachusetts.[5] On April 22, 1774, the New York Sons of Liberty received word from Philadelphia that the *London*, rather than return to England as the mob had demanded, was going to attempt to sneak the tea into America through the port of New York. Upon arrival, the Sons of Liberty boarded the ship and escorted its captain, James Chambers, to what was then known as the Queen's Head Tavern (see Fraunces Tavern, page 92) for questioning. There, Chambers confessed to possessing eighteen chests of tea. As in

LEFT *"Fraunces Tavern, Corner of Broad & Pearl Streets," by George Hayward, New York, 1853.*

Colonial Cocktails

FLIP

INGREDIENTS

3 oz. eggnog (Traditional: Substitute eggnog with 2 oz. cream and 1 egg)

1 tbsp. brown sugar or molasses

10 oz. beer

1.5 oz. rum

1 tbsp. of dried pumpkin, apple, nutmeg, or cinnamon

SOURCE
Author's own variation. "November. 25th. 1760," in *The Adams Papers: Diary and Autobiography of John Adams*, vol. 1: *1755. 1d*, ed. L. H. Butterfield (Cambridge, MA: Harvard University Press, 1961), 172–73.

FLIP WAS PROBABLY THE MOST POPULAR DRINK in colonial America. A twenty-five-year-old John Adams wrote of a party at Thayer's Tavern that included "a wild Rable of both sexes, and all Ages, in the lower Room, singing, dancing, fiddling, drinking flip. . . . This is the Riot and Revelling of Taverns And of Thayers frolicks." This mealy beverage, sometimes known as a bellow-stop, perfectly illustrates the colonial view of drinking as a calorie supplement.

DIRECTIONS

In a small bowl combine the eggnog, rum, and sugar or molasses; whisk until frothy and pour into pint glass.

Pour the beer into a saucepan and heat over medium flame until steaming. Do not boil.

Once steaming, pour the heated beer back and forth into the pint glass with the eggnog/rum/sugar mix and back into saucepan several times to blend (once fully blended in the pint glass, the traditional recipe calls for a red hot iron to be plunged into the drink to froth the egg).

Garnish with the dried spice.

Fraunces Tavern

EST. 1762 AS THE QUEEN'S HEAD TAVERN ✱ TODAY OPERATES AS A RESTAURANT, BAR, AND MUSEUM ✱ FREQUENTED BY GEORGE WASHINGTON, JOHN ADAMS ✱ NEW YORK, NEW YORK

Originally known as the Queen's Head Tavern, Fraunces Tavern is today the oldest building in Manhattan. The tavern was built in 1719 and sold to Samuel Fraunces in 1762. Fraunces immediately had the house refitted for tavern keeping, adding an ale room and an assembly space for as many as seventy guests. The tavern assumed a central role in New York society as a place of entertainment, news, politics, business, and food (Fraunces is said to have invented take-out dining). Its "plain but genteel style" appealed to Washington's republican sensibilities, and he would go on to cultivate a close relationship with Fraunces and his tavern.

Interior detail of Fraunces Tavern dining room.

The tavern's first brush with revolution occurred in 1774. News of the Boston Tea Party had spread across the colonies, inspiring similar raids in Charleston and Philadelphia. When New York's Sons of Liberty received intelligence that the British ship *London* was hiding tea, the Sons escorted the captain to Fraunces Tavern, where he confessed. As in Boston, patriots disguised themselves as native Americans and dumped the tea overboard. Some months later, local Sons of Liberty leader John Lamb attempted to steal a dozen cannons from the New York Battery. The raid resulted in a firefight with a British ship of the line, the HMS *Asia*, which pummeled New York throughout the night, sending an 18-pound cannon ball through the roof of Fraunces Tavern.

Following the British occupation of New York, Fraunces fled with other patriots, leaving the tavern with his Tory son-in-law. Fraunces is believed to have returned to New York shortly after to work in the tavern as a spy. During this time, Thomas Hickey, a member of Washington's personal guard, and two coconspirators

Portrait of Samuel Fraunces.

accepted an unknown sum from Tory agents to assassinate Washington and General Putnam and sabotage the American position. Washington and his guards were stationed about a mile and a half from New York City in the Mortier House on Harlem Heights. Hickey was eventually jailed for counterfeiting colonial currency. While in confinement, he disclosed the plot to his cellmate, who promptly informed patriot authorities in exchange for leniency on his own crimes. Hickey was hanged as a traitor. While the record matches the story's validity, it was once rumored that Hickey had revealed the plot to his lover, Mortier's housekeeper, who was suspected of being either the slave or daughter of Samuel Fraunces. What is certain is that after the war, Congress awarded Fraunces £2,000 and Fraunces became Washington's personal chef.

Following the British surrender at Yorktown, Congress began debating the issue of promised pensions and back pay for American Continental officers. The nation was broke, and with the Constitution still years away, Congress had not yet assumed the powers of the purse. Patience was running thin among the ranks, and broadsides began circulating among American regiments suggesting armed conflict with Congress. Against this backdrop, Washington took the floor at Fraunces Tavern to address the "cold and angry faces" of his officers. As he began, he pulled out his glasses to read a letter, saying, "Gentlemen, you will permit me to put on my spectacles, for I have not only grown grey but almost blind in the service of my country." According to historian Thomas Fleming, "A rustle of unease, a murmur of emotion swept through the audience. . . . Tears began to stream down Washington's cheeks. The officers' anger . . . dissolved."

Following the war, tens of thousands of loyalists, from wealthy Tories to runaway slaves, descended on New York City to prove their wartime loyalty to the Crown and evacuate with British troops. Weekly trials were held at Fraunces Tavern by British General Birch to consider each case.

Following the Revolution Congress would locate the Departments of State, War, and Treasury in the tavern from 1785 to 1790. With the 1790 relocation of the American capital to Philadelphia, Fraunces once again became a tavern. The building was acquired and saved from demolition by the Sons of the Revolution in 1904 and is today a museum, restaurant, and bar.

SOURCES

John Buescher, "Are There Instances of Raids Similar to the Boston Tea Party?" TeachingHistory.org.

Henry Russel Drowne, "A Sketch of Fraunces Tavern and Those Connected with Its History" OpenLibrary.org (New York, 1919).

"54 Pearl Street History," Fraunces Tavern Museum, http://fraucestavernmuseum.org.

Tom Fleming, "Why Washington Wept," *New York Sun*, December 4, 2007.

Kym Rice, *Early American Taverns: For the Entertainment of Friends and Strangers* (Chicago: Regnery Gateway, 1983, 128, 129.

Boston, patriots disguised themselves as Mohawks and proceeded to steep the harbor in the "King's vile bohea."[6, 7]

Boston's leaders immediately recognized the implications of the "Destruction of the Tea in Boston" (the phrase "Boston Tea Party" wouldn't be coined for decades). John Adams recorded the event in his diary:

> Last Night 3 Cargoes of Bohea Tea were emptied into the Sea. This Morning a Man of War sails. This is the most magnificent Movement of all. There is a Dignity, a Majesty, a Sublimity, in this last Effort of the Patriots, that I greatly admire. The People should never rise, without doing something to be remembered—something notable. And striking. This Destruction of the Tea is so bold, so daring, so firm, intrepid and inflexible, and it must have so important Consequences, and so lasting, that I cant but consider it as an Epocha in History.[8]

In a letter to James Warren written that same night, Adams invoked Julius Caesar: "The die is cast. The people have passed the river and cut away the bridge. Last night three cargoes of tea were emptied into the harbor. This is the grandest event which has ever yet happened since the controversy with Britain opened."

Samuel Adams gushed to his friend Arthur Lee that the Boston Tea Party was "as remarkable an event as has yet happened since the commencement of our struggle for American liberty." "You cannot imagine," Adams wrote, "the height of joy that sparkles in the eyes and animates the countenances as well as the hearts of all we meet on this occasion; excepting the disappointed, disconcerted Hutchinson and his tools." This was putting it mildly. Hutchinson was reviewing the possibility of charging patriot leaders with treason, an offense punishable by death. Since the tea was private property, and not the property of the British government, some patriot leaders felt the Boston Sons crossed the line. Ben Franklin and George Washington believed the East India Company deserved to be repaid. Some feared that mob violence against the Crown could spiral out of control and that both Parliament and the king would feel forced to respond.

Morning in America: The Rise of Coffee

PRIOR TO INDEPENDENCE, Americans considered themselves British subjects and largely adopted British customs, including fashion, cuisine, and the preference for tea. Beginning in 1765, however, the British Parliament began taxing Americans to help pay debts incurred during the French and Indian War. Americans' outrage ultimately led to a conflict between a Boston mob and occupying British soldiers in which five Americans were shot dead. Soon after, on April 12, 1770, a sympathetic Parliament repealed most of the American taxes except those on tea. With American ire concentrated almost entirely against the tea taxes, English tea became heavily politicized, culminating in the Boston Tea Party (smuggled Dutch tea was still popular). Though tea made a comeback following independence, the War of 1812 delivered the knockout blow. Between tea's lingering association with Britain and the much safer Caribbean and South American coffee trade, coffee conquered American markets.

SOURCE
Norman Berdichevsky, "The Cultural Geography of Consumption," *New English Review* (May 2008).

Old '76 House

EST. 1755 AS THE CASPARUS MABIE HOUSE ✻ TODAY OPERATES AS A BAR AND RESTAURANT ✻ FREQUENTED BY GEORGE WASHINGTON, ALEXANDER HAMILTON, MARQUIS DE LAFAYETTE, BRITISH MAJOR JOHN ANDRÉ ✻ TAPPAN, NEW YORK

Located in the old Dutch hamlet of Tappan, the Old '76 House is one of the most famous taverns in the United States. There's some debate on the building's exact age, but most sources believe it was built in the 1750s. The building was known during the Revolutionary era as the Casparus Mabie House and, later, Mabie's Tavern. Mabie's was one of the most popular taverns in the region. Other than a brief interval of neglect and decay in the late nineteenth century (when it became known as the Old '76 House), it has remained in operation as a bar and restaurant ever since.

The story of the Old '76 House includes some of the most riveting drama among taverns involved in the Revolutionary War. It begins with the nearby Hudson River, whose capacity for transport and agriculture first made the region attractive to seventeenth-century Dutch settlers, who named it Orangetown after the Dutch royal family. The area's Dutch influence remained strong, and on July 4, 1774, exactly two years before the Continental Congress adopted the Declaration of Independence, Orangetown's independent-minded leaders convened at the Old '76 House and adopted the Orangetown Resolutions. Though affirming

the "wish to be true and loyal subjects" to the king, the resolutions expressed the town's "abhorrence" at the Crown's tax policies and occupation of Boston, and pledged to suspend all trade "to and from Great Britain and the West Indies" until the aggression stopped.

But it was the Hudson's military value, particularly the critical juncture at West Point, that eventually brought the Old '76 House fame. Stretching north 300 miles from New York City, the Hudson River neatly separates New England from New York and the rest of the United States. With control of the Hudson, the British could isolate New England and possibly negotiate an end to the war on their own terms. The obvious military value made the Tappan area among the most contested and battle-hardened regions of the United States during the Revolution, culminating in the events of September 22, 1780. On that date, American hero Benedict Arnold secretly met with British Major John André behind American lines and affirmed the sale of his loyalty to the British for £20,000 and a brigadier generalship in the Royal Army. Arnold provided André with detailed plans of West Point's defenses and a disguise and passport to safely return to the British line. With the West Point plans hidden in his boot, André was captured en route by American soldiers, who imprisoned him in the tavern's north reception room. After admitting his true identity, André was tried as a spy and hanged in the field behind the tavern. The execution of André, a British gentleman of high rank, affirmed Washington's commitment to equal treatment under the law and was seen by some as vengeance for the British execution of beloved American spy Nathaniel Hale several years earlier.

Soon after the plot was uncovered, Washington himself arrived in Tappan and made his headquarters at the nearby DeClark-DeWint House. Upon entering the tavern, Washington is believed to have had the portrait of Arnold hanging over the fireplace turned upside down in shame. In addition to Washington, both Alexander Hamilton and the marquis de Lafayette are believed to have dined at the tavern, served by Washington's personal chef, Samuel Fraunces (see Fraunces Tavern page 92). Washington may have even leaned on the very bar that's still in use today.

ABOVE *Fireplace at the Old '76 House. Note the portrait of Benedict Arnold hung upside down in shame.*

Today the Old '76 House has been expertly restored under the ownership of Robert Norden, who purchased the property in 1987. The tavern's low ceilings, diverse menu, and original fireplaces and taproom make it one of the best-preserved taverns from the Revolutionary era.

SOURCES

Benson J. Lossing, *The Two Spies: Nathan Hale and John Andre* (New York: Appleton, 1909), 97.

The Orangetown Historical Museum and Archives estimate in *Orangetown* (Arcadia, Charleston 2011) that the tavern was built in 1753 (p. 11). In *The Crisis of the Revolution* (1899), author William Abbat estimates it was built in 1755. The tavern's current ownership believes the building was constructed around 1668.

Arthur Tompkins, *History of Rockland County, New York* (New York: Van Deusen & Joyce, 1902), 352.

INTOLERABLE ACTS

British Prime Minister Lord North had had enough. Addressing the House of Commons on April 22, 1774, he declared, "The Americans have tarred and feathered your subjects, plundered your merchants, burnt your ships, denied all obedience to your laws and authority; yet so clement, and so long forbearing has our conduct been, that it is incumbent on us now to take a different course."[9] That "different course" was the Coercive Acts, known in America as the Intolerable Acts. The measures closed the Port of Boston, established military rule in Massachusetts, provided for the quartering of British troops in American homes, prohibited town meetings, and reaffirmed the right of royal officers accused of crimes to be tried in Britain.[10]

ABOVE *"The patriotick barber of New York, or the Captain in the suds," by Philip Dawe, London, 1775. Cartoon shows a New York barber refusing to finish shaving a customer after learning of his British identity.*

When news of the Intolerable Acts reached Virginia, the outraged House of Burgesses proclaimed June 1—the date the Boston blockade would take effect—"a day of fasting, humiliation, and prayer."[11] Royal Governor Dunmore dissolved the Burgesses for their pro-Boston sentiments and for not toeing the Crown's line. "The day after this event," wrote George Washington, "the Members convend themselves at the Raleigh Tavern" and resolved "that Americans will never be tax'd without their own consent, that the cause of Boston considerd as the cause of America" and that the Committees of Correspondence for each colony should put forward delegates for a Continental Congress.[12]

Ten years had passed since Parliament had passed the Molasses Act, setting off an escalating cycle of overreach and resistance that was finally poised to break into open war. Until this point, the American opposition had been chiefly organized from America's urban centers in Boston, Philadelphia, and Williamsburg.

In the days before polling, one of the best ways a political leader could consult the opinion of the country was to visit taverns. In 1774, John Adams recounted the pivotal moment in which yeoman farmers at a country tavern realized they too had a stake in the budding conflict:

> Within the course of the year before the Meeting of Congress in 1774 on a Journey to some of our Circuit Courts in Massachusetts, I stopped one night at a Tavern in Shrewsbury about forty miles from Boston: and as I was cold and wett I sat down at a good fire in the Bar room to dry my great coat and saddlebags, till a fire could be made in my Chamber. There presently came in, one after another half a dozen or half a score substantial yeoman of the Neighborhood, who, sitting down to the fire after lighting their Pipes, began a lively conversation upon Politicians. As I believed I was unknown to all of them, I sat in total silence to hear them. One said "The People of Boston are distracted." Another answered "No wonder the People of Boston are distracted, oppression will make Wise men mad," a third said, "what would you say, if a Fellow should come to your house and tell you he was come to take a list of your cattle that Parliament might tax you for them at so much a head? and how shall you feel if he shall go and break open your barn, to take down your oxen cows horses and sheep? What would I say?" replied the first, "i would knock him in the head. Well, said a fourth, "if Parliament can take away Mr Hancocks wharf and Mr Revere's wharf they can take away your Barn and my House." After much more reasoning in this Style, a fifth who had as yet been silent, broke out "Well it is high time for us to rebel. We must rebel some time or other: and we had better rebel now than at any time to come. If we put it off for ten or twenty years, and let them go on as they have begun, they will get a strong Party among us, and plague us a great deal more than they can now. As yet they have but a small party on their side." I was disgusted by his word "rebel," because I was determined never to rebel, as much as I was to resist rebellion against the fundamental principles of the Constitution when our British Generals or Governor Generals begin it. I mention this Anecdote to show that the Idea of Independence was familiar even among the common People much earlier than some persons pretend.[13]

With the support of the common people, political conflict between Britain and America became increasingly martial. In September, Boston patriots stole four brass cannons from under British guards and smuggled them to the militia storehouse at Concord, twenty miles west of Boston.[14] That same month, the First Continental Congress was convened in Philadelphia, ushering in the first meeting of many of America's eventual founding fathers. In session for barely a month, the Congress resolved to establish and enforce a universal boycott of all imported British goods so long as the Intolerable Acts remained in place, and for the eventual prohibition of all exports to Britain should the acts not be repealed by the following September. Before the Congress adjourned on October 26, it resolved to convene again on May 10, 1775.

Another result of the First Continental Congress was the rise to prominence of a new Philadelphia establishment, the City Tavern (see page 66). Opened barely a year earlier by a collection of the city's leading merchants, the City Tavern was, according to John Adams, "the most genteel in America."[15] Following the congressional session, the congressmen were treated to a night's entertainment at the statehouse followed by a massive feast at the City Tavern. An estimated five hundred people attended the banquet, which was accompanied by toasts, music, and gun salutes.[16]

In Massachusetts, no celebrations commemorated the new Provincial Congress. Following the Intolerable Acts, Britain replaced the Massachusetts civilian governor, Thomas Hutchinson, with a military governor, Thomas Gage, who had served as a British general during the French and Indian War. While the Continental Congress was meeting in Philadelphia, Gage invoked the Intolerable Acts to dissolve the Massachusetts Provincial Assembly. The assembly instead retreated to Concord, where on October 7, the three hundred delegates declared themselves the first Massachusetts Provincial Congress, with John Hancock as acting president. Massachusetts was thus split into two administrative regions, with Boston under the control of occupying British forces and all areas outside Boston under the control of the Provincial Congress. Many of the Congress's first committees on military, safety, and tax collections met at the Wright Tavern, a stately clapboard building that still stands today as various offices (see page 111).[17]

Following years of mob intimidation, vandalism, and now the theft of military supplies and a blatantly illegal shadow

RIGHT *Color reproduction of Philadelphia's City Tavern by Robert Smith Ale Brewing Co., 1908.*

government, many British officers were frustrated by the sense that the Americans were taking the advantage and that General Gage was being far too soft. This sense of embitterment was exacerbated by Boston's patriotic demonstrations and orations commemorating the March 5 anniversary of the Boston Massacre, which left British officers offended and hungry for revenge. In the days following one such commemoration, British officers finally reacted. "A simple Country man" apparently approached a British regular to purchase a firing lock for a musket. Once the money changed hands, the unsuspecting fellow was taken into custody (trade with soldiers was strictly prohibited). The following day, British officers had the man tarred and feathered and hung a sign reading "AMERICAN liberty, or a specimen of democracy" over his neck. They then carted the man through Boston accompanied by the drums and fifes of the Forty-Seventh Regiment playing "Yankee Doodle." The patriots were disgusted. "See what indignities we suffer, rather than precipitate a crisis," wrote Samuel Adams of the incident.[18, 19] In fact, the crisis was barely a month away.

BATTLES OF LEXINGTON AND CONCORD

On April 19, 1775, the decade-long standoff over taxation without representation erupted into war, and with it the immortal fame of several American taverns. Massachusett's military governor, Thomas Gage, was still smarting over the theft of the four bronze cannons from Boston the previous September and had received intelligence from British spies that "a quantity of Ammunition, Provisions, Artillery, Tents and small Arms have been collected at Concord, for the Avowed Purpose of raising and supporting a Rebellion against His Majesty."[20] Gage ordered Lieutenant Colonel Smith to march seven hundred men to Concord the night of April 18 so as to arrive by surprise the morning of April 19. But Massachusetts patriots had been awaiting this "surprise" expedition for weeks, and were ready. With Sam Adams and John Hancock staying in Lexington, midway between Boston and Concord, the physician Joseph Warren was the most senior patriot still residing in Boston (see Warren Tavern page 72). When he learned that the British were planning to march, he assumed the objective was the arrest of Hancock and Adams and sent Paul Revere to ride to Lexington to sound the alarm (although Revere successfully warned Lexington, he was captured and arrested by British scouts before reaching Concord). Boston at the time was a

On April 18, 1775, the decade-long standoff over taxation without representation erupted into war, and with it the immortal fame of several American taverns.

ABOVE *An unknown artist's depiction of Paul Revere's ride on the night of April 18, 1775.*

peninsula connected to the mainland via a narrow, heavily guarded isthmus called the Boston Neck, so Revere took a small vessel across the Charles River to Charlestown, where several other riders had already been alerted to the march. Boston patriots had told the Charlestown riders to look for lanterns over the North Church in the North End of Boston, "one if by land, two if by sea," to indicate which route the British were taking out of Boston (overland across the Boston Neck, or oversea across the Charles River).

> *One if by land, and two if by sea;*
> *And I on the opposite shore will be,*
> *Ready to ride and spread the alarm*
> *Through every Middlesex, village and farm,*
> *For the country folk to be up and to arm.*[21]

When Revere reached Lexington at around 1:00 a.m., Munroe Tavern proprietor and Minuteman sergeant William Munroe ordered a squad of men to surround the Jonas Clarke house where Adams and Hancock were posted, until Revere finally convinced both Adams and Hancock to flee (see Munroe Tavern page 114). Within minutes, thirty militiamen were gathered at the nearby Buckman Tavern, awaiting orders from Captain John Parker, who made the tavern his headquarters for the night (see Buckman's Tavern page 107).[22]

Colonel Smith's mismanagement slowed the British march to such an extent that some militiamen decided the British weren't coming after all and headed home. By around 5:00 a.m. however, advance riders confirmed the British were near, and orders rang from Buckman Tavern that the sixty to seventy militiamen assume formation on Lexington Green. In his deposition to the Continental Congress, Captain Parker swore that at this point, he "ordered our Militia to meet on the Common in said Lexington to consult what to do, and concluded not to be discovered, nor meddle or make with said Regular Troops (if they should approach) unless they should insult or molest us; and, upon their sudden Approach, I immediately ordered our Militia to disperse, and not to fire."

When the first British soldiers arrived in Lexington, they found Smith and his men in formation on the Lexington Green, the road to Concord unobstructed. Accounts differ over what happened next. John Robins, on the American front line, claimed the British regulars immediately charged:

> Huzzaing . . . on full Gallop towards us, the foremost of which cryed, "throw down your Arms ye Villains, ye Rebels!" upon which said Company Dispersing, the foremost of the three Officers order'd their Men, saying, "fire, by God, fire!" at which Moment we received a very heavy and close fire from them, at which Instant, being wounded, I fell, and several of our men were shot Dead. . . . Captain Parker's men I believe had not then fired a Gun.

Elijah Saunderson, another eyewitness, claimed he heard

> one of the Regulars, whom I took to be an officer, say, "Damn them, we will have them," and immediately the Regulars shouted aloud, Run and fired upon the Lexington Company, which did not fire a Gun before the Regulars Discharged on them; Eight of the Lexington Company were killed while they were dispersing, and at a Considerable Distance from each other, and Many wounded, and altho' a spectator, I narrowly Escaped with my Life.

BELOW *Wood engraving after plate II of the engravings by Amos Doolittle from drawings by Ralph Earle, published at New Haven in December 1755. Engraving shows British Troops entering Concord, Massachusetts.*

1. Companies of the Regulars marching into Concord. 2. Companies of the Regulars drawn up in order. 3. A Detachment destroying the Provincial Stores. 4, 5. Colonel Smith and Major Pitcairn viewing the Provincials, who were mustering on an East Hill in Concord. 6. The Court and Town House. 7. The Meeting-House.

THE BRITISH TROOPS ON CONCORD COMMON.—[FAC-SIMILE OF AN OLD ENGRAVING.]

Edward Thoroton Gould, a British lieutenant, confirmed that the British "Troops rush'd on shouting, and huzzaing, previous to the firing," although "which party fired first, I cannot exactly say."[23] British Lieutenant William Sutherland had no such misgivings and swore to General Gage that the first shots were fired by Americans, possibly from behind Buckman Tavern.[24] Regardless of who fired first, the encounter at Lexington left eight Americans dead and nine wounded.

With only one Briton wounded, Colonel Smith and the redcoats continued on to Concord, about 7 miles farther west into patriot territory. Like Lexington, Concord received advance warning from a patriot rider, Samuel Prescott, who alerted local militia at Wright Tavern.[25] Colonial militia began assembling on the far end of the North Bridge, a half-mile from the center of town, which was soon secured by about one hundred British soldiers, while the bulk of British troops scoured Colonel James Barrett's farm and other locations suspected of hiding militia supplies. At Wright Tavern, British Major Pitcairn is believed to have employed a touch of flair by stirring a glass of brandy with his bloody finger, saying, "I mean to stir the damned Yankee blood as I stir this, before night!"[26] What little military supplies the British found were burned, destroyed, or dumped in the river. Smoke from the fires, however, sounded the alarm throughout the region, and militiamen kept arriving, believing the British were torching Concord to the ground. One company of men arrived from the town of Sudbury, 6 miles south of Concord, under the leadership of Lieutenant Ezekiel Howe, owner and proprietor of Howe's Tavern (see Longfellow's Wayside Inn on page 38). Lieutenant Joseph Winn, owner of Winn Tavern, rode 15 miles at 2:00 a.m. from his home in Woburn to defend the town.[27] twenty miles away in the town of Shirley, militia rallied at Bull Run Tavern (then Sawtell's Tavern) before marching to the relief of Concord.

With militia pouring in from the surrounding areas, colonial ranks at North Bridge swelled to about four hundred men. The colonists, with superior numbers and believing the British to be torching the town, marched on the bridge "with as much order as the best discipline Troops," recounted a British officer.[28] Whereas the

Whereas the conflict on the Lexington Green earlier that morning was less of a battle and more of a confused skirmish, what occurred on Concord's North Bridge was crystal clear to the participants: this was war.

TAVERNS OF THE BATTLES OF LEXINGTON AND CONCORD

Buckman, Hartwell, Wright, and Munroe Taverns

By spring 1775, British-American relations reached crisis levels. The British refusal to repeal import duties on tea sparked the Boston Tea Party and other tea protests across the colonies, resulting in the destruction of millions of dollars of British property. Britain responded by closing the port of Boston, prohibiting town meetings, and establishing military rule in Massachusetts. The Crown's assault on basic freedoms emboldened American claims of tyranny, and what began as a political conflict became increasingly militant. Boston's Sons of Liberty were suspected of stealing four bronze cannons from British garrisons months earlier, and on April 18, Military Governor Thomas Gage received intelligence from British spies that "a quantity of Ammunition, Provisions, Artillery, Tents and small Arms have been collected at Concord, for the Avowed Purpose of raising and supporting a Rebellion against His Majesty." In response, Gage sent seven hundred men on a 20-mile nighttime march to Concord, so as to arrive by surprise the morning of April 19. Boston's Sons of Liberty discovered a march was imminent, but the purpose remained unclear. Dr. Joseph Warren, the most senior patriot leader left in Boston, believed the British were out to capture Sam Adams and John Hancock, hiding in Lexington, and sent Paul Revere on his famous ride to sound the alarm. Colonial militias used the advanced warning to rally at local taverns, eventually confronting British soldiers in what became the opening conflict of the American Revolutionary War.

Buckman Tavern

EST. 1713 AS MUZZY TAVERN ✻ TODAY OPERATES AS A MUSEUM ✻ LEXINGTON, MASSACHUSETTS

Established in 1713, the Buckman Tavern was headquarters to one of the most significant events in American history and is today the oldest building in Lexington. It underwent several renovations until being brought mostly to its current Georgian appearance in 1755 by owner John Muzzy (two small wings were added in the 1800s). In 1768 the tavern fell to the ownership of John Buckman, who ran it throughout the Revolution.

Soon after Paul Revere arrived in Lexington with word that the British were coming, Samuel Adams and John Hancock fled for safety. Local militia were soon rallying at the Buckman Tavern under the leadership of Captain John Parker, who ordered the militiamen into formation outside the tavern on Lexington Green. Upon the arrival of the British regulars, he ordered the militia not to "meddle or make with said Regular Troops (if they should approach) unless they should insult or molest us" in which case they were to "disperse, and not to fire."

As he approached Lexington, it became clear to British Colonel Francis Smith that the countryside had been alerted and the element of surprise lost. Smith sent for reinforcements from Boston, which arrived at the Lexington Green at 5:00 a.m., resulting in a tense standoff with American militia. What is certain is that the British ordered the Americans to stand down, the Americans refused, and an uproar of shouting and confusion ensued. A shot, suspected by many historians to have come from behind the Buckman Tavern, was fired, resulting in a British charge that left eight Americans dead, nine wounded, and a musket hole in the door of the Buckman. Hours before the famous "shot heard 'round the world" at Concord's North Bridge, the first shot of the American Revolution may have been fired from the Buckman Tavern.

Tavern operations ceased in 1815, and the building became part of a large farm operation. In 1914, the Lexington Historical Society partnered with the Town of Lexington and the American Red Cross to repurpose the building as a community and support center for the war effort during World War I. Following the war, the building was restored to its colonial appearance and converted to a museum complete with period furniture and artifacts. Today, tours provided by the Lexington Historical Society offer an authentic glimpse of the tavern that may have started it all.

Hartwell Tavern

EST. 1756 ✻ MINUTE MAN NATIONAL PARK, LINCOLN, MASSACHUSETTS

The Hartwell Tavern was erected in 1732 and converted to a tavern by Ephraim Hartwell in 1756. After warning the people of Lexington that the British were coming, Paul Revere, William Dawes, and Samuel Prescott pressed on to warn the people of Concord. An advance British guard captured and arrested Revere and Dawes, while Prescott was able to escape and continue along the Old Bay Road toward Concord. According to lore, Prescott made a brief stop at Hartwell Tavern along the way to warn owner Ephraim Hartwell, whose three sons were part of the Lincoln Minutemen. Soon after, British troops marched directly past the Hartwell en route to Concord. With Prescott's advance warning, the Lincoln Minutemen, including the Hartwell boys, were assembled in time to engage the British at North Bridge. For most of its history since the Revolutionary War, the Hartwell Tavern served as a private residence. It was purchased by the National Park Service in 1967 and restored to its 1775 appearance with much of the original building intact. Today, the Hartwell is part of the Minute Man National Park and is available for tours.

conflict on the Lexington Green earlier that morning was less of a battle and more of a confused skirmish, what occurred on Concord's North Bridge was crystal clear to the participants: this was war. When the Americans reached the bridge's west end, the British opened fire. The American line took the volley, after which American Major John Buttrick screamed, "Fire, for God's sake, fellow soldiers, fire!"[29] The outnumbered and outmaneuvered British broke ranks and fled while the Americans pushed forward, using guerrilla tactics to force the British line into a long, hectic, and bloody withdrawal back toward Boston (some Americans reportedly taunted the British with shouts of "King Hancock forever!").[30] Americans wounded in Concord were brought to the home of Dr. Timothy Minot, which survives today as Concord's Colonial Inn (see page 81). Gruesome operations took place in room 24, and those who didn't survive were sent to room 27, set up as a morgue. By nightfall, forty-nine Americans and seventy-three British, were dead, and Boston was surrounded on three sides

BELOW *"The battle of Lexington April 1775," by Amos Doolittle, 1775. Print shows Minutemen being fired upon by British troops in Lexington, Massachusetts. Notice the Buckman Tavern (middle left).*

by thousands of militiamen from all over Massachusetts, with more on the way from the surrounding colonies, resulting in the siege of Boston. The Revolutionary War had begun.

Surveying the Concord battlefield, John Adams again invoked Caesar, writing, "The Die was cast, the Rubicon passed."[31] Ben Franklin described the event as "the Commencement of a Civil War."[32] And so when Adams, Franklin, and the other founders met in Philadelphia barely two weeks later to convene the Second Continental Congress, the discussion was dominated by how best to present a united response to Britain. While Congress was discussing the matter, the British tried to break the American siege on Boston by taking the high ground guarding Boston Harbor: Bunker Hill. On June 17, the British crossed the Charles River from Boston and, after coming under sniper fire, burned Charlestown to the ground and continued marching toward Bunker Hill. However, the American position was heavily fortified, and the disciplined colonists were ordered not to "shoot until you see the whites of their eyes" to save gunpowder. The Americans were eventually pushed back, though not before exacting huge British losses. The battle took its toll on both sides, leaving 140 Americans dead and 271 wounded, but the British suffered the greater loss with 226 killed and 828 wounded.[33]

BELOW *General George Washington's attack on Germantown, Pennsylvania, October 4, 1777.*

Wright Tavern

EST. 1747 ✶ TODAY OPERATES AS VARIOUS OFFICES ✶ CONCORD, MASSACHUSETTS

Wright Tavern was built by Ephraim Jones in 1747 and takes its name from Amos Wright, the landlord at the time of the outbreak of the American Revolution. The tavern is famous for two key political and military events running up to the Revolutionary War.

In 1774, Parliament responded to the Boston Tea Party by enacting a series of punitive measures known collectively by Americans as the Intolerable Acts. One of these measures, the Massachusetts Government Act, dissolved the colony's elected government and installed a military governor. However, only Boston was under British control, making the act a dead letter everywhere else. The Massachusetts legislature instead convened at Wright Tavern in Concord. There, the delegates declared themselves the Massachusetts Provincial Congress and became the de facto colony government.

The tavern also played an important role during the Battles of Lexington and Concord. With advance warning from patriot rider Samuel Prescott, the Concord Minutemen rallied in the early hours of April 19 at Wright Tavern to await instructions. At 7:00 a.m., after a nine-hour comedy of errors in which the slow-moving British killed eight Lexington militiamen and completely forfeited the element of surprise, British soldiers finally arrived in Concord. They immediately secured the two bridges into town and began searching the tavern and Colonel Barrett's farm for suspected militia supplies, burning whatever they found. The Concord Minutemen had already withdrawn to the far side of North Bridge, where their ranks began to swell with volunteers from the surrounding countryside. Seeing the smoke, the militia feared the British were setting the town to torch and decided to use their superior numbers to confront the British troops guarding North Bridge. The two sides assumed battle formations opposite each side of the bridge and volleyed the famous "shot heard 'round the world." While British forces were busy losing North Bridge to American militia, British officers were making themselves comfortable a mile away at Wright Tavern. Major Pitcairn is believed to have employed a touch of flair by helping himself to a glass of brandy from behind the bar, which he stirred with his bloody finger saying, "I mean to stir the damned Yankee blood as I stir this, before night!"

The tavern was converted to a residence and bakery after the Revolution and became an inn once again in 1886. It was then converted to office space in the mid-twentieth century by its current owner, the First Parish Church.

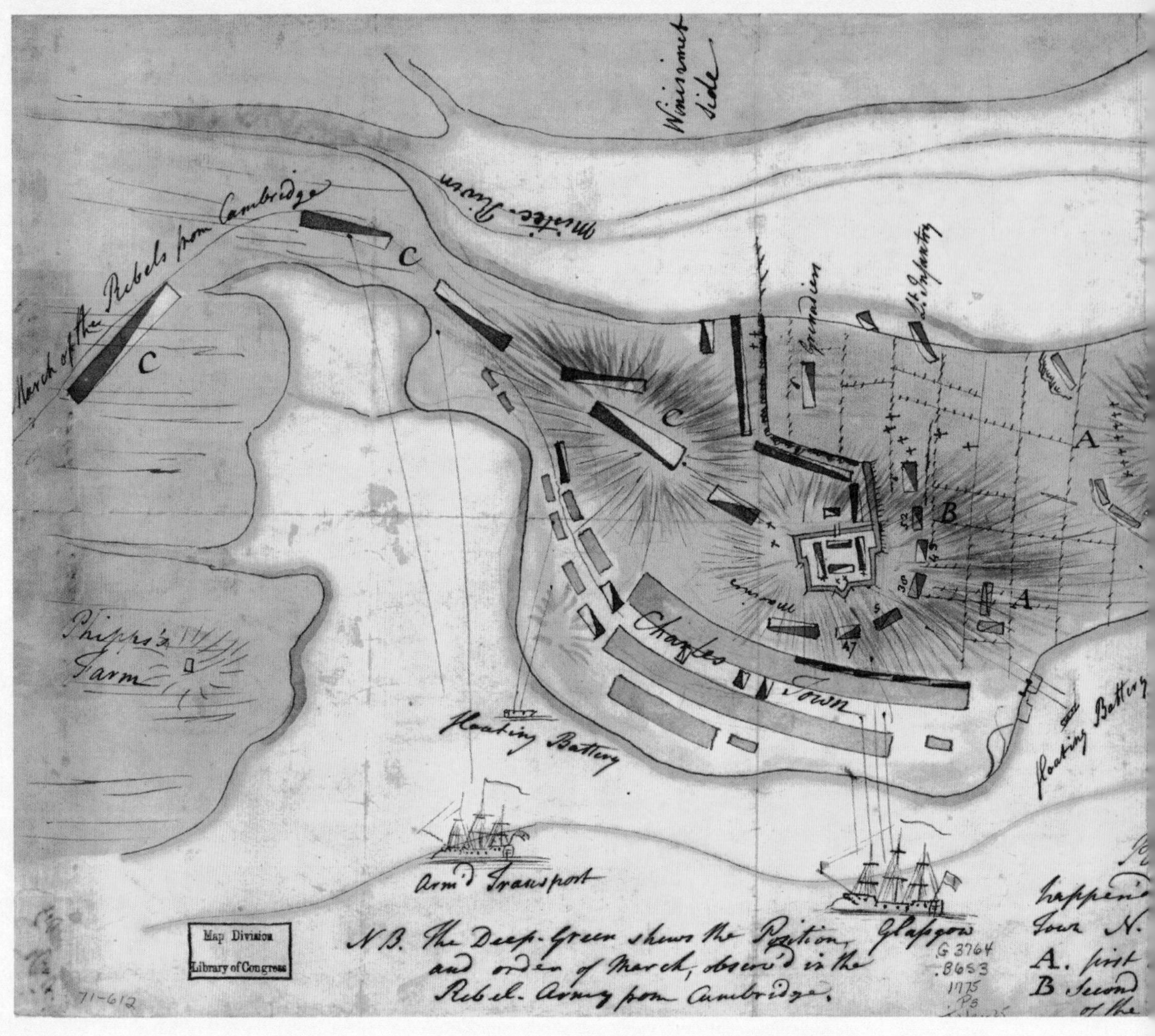

ABOVE *"Plan of the action which happen'd 17th. June 1775, at Charles Town, N. America," by Sir Thomas Hyde Page, c. 1775. Map depicts plan of action for the Battle of Bunker Hill.*

Among the American dead was Joseph Warren, who almost certainly would have become as revered in the American pantheon as Samuel Adams, Benjamin Franklin, or even Washington himself had he survived. In the years leading up to the outbreak of violence, the Harvard-educated physician was a well-known pamphleteer and leader of the Boston Sons of Liberty. His stirring oration at the anniversary commemoration of the Boston Massacre helped galvanize both Bostonians and British officers for conflict. He was the one who sent Paul Revere on his famous ride, and when alerted to the outbreak of hostilities on Lexington Green, he shouldered his

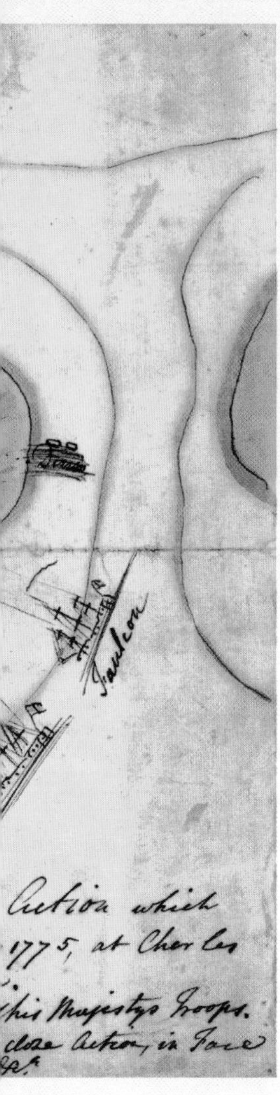

musket and rode out to defend the countryside. When Charlestown was eventually rebuilt following the British assault, one of the first establishments was named in his honor, the Warren Tavern, which still exists today as the oldest in Massachusetts (see Warren Tavern on page 72). Israel Putnam, another American hero of the Battle of Bunker Hill, also has a tavern named after him: Putnam Cottage in Greenwich, Connecticut.[34]

The Battles of Lexington and Concord, and now Bunker Hill, were making a powerful case for independence, and John Adams became "convinced that the Cancer is too deeply rooted, and too far spread to be cured by any thing short of cutting it out entire."[35] The majority of the Continental Congress, however, opted to at least make a show of an appeal for peace by sending the Olive Branch Petition to King George. Perhaps indicative of their true intentions, however, the delegates adopted the Declaration of the Causes and Necessity of Taking Up Arms on the very next day. The overtures were moot because King George considered the Continental Congress an illegal assembly and therefore refused to hear its petitions. With blood being shed and the king refusing to negotiate with America's chosen leaders, there was little room left for diplomacy. George Washington was named commander in chief of the new Continental Army, and George III declared the American colonies to be in a state of rebellion.

RIGHT *"View of the attack on Bunker's Hill, with the burning of Charles Town, June 17, 1775," by John Lodge, c. 1783. Print shows four British warships landing troops and firing on Charlestown, a British battery on Copp's Hill in Boston firing on Charlestown, which is in flames, and the assault on Bunker's Hill.*

Munroe Tavern

EST. 1735 ✵ TODAY OPERATES AS A MUSEUM ✵ LEXINGTON, MASSACHUSETTS

First erected in 1735, the Munroe Tavern is one of the first buildings that travelers from colonial Boston would have encountered on arriving in Lexington. William Munroe acquired the tavern in 1770 from John Buckman, who owned the nearby Buckman Tavern. The tavern's location ensured it a prominent role during the Battles of Lexington and Concord.

Following the battle on the Lexington Green, British Colonel Francis Smith pressed on toward Concord, where his men discovered and destroyed militia provisions until militia reinforcements forced a hasty and bloody British retreat back toward Boston. As Smith and his men passed again through Lexington, they found British Brigadier General Hugh Percy and his twelve hundred reinforcements near Munroe Tavern, which had been converted into a field hospital. Before withdrawing to Boston, Percy's men killed the disabled caretaker, John Raymond, while Munroe's wife and children hid in the woods nearby. Years later, on November 5, 1789, George Washington dined at the Munroe during his presidential tour of New England.

The Munroe Tavern remained in the Munroe family until 1911, after which it was acquired by the Lexington Historical Society. Today, it is maintained as a history museum and boasts a well-preserved taproom, authentic colonial-era furniture, and an educational focus on the British perspective of the Battles of Lexington and Concord.

TAVERNS MOBILIZE FOR WAR

With the spirit of resistance sweeping the colonies, America's taverns became part of the mobilization effort. On June 10, patriots organized at Burnham Tavern in Machias, Maine, before sailing out to capture the British schooner *Margaretta* in the first naval battle of the war. On August 23, 1775, John Lamb, a prominent wine merchant and local Sons of Liberty leader, attempted a daring theft of a dozen cannons from the New York Battery. The raid resulted in a firefight with a British ship of the line, the HMS *Asia*, which pummeled New York throughout the night, eventually sending one of its 18-pound cannon balls through the roof of Fraunces Tavern.[36] On November 10, the Continental Congress in Philadelphia passed resolutions creating the Continental Marines, which would later become the U.S. Marine Corps. First Commandant Samuel Nichols immediately marched over to the Tun Tavern, a well-known Freemason lodge, and began soliciting volunteers with tavern keeper—and first recruiter—Robert Mullan.[37]

With the spirit of resistance sweeping the colonies, America's taverns became part of the mobilization effort.

ABOVE *The Old Tun Tavern. It was here that the first lodge of Freemasons was organized in North America.*

Mill Street Hotel & Tavern

EST. 1723 AS THE THREE TUN TAVERN ✲ TODAY SERVES AS A BAR AND INN OFFERING MEDIUM- AND LONG-TERM RENTALS ✲ MOUNT HOLLY, NEW JERSEY

In the centuries since 1776, the United States has been transformed from Western civilization's frontier curiosity into the world's indispensable economic, cultural, and military power—surviving slavery, civil war, prohibition, depression, and two world wars. In the face of such monumental change, the wonder is that anything survives from the colonial era at all. For most taverns, survival came only with catering to new markets and new tastes: fancier drinks, finer dining, and more comfortable rooms (when rooms are still offered at all)—all of which makes the Mill Street Hotel & Tavern stand out from the pack. It might not be the oldest or the fanciest, but it is the oldest building in Mount Holly and quite possibly the most authentic colonial tavern in America.

The Mill Street Hotel & Tavern first opened its doors in 1723 as the impressively named Three Tun Tavern, signifying the tavern was permitted to store up to three tuns (about 750 gallons) of liquor onsite. Following the Declaration of Independence, the British seized New York and pushed Washington across the Delaware River out of New Jersey and into Pennsylvania. British and Hessian troops established defenses in Trenton and Mount Holly to hold the line, during which time British commanders are believed to have used the Mill Street Hotel as headquarters during the Mount Holly occupation. On December 22 and 23, American forces attacked Hessian positions in what came to be known as the Battle of Iron Works Hill, with the primary objective

being to provoke Hessian forces in Trenton into sending reinforcements at the expense of their own defense. The plan worked, culminating in Washington's dramatic crossing of the Delaware River and surprise attack on the Trenton Hessians.

Today the tavern's outside appearance is sturdy and plain, with a broad brick base and thick porch that give it a massive and permanent presence. Nearly a third of the tavern, clearly an addition, is wood. The tavern's location along the outer boundary of town makes it easy to miss but also makes it a haven for local residents. The bar is tended by the current owners, whose family has owned the tavern for nearly seventy years. The clientele is so thoroughly local that the entire bar is sometimes taken by a single conversation involving virtually every patron. Entertainment consists of a corner jukebox and lone television set, and the front door's sensor squeal is so meekly annoying it's charming. Nothing—not the floors, not the ceilings, not the bar itself—appears original, and the tavern has the distinction of being perhaps the only Revolutionary tavern with beer neon signs in its windows. The tavern still rents out rooms, seven in total. But without a website or a social media account, even the hotel guests tend to be local: tow truck drivers or other working people between jobs and between homes.

The Mill Street Hotel & Tavern is a place to get a good drink, see familiar faces, and even secure an affordable bed when times get tough or just when passing through. What the bar lacks in polished mahogany or post-and-beam ceilings, it makes up for with a sense of deep socioeconomic continuity and a feeling that its current state is the result of an unbroken line of repairs and tweaks made by proud tavern keepers going back three hundred years. Even so, the history is there. A modest sign near the bar signals the establishment's 1723 construction, and the owners keep behind the bar a framed copy of each of the building's liquor licenses going back to 1887.

By the time Thomas Jefferson is said to have sat in Philadelphia's Indian Queen Tavern to pen the first draft of the Declaration of Independence, the air of revolution was beginning to affect popular culture.

ABOVE *Portrait of Thomas Jefferson.*

OPPOSITE *Thomas Paine, author of* The Rights of Man. *Portrait by George Romney, c. 1790.*

Taverns also played a critical role in the propaganda wars, whose greatest tactician was the English-born former corset maker, Thomas Paine. On January 10, 1776, Paine's *Common Sense* used plain language to condemn hereditary monarchy and argue for the independence of the American colonies (Paine is even suspected of having coined the name "United States of America"). Historians differ on how many copies of *Common Sense* sold, but it was probably in the middling tens of thousands and is often considered the best-selling book in American history relative to the population at the time. Paine's work would have reached even more people than its impressive sales implied, as the pamphlet was read aloud in taverns throughout the colonies. George Washington had *Common Sense* read to his troops during the siege of Boston. Paine even used the example of a tavern keeper to illustrate the morality of immediate war with Britain, dismissing the character's desire to postpone any conflict with Great Britain until after his death, and arguing that the honorable choice would be for the tavern keeper to fight now and secure peace for his children. For all of Paine's influence among the commoners, some of America's elite were less impressed. With a whiff of jealousy, John Adams dismissed Paine as having "a better hand at pulling down than building" and his fans as "Men of very little Conversation with the world and Men of very narrow views and very little reflection."[38] Adams's elitist sneer notwithstanding, *Common Sense* helped the young nation discover its identity and still holds up today as one of the most powerful arguments ever made against monarchy.

By the time Thomas Jefferson is said to have sat in Philadelphia's Indian Queen Tavern to pen the first draft of the Declaration of Independence,[39] the air of revolution was beginning to affect popular culture. Taverns with signs depicting symbols of British heraldry, such as the Red Lion or the King George, seemingly changed overnight to such names as the Blue Bell (the symbol of liberty) and the George Washington. Tavern signs politically associated with one side or another were often subjected to attack by opposing forces. Portsmouth, New Hampshire's Earl of Halifax Tavern was the scene of one such encounter. The Sons of Liberty surrounded the tavern, a known Tory establishment, in 1775 and took an axe to its sign.

Rights
of
Man

The Designer of the American Flag Wanted Payment in Wine

BETSY ROSS may (or may not) have sewn the first American flag, but historians are pretty certain she didn't design it. That honor goes to Francis Hopkinson, a lawyer, congressman, and signer of the Declaration of Independence. As acting secretary of the U.S. Navy, Hopkinson laid out a design for the U.S. Navy flag consisting of thirteen alternating red and white stripes with a blue canton filled with thirteen white stars with six points. With only a slight modification (the six-point stars became five points), the design eventually became the flag of the United States. In a May 25, 1780, letter to the Continental Congress, Hopkinson asked "whether a Quarter Cask of the public Wine will be a proper & a reasonable Reward" for his design. Hopkinson's political enemies in Congress blocked his request, and he was never paid.

ABOVE *"Betsy Ross, 1777," by Jean Leon Gerome Ferris, depicts Betsy Ross showing Major Ross and Robert Morris how she cut the stars for the American flag; George Washington sits in a chair on the left.*

SOURCE

Samuel Hughes, "The Artful Rebel," *Pennsylvania Gazette*, May/June 2012.

The innkeeper, a man named Stavers, instructed one of his slaves to attack the men, who struck one of the patriots with such a blow that his faculties never fully recovered. The enraged mob responded by smashing the windows and forcing Stavers to flee town. Stavers was later caught and jailed but eventually freed after swearing an oath of allegiance and renaming his tavern after the friend of America, William Pitt.[40]

Other tavern keepers didn't require such difficult convincing. One Lancaster, Pennsylvania, tavern named after famed British Admiral Peter Warren was renamed after the patriot hero of Bunker Hill, Joseph Warren (on the signboard, Peter Warren's red coat was painted blue to make the transition clear).[41] Perhaps the clearest indication that the American public was culturally breaking from England came in Boston, where a mob gathered the city's heraldic tavern signs for a bonfire outside the pro-American Bunch of Grapes Tavern. One contemporary recounted, "When the Declaration of Independence had been promulgated, this gilt emblem flashed and gave back ruddy beams of a bonfire built in front of the Bunch of Grapes Tavern—a bonfire which consumed crowns, lions, and unicorns."[42]

RIGHT *The London Coffee House in Philadelphia, created by Robert Smith Ale Brewing Co., c. 1908.*

General Warren Inne

EST. 1745 AS THE ADMIRAL VERNON INNE ✱ TODAY OPERATES AS A RESTAURANT, BAR, AND INN ✱ MALVERN, PENNSYLVANIA

Twenty miles west of Philadelphia, the General Warren Inne lies hidden within the wooded hills of the old Lancaster Turnpike. The inn's story begins in 1745 when John Penn, grandson of Pennsylvania founder William Penn, opened its doors for business as the Admiral Vernon Inne, after British naval officer Edward Vernon. The much admired Vernon was nicknamed "Old Grog" for having invented the grog cocktail–rum, water, and lemon—which became a naval staple and the bane of law and order (rowdy taverns frequented by seamen became known as "grog shops"). In 1758, the inn was renamed in honor of another British officer, Admiral Peter Warren, a hero of the French and Indian War. A staunch Tory and dedicated Anglophile, John Penn sided with the British during the Revolutionary War and lent his inn to assist the loyalist cause.

ABOVE *Interior detail of Warren Inne taproom.*

The inn's brush with history is tied to the military campaign under British General Howe during the summer of 1777. Howe had agreed to a joint operation with General John Burgoyne to isolate New England by seizing control of the Hudson River. According to the plan, Howe's forces would march north to Albany from Manhattan, where they'd rendezvous with Burgoyne's forces marching south from Montreal. In a stunning turn of events, Howe instead decided to march on Philadelphia. Burgoyne's abandoned forces were routed at Saratoga, convincing France to enter the war on the American side.

At the Warren, meanwhile, loyalists were drawing up maps of the region to aid Howe's capture of Philadelphia. Rather than marching south from New York through American lines, Howe landed his troops in Chesapeake Bay south of Philadelphia and marched north. Washington engaged Howe at the Battle of Brandywine, during which Americans lost thee hundred men in a stinging defeat. Washington, however, left behind a force of about fifteen hundred men under the command of Brigadier General "Mad Anthony" Wayne to monitor Howe's movements and harass the British rear. By the night of September 20, 1777, British forces had marched into Malvern and captured a local blacksmith suspected of possessing intelligence on Wayne's whereabouts. According to legend, the blacksmith was dragged to the Warren and tortured in a room on the third floor until he confessed: the Americans were camped near the Paoli Tavern, about a mile away. At around midnight, British General Charles Grey marched to Paoli for a surprise attack, going so far as to remove the flints from his soldiers' muskets to

ensure the Americans weren't alerted by a stray shot. The result came to be known as the Paoli Massacre: fifty-three Americans killed, two hundred wounded or captured, and stories of surrendering Americans run through by merciless British bayonets. Howe captured Philadelphia on September 26, to little avail. Burgoyne was defeated, the French declared themselves America's ally, and Philadelphia was of limited military value in any case and was abandoned only eight months later.

John Penn relocated to England after the war and sold the tavern to German Seventh Day Adventist Casper Faumstalk. Washed of its loyalist stain, the tavern returned to prosperity and was (slightly) renamed to the *General* Warren Inne after the Boston patriot and hero of the Battle of Bunker Hill. Like many other country taverns, business went into a steep decline following the advent of railroads. Faumstalk's heirs lacked his business acumen and converted the inn into a temperance hotel in the 1830s. The inn was a private residence for much of the remaining nineteenth century, reopening again as an inn during the 1920s.

Today the Warren boasts an elegantly restored restaurant, tavern, and eight guest rooms (combined from the original fifteen). Behind the inn, a recently renovated all-weather patio shows off the building's original masonry and the vine-covered ruins of the old springhouse. The Warren's excellent condition and its Tory history make it one of the most fascinating and well-preserved inns of the mid-Atlantic.

SOURCE

General Warren Tavern, "History," retrieved October 12, 2015, from http://www.generalwarren.com.

ABOVE *A view of New York in 1776 from the west bank of the Hudson River.*

SIEGE OF NEW YORK

John Adams is said to have estimated that at the outbreak of revolution, one-third of Americans supported the patriots, another third supported Britain, and the final third were neutral. Americans who supported Britain were known as loyalists, or Tories, and no other colony had more Tories than New York. The state is estimated to have contributed 23,500 troops to the British cause, more than all other colonies combined.[43] After Washington liberated Boston from the British occupation, he and the Continental Army began marching toward New York City, calling it "a post of infinite importance."[44]

Washington found that the city's elites were firmly with the Tories. The wealthy James and Oliver DeLancey, sons of the man who built the home that would later become the Fraunces Tavern, would go on to raise three battalions of fifteen hundred American loyalists and a group called DeLancey's Cowboys to fight Washington's forces and raid the homes of their patriot neighbors in Westchester County.[45] Washington, ultimately outnumbered by British forces under General Howe, was forced to flee and regroup outside the city. Before leaving, Washington considered burning New York to the ground rather than let it become Britain's continental stronghold.[46] Ordered by Congress to leave New York unharmed, Washington's fears ultimately played out as the city fell to British forces swiftly following the Declaration of Independence and became the headquarters for Britain's North

American command until the end of the war. (New York would mysteriously catch fire shortly after Washington's withdrawal.)

Tavern keeper Samuel Fraunces sided with the patriots, leaving the city with General Putnam[47] and his tavern with his Tory son-in-law. The year was 1776, and yet records indicate Fraunces didn't officially enlist in the Continental Army until 1780 or 1781. It is assumed that he returned to New York shortly after leaving and worked as a spy in the tavern during the intervening years, during which time the tavern provided food, drink, and community to both sides. According to the Fraunces Tavern museum, in 1780, Tory Governor William Tryon hosted a dinner for seventy at Fraunces Tavern, attended by the city council and several British generals.[48]

Bribes were common during the war, and New York's Tory establishment, including Governor Tryon, Mayor David Matthews, and the DeLancey family, raised money to purchase colonial loyalties. The spectacular betrayal of American General Benedict Arnold, which the British secured for £20,000 and a brigadier generalship in the Royal army, was nevertheless an aberration as such bribes mostly failed to entice American higher officers. Officers of lower rank, however, such as the lowly Thomas Hickey, were more easily tempted. Hickey, an Irishman and British deserter before becoming a member of Washington's personal guard, was eventually caught counterfeiting colonial script, a serious crime punishable by death. While imprisoned, Hickey boasted of a nefarious plot to his cellmate, Isaac Ketchum, who sent letters to New York's Provincial Assembly seeking to exchange information for leniency. In an astonishing episode, Ketchum revealed that Hickey and two coconspirators had accepted an unknown sum to assassinate Washington and General Putnam, disable American cannons, set fire to American positions, and signal the British to attack during the ensuing confusion.

ABOVE *Sketch of New York's Bull's Head Tavern in the Bowery.*

Solomon Drowne Jr., a New York-based patriot war doctor, wrote as news of the conspiracy broke:

> A most infernal plot has lately been discovered here, which, had it been put into execution, would have made America tremble. . . . The hellish conspirators were a number of Tories (the Mayor of [New York] City among them) and three of General Washington's Life Guards. The pretty fellows are in safe custody.[49]

Hickey was court-martialed and executed four days later on June 28, 1776. It is here where Samuel Fraunces might be something of a hero. An alternate, rumor-based explanation of the Hickey affair involves a romantic relationship between the traitor and a housekeeper at the home of Abraham Mortier, where Washington was headquartered. According to the rumor, Hickey tried to impress the housekeeper by telling her of his plot, believing her to be a loyalist. Instead, she was the slave (some suspect the daughter) of New York City tavern keeper Samuel Fraunces. The housekeeper alerted Fraunces, who in turn informed Washington. Historians dismiss this romantic version of events. But what is beyond dispute is that after the war, Congress declared Fraunces "instrumental in discovering and defeating" the assassination plot, and awarded him £2,000, with interest, to help offset debts he had incurred during the war. The generous handout to Fraunces is made more notable given Congress's simmering pay disputes with army officers, which would itself culminate in Washington's teary-eyed farewell address to his disappointed officers seven years later at Fraunces Tavern.

Washington's assassination was thwarted, but his defeat in New York City forced the Continental Army to beat a strategic retreat through New Jersey into Pennsylvania. Believing Washington crushed, British General Howe established a series of military outposts stretching from Manhattan to New Jersey, setting up one of the most iconic events of the Revolution. Washington celebrated Christmas dinner, 1776, beside the warm fire of McConkey's Tavern, located just across the Delaware River from the Hessian garrison at Trenton. That night, Washington led his troops quietly across the Delaware in a surprise attack that left twenty-two Hessians dead, ninety-eight wounded, and over nine hundred captured, along with their munitions and other supplies.[50] The surprise attack invigorated American morale and capped a momentous year for the American cause.

Origin of "Bar"

ASK ANY AMERICAN TO PICTURE the interior of a bar, and chances are that person will imagine a narrow countertop stretching down the length of a room. This classic American-style bar layout, however, is an innovation of the nineteenth-century saloon, and neither the layout, nor even the word *bar*, is believed to have been in common use in colonial taverns. America's first bars were instead known as the tavern taproom, and typically consisted of a restaurant-style arrangement of tables and chairs and a fireplace around which men, and sometimes women, would mill about, play cards, smoke pipes, and discuss business and politics. Rather than stretch the length of the room, the "bar" was squeezed into a corner at 90 degrees. When the tavern keeper stepped out, he or she would protect the liquor from greedy patrons by lowering a hinged barrier from the ceiling and locking it to the countertop. Together, the "barrier" and its design—consisting of evenly spaced bars reminiscent of a prison window—are thought to be the origin of the term *bar*. Many of America's surviving colonial taverns still have these "bars" hinged to the ceiling.

ABOVE *Bar at the Colonial Inn in Concord, Massachusetts.*

SIEGE OF PHILADELPHIA

At the beginning of 1777, Britain's military presence in North America was centered in New York City under General William Howe and in Montreal under General John Burgoyne. The two generals appeared to be hatching a plan to cut off the rebellious New England from the rest of the colonies by marching from their respective positions and converging in Albany, New York. Washington was confounded. Staying in Pennsylvania meant losing New England, and yet relieving New England meant abandoning Philadelphia, the patriot capital.[51] The problem was eventually alleviated by British incompetence: Howe abandoned Burgoyne to pursue Philadelphia by sea, allowing American General Horatio Gates to surround and defeat Burgoyne at Saratoga, New York. Washington, meanwhile, moved to engage Howe's forces outside Philadelphia, setting up what became known as the Paoli Tavern Massacre—one of the most gruesome scenes of the war.

Washington, meanwhile, moved to engage Howe's forces outside Philadelphia, setting up what became known as the Paoli Tavern Massacre—one of the most gruesome scenes of the war.

After spending several days camped at Aiken's Tavern near Elkton, Delaware,[52] General Howe's troops moved on Washington in the Battle of Brandywine on September 11. With Washington's right flank exposed, Americans suffered a stinging defeat, losing three hundred men compared to just ninety-eight British. In retreat toward Chester, Pennsylvania, Washington ordered "A gill of rum or whiskey is to be served out to each man"[53] following the loss. American and British forces engaged in several minor skirmishes in the following days, and on September 18, Washington departed the Seven Stars Tavern (whose proprietor, Benjamin Gerhard, was a local militiaman) to lead the army across the Schuylkill River.[54]

The campaign wasn't over. Washington had left behind a force of about fifteen hundred men under the command of Brigadier General "Mad Anthony" Wayne to monitor Howe's movements and harass his rear. On the night of September 20, 1777, British forces occupying Malvern captured the local blacksmith, tortured him on the third floor of the General Warren Inne (see page 122), and discovered Wayne's division was camped only a mile away near the Paoli Tavern.[55] British General Charles Grey marched his troops under cover of nightfall and made a surprise attack just after midnight, after having removed

OPPOSITE *"Surrender of General Burgoyne at Saratoga N.Y. Oct. 17th. 1777," by John Trumbull, shows British General Burgoyne surrendering his sword to General George Washington after the Battle of Saratoga.*

the flints from his soldiers' muskets to ensure the Americans weren't alerted by a stray shot. The result was a complete British victory, with fifty-three Americans dead and almost two hundred wounded or captured. Only four British were killed. According to several eyewitness accounts, unarmed American soldiers attempting to surrender were mercilessly run through by British bayonets, and the "battle" became known as the Paoli massacre.

Following Brandywine and Paoli, the superior British forces under Howe were unobstructed in marching on Philadelphia, which the Continental Congress had already fled from. With winter approaching and with a string of recent defeats behind him, Washington launched an audacious assault on the British stronghold in Germantown, today a Philadelphia neighborhood but then a distant outpost from downtown. Although Germantown resulted in another British victory, the win was hard fought, and a turn in the weather could have tipped the scales.[56] According to historian Sir George Otto Trevelyan,

OPPOSITE *"Washington's Head Quarters—Brandywine," by Frederic Stevenson, 1856. Landscape drawing shows the house that served as Washington's headquarters at Brandywine, Pennsylvania, during the American Revolution.*

BELOW *"Battle of the Brandywine," by Frederick Coffay Yohn, Pennsylvania, 1777, depicts the battle at Chadd's Ford, Pennsylvania.*

> That the battle had been fought unsuccessfully was of small importance when weighed against the fact that it had been fought at all. Eminent generals, and statesmen of sagacity, in every European Court were profoundly impressed by learning that a new army, raised within the year, and undaunted by a series of recent disasters, had assailed a victorious enemy in his own quarters, and had only been repulsed after a sharp and dubious conflict. . . . The French Government, in making up its mind on the question whether the Americans would prove to be ficient allies, was influenced almost as much by the battle of Germantown as by the surrender of Burgyone.[57]

Following the defeat at Germantown, Washington made preparations for the army to winter in Valley Forge, whose surrounding area featured several taverns where Washington is likely to have visited, including the Broad Axe, Wheel Pump Inn, Wagon and Horses, and Michie Taverns.[58]

BENEDICT ARNOLD AFFAIR

ABOVE *Portrait of Benedict Arnold.*

OPPOSITE TOP *Engraving by Daniels Chodowiecki shows Major John André being taken into custody by three men, John Paulding, Isaac Van Wart, and David Williams, near Tarrytown, New York.*

THESE PAGES *A view of West Point in 1780.*

Between 1778 and 1780, the United States entered into an alliance with France, and the war spread into the American South with the British capture of Savannah. Amid the uneasy stalemate setting in between American and British forces, tension within American ranks over the prospect of victory and pay began testing American cohesion.

On the morning of September 22, 1780, British spymaster John André boarded the man-of-war *Vulture* and sailed up the Hudson River for a secret rendezvous with American General Benedict Arnold. Arnold had agreed to accept £20,000 and a brigadier generalship in the royal army in exchange for surrendering West Point, New York, which would have allowed the British to cut off New England from the rest of the United States. While discussing the terms of Arnold's betrayal, the *Vulture* came under American fire, forcing André and Arnold to flee on horseback several miles to West Haverstraw. There, Arnold provided André with civilian clothes and a fake passport to cross American territory back to occupied New York City. André was intercepted by three American patriots whom he mistook for loyalists and confided his rank as a British officer. At this the Americans searched him and, finding documents detailing the fortifications at West Point hidden in his boot, took him prisoner.

André was marched to the Continental Army headquarters in Tappan, New York, and imprisoned at Mabie's Tavern (see the Old '76 House on page 96). Presiding officer Lieutenant Colonel John Jameson, not suspecting Arnold's treason, decided the best course was to send the West Point papers to Washington and André back to Arnold under American guards. André was thus en route to freedom when the head of Continental intelligence, Major Benjamin Tallmadge, learned of the situation and immediately suspected a traitorous plot involving Arnold. Tallmadge sent riders to bring André back to Mabie's Tavern. The riders were able to retrieve André, though one rider, unaware of the suspected treason, continued on to inform Arnold of the arrest. Arnold received the note at breakfast, then politely excused himself and fled on horseback. When Washington received the papers, he immediately made the 18-mile journey to West Point to investigate. Washington found West Point's defenses in shambles and was irritated that Arnold had not greeted him according to protocol. When it became clear that Arnold had fled under the disgrace of treason, patriot despair was alleviated only by the fact that André was in custody. In the end, a board of senior American officers at Mabie's Tavern argued that André was a spy and deserved death by hanging. Washington agreed, and the punishment was carried out on October 2, 1780, behind the tavern.[59]

To Your Health: Toasts

TOASTS WERE A BIG DEAL in colonial America, allowing for displays of wit and oratory. During the Revolutionary War, Captain William Watson at the Eagle Tavern at East Poultney, Vermont, is said to have famously toasted to "the enemies of our country; May these have cobweb breeches, a porcupine saddle, a hard trotting horse, and an eternal journey." The number of toasts given during a meal was often considered the most serious measure of an evening's festiveness. In his letter to James Madison about the 1800 Independence Day party at the Raleigh Tavern, Thomas Jefferson took great care to enumerate to whom each of the night's eight toasts was given. Others were less impressed. One French visitor found it an "absurd and truly barbarous practice" to have to drink a toast to every man present before dining, exclaiming that a man could "die of thirst, whilst he is obliged to inquire the names, or catch the eye of five and twenty persons" before taking the quenching gulp.

SOURCES

Sharon V. Salinger, *Taverns and Drinking in Early America* (Baltimore: John Hopkins University Press, 2004), 220.

Helene Smith, *Tavern Signs of America* (Greenburg, PA: MacDonald/Swärd Publishing Company, 1989), 20.

"Thomas Jefferson to James Madison, 20 July 1800," in *The Papers of Thomas Jefferson*, vol. 32: *1 June 1800-16 February 1801*, ed. Barbara B. Oberg (Princeton, NJ: Princeton University Press, 2005), 59–61.

AMERICAN VICTORY AND MUTINY

From here the remaining action of the war mostly turned to the South, where battles at Charleston, Waxhaws, and Camden put Americans on the run. The role taverns played in the southern campaign isn't as well documented as the northern theater, though the reasons aren't clear. Enslaved Southerners clearly didn't do much traveling, and the freemen who did could likely find generous hospitality at other plantation homes, undermining the economic basis for taverns. One exception is the Michie Tavern, established in 1784 in Charlottesville, Virginia. Located across from Monticello, the Michie Tavern today hosts a restaurant and taproom, metalsmith, and museum. Another is the Pirates' House in Savannah, Georgia. Built in 1753 along the Savannah River, the Pirates' House was known as a rough grogshop frequented by all stripes of sailors—fishermen, merchants, and pirates. A secret tunnel beneath the tavern supposedly still connects to the nearby harbor and was used to shanghai unsuspecting drunkards to far-flung locales.

Finally, on September 28, 1781, American forces under George Washington and French forces under comte de Rochambeau and comte de Grasse converged on General Cornwallis at Yorktown, Virginia, for the decisive battle in the war. After a three-week siege during which time the trapped Cornwallis sunk over a dozen of his own ships rather than see them fall into the hands of the enemy, the British finally surrendered on October 19. Although the Treaty of Paris was still two years out, Cornwallis's defeat ensured the inevitability of American independence.

ABOVE *"The British surrendering their arms to Gen. Washington after their defeat at YorkTown in Virginia October 1781," by John Francis Renault, c. 1819. Print shows British officers on the right, with Cornwallis presenting his sword to Washington.*

As Ben Franklin would later warn, the American people had their republic, "if they could keep it." Even before the war was over, the new nation faced enormous domestic political and economic challenges. The first signs of trouble appeared on January 1, 1781, when over twenty-five hundred Continental soldiers of the Pennsylvania Line (the eleven regiments under General Wayne's command) mutinied over back pay. The powers of the Continental Congress were few and vague, and depended on the uneven generosity of the respective states to pay the army. Although the Pennsylvania mutiny was eventually resolved, the issue of national government was just beginning.

After the war, Congress began debating the issue of promised pensions and back pay for American army officers. The nation was broke, and with the Constitution still years away, Congress had not yet assumed the power of the purse. The young country was beginning its republican experiment cash poor and with thousands of aggrieved men under arms. Conspiracy was in the air. Months earlier, anonymous broadsides began circulating among American regiments suggesting armed conflict with Congress, and mutinous troops had even forced Congress to flee Philadelphia.[60]

It was against this backdrop that Washington took the floor at Fraunces Tavern to address the "cold and angry faces" of his Continental officers in what is the most celebrated event of that tavern's history.

It was against this backdrop that Washington took the floor at Fraunces Tavern to address the "cold and angry faces" of his Continental officers in what is the most celebrated event of that tavern's history. According to historian Thomas Fleming:

> Washington pulled out a letter from a Virginia delegate who claimed Congress was trying to meet the officers' demands. As the general started to read it, he blinked, rubbed his eyes wearily, and drew a pair of glasses from his pocket. It was the first time anyone except a few aides had seen him wearing them. "Gentlemen," he said. "You will permit me to put on my spectacles, for I have not only grown grey but almost blind in the service of my country." A rustle of unease, a murmur of emotion swept through the audience. . . . Tears began to stream down Washington's cheeks. The officers' anger at this man—if not at Congress—dissolved. . . . They understood that the chief reason for those tears was regret. He had failed to get them the rewards they needed and deserved.[61]

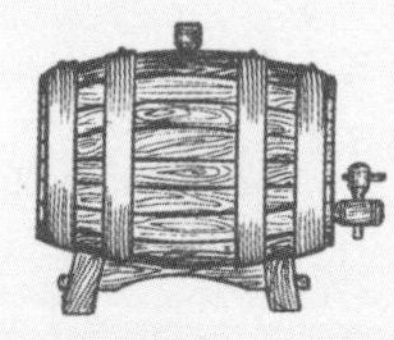

Washington's Farewell Blowout

RATHER THAN SEIZE POWER FOR HIMSELF, George Washington voluntarily resigned his military post at the end of the war, astonishing Europe's rulers and instantly making him a hero of republicanism. Upon hearing of Washington's resignation, King George was said to have gaped, "If he does that, he will be the greatest man in the world." Washington's resignation legitimized the Continental Congress, whose members expressed their gratitude by throwing Washington a bender fit for a would-be king. According to the evening's surviving receipt, Washington and fifty-four other gentlemen crammed into the City Tavern and conquered seven bowls of rum punch, eight bottles of cider, thirty-four bottles of beer, fifty-four bottles of madeira, and sixty bottles of French bordeaux. The total cost in today's dollars has been estimated at $15,400.

ABOVE *"Washington's Farewell to Officers," by H. A. Ogden, c. 1893, shows George Washington shaking hands with an officer, among other officers of the Continental Army, as he bids them farewell in 1783, at the end of the American Revolution.*

SOURCES

Gordon Lloyd, "Entertainment of George Washington at City Tavern, Philadelphia," September 1787, *Teaching American History*.

State of Maryland, "George Washington's Resignation," Maryland State House, retrieved October 24, 2015.

PRECEEDING PAGES *"Washington's triumphal entry into New York, Nov. 25th," by Christian Inger, c. 1860. Print shows George Washington and other military officers riding on horseback as spectators line the street and others observe from balconies and windows. Note the tavern sign in the background, possibly for Fraunces Tavern.*

LEFT *George Washington bidding farewell to a crowd in New York.*

With conflict averted, Washington departed for Annapolis to resign his post before the Congress. While in Annapolis, Washington, Adams, Jefferson, Franklin, and other founders are believed to have visited the Middleton Tavern. Upon learning that Washington intended to retire to Mount Vernon rather than seize power for himself, King George is reported to have gaped "If he does that, he will be the greatest man in the world."

Between the signing of the Treaty of Paris and the departure of the last British troops from American soil, tens of thousands of loyalists descended on British headquarters in New York City to prove their wartime loyalty to the Crown and flee the United States alongside British soldiers. These included wealthy Tories whose property had been confiscated and thousands of runaway slaves whose loyalty to Britain had earned them their freedom. Weekly hearings were held at Fraunces Tavern by British General Samuel Birch to consider each case. By the time the evacuation was complete, an estimated thirty thousand people had fled the United States, mostly for lands elsewhere within the British Empire.[62]

Following the Revolution, George Washington would go on to hire Fraunces as his personal cook, and Congress would go on to locate a sizable portion of the American government in his tavern. Between 1785 and 1790, Fraunces Tavern would house the Departments of State, War, and Treasury and serve as the venue for celebrating the opening of the U.S. Supreme Court.[63] With the 1790 relocation of the American capital to Philadelphia, Fraunces once again became a tavern. The building was acquired and saved from demolition by the Sons of the American Revolution in 1904.

LAST CALL

Within barely a decade, a shockingly improbable series of events drove once-loyal British subjects into rebellion and union. Men were motivated by bravery, virtue, and freedom, with additional nudging from the rum tax, the tea tax, and tavern meetings. Taverns were vital to the Revolutionary War: the Green Dragon, where the Sons of Liberty met; Raleigh Tavern, where Jefferson made common cause with Massachusetts; and City Tavern, where Washington celebrated his victory. There was the first shot fired from the Buckman, the founding of the Marine Corps at the Tun, the hanging of Major John André at the Old '76 House, and the reading of Thomas Paine's *Common Sense* in hundreds, if not thousands, of taverns throughout the country. The United States owes its existence to passions first unleashed when a foreign power tried to make alcohol too expensive and to the unsung tavern keepers who lent their homes and businesses to the cause of educating, recruiting, and at times leading their brothers and sisters into the War for Independence.

CHAPTER 4

MISTS OF INTOXICATION AND FOLLY

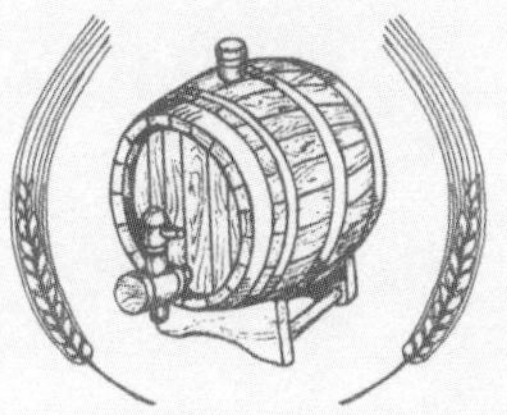

With the war over, Americans had to prove they were capable of self-government. Success was not assured. Internal rebellion over new land and liquor taxes nearly broke the weak confederation government, leading to the creation of a new federal Constitution. Change was in the air. Rum, America's most popular spirit for 150 years, was finally displaced by whiskey, sparking a spectacular half-century binge. Meanwhile, a combination of new wealth and urbanization led to new options for American travelers, and taverns were gradually displaced by modern hotels and restaurants.

No sooner had American independence been recognized by Britain than key members of the leadership class of '76 left the scene. George Washington resigned his military post and retired to Mount Vernon, while John Adams, Thomas Jefferson, and Benjamin Franklin were serving as ambassadors in Britain and France. These were the years under the Articles of Confederation, a preconstitutional government presided over by men such as Cyrus Griffin and Nathaniel Gorham, largely forgotten by history. Federal operations under the Articles depended on voluntary financial contributions from the states, which, unsurprisingly, rarely came, and the government's lack of resources began to undermine political stability at a crucial point in the young nation's development. "Thirteen sovereignties pulling against each other" warned Washington, "and all tugging at the federal head will soon bring ruin on the whole."[1] Barely three years after the last British soldier left the United States, an armed insurrection in Massachusetts known to history as Shays' Rebellion would fundamentally alter the course of American history.

PRECEEDING PAGES *"American Scenery—The Inn on the Roadside," by an unknown artist, c. 1872, depicts a busy day outside an American tavern at a crossroads.*

LEFT *Satirical engraving by Amos Doolittle highlighting issues in Connecticut politics on the eve of the ratification of the U.S. Constitution, 1787.*

A series of remarkably familiar events began to unfold. In late August 1786, bands of militant farmers, opposed to tax policies and radicalized by tavern politics, swept rural Massachusetts and seized state government buildings across five counties. The rebels established Committees of Correspondence and coordinated the rebellion through a network of taverns, including Conkey's Tavern in Pelham, Upton Tavern in Fitchburg, the Old Goldsury Inn in Warwick, and Fuller's Tavern in Ludlow.[2] When the state militia was sent in to put the rebels down, many of those men bucked the law and joined the rebels. In a letter to George Washington, Lieutenant Colonel Henry Lee estimated "the five seditious countys possess 40,000 [rebels]. . . . Upon a fair calculation I believe we may reckon that state divided for & against Government"[3] (in reality the rebels had about four thousand men, and about half of those "armed" had little more than pitchforks). Even more worrying to the government was that the rebellion's apparent leader, Daniel Shays, was a respected veteran of both Bunker Hill and Ticonderoga.

Rumors that the rebels planned to seize the federal munitions cache at Springfield spread fears of everything from a military coup to a conspiracy to return New England to George III. As recounted in Leonard Richard's history of the rebellion, an alleged interview with Shays printed in the *Massachusetts Centinel* claimed the rebel plan was to seize the federal munitions and "march directly to Boston, plunder it, and then . . . burn it and lay the town of Boston in ashes" in order to "overthrow the present constitution."[4] John Adams feared that unless the situation was addressed, it would "infallibly lead to a civil war, with all its horrors."[5]

Reactions from key founders were varied. Thomas Jefferson, writing from Paris and unburdened by responsibility, reacted with some of his most famously dismissive rhetoric regarding law and order. After briefly affirming an unconvincing disapproval, Jefferson spent considerable ink justifying the rebels:

> Even this evil is productive of good. It prevents the degeneracy of government and nourishes a general attention to the public affairs. I hold it that a little rebellion now and then is a good thing, and as necessary in the political world as storms in the physical. Unsuccessful rebellions, indeed, generally establish the encroachments on the rights of the people which have produced them. An observation of this truth should render honest republican governors so mild in their punishment of rebellions as not to discourage them too much. It is a medicine necessary for the sound health of government.[6]

Washington, however, would have none of it. Writing to Henry Lee, Washington said the rebellion left him "mortified beyond expression." Washington took republican ideals with profound seriousness and was eager to showcase a stable self-government to sneering European elites. He considered the "mist of intoxication and folly"[7] in Massachusetts a clear threat:

> How melancholy is the Reflection, that in so short a space, we should have made such large strides towards fulfilling the prediction of our transatlantic foe! "Leave them to themselves, and their government will soon dissolve." Will not the wise & good strive hard to avert this evil? Or will their supineness suffer ignorance and the arts of self interested designing disaffected & desperate characters, to involve this rising empire in wretchedness & contempt?[8]

Publick House Historic Inn

EST. 1771 AS CRAFTS' TAVERN ✻ TODAY OPERATES AS AN INN, RESTAURANT, TAPROOM, BAR, AND BAKERY ✻ STURBRIDGE, MASSACHUSETTS

The story of the Publick House Inn offers a brief glimpse into the spartan grit of eighteenth-century American life. Of the fifteen children born to Royal Navy Captain Joseph Crafts and his wife, Susannah Warner, only three survived to adulthood. The youngest of these, Ebenezer, shunned his father's military service to pursue theology at Yale. Ebenezer is believed to have been a bullish young man, and despite his ecclesiastic calling, he was known for lifting cider barrels overhead to drink from the bunghole. Perhaps unsurprisingly, the Sturbridge congregation ultimately denied Ebenezer's attempt to take the pulpit, favoring instead his best friend, Joshua Payne.

Portrait of Samuel Crafts

The disgruntled Ebenezer joined the militia in Massachusetts, where his combination of brains and brawn enabled him to rise in the ranks. He married Mehitabel Chandler, and they moved into a single-room dwelling on a lot at the edge of town that Ebenezer won in a game of cards. The dwelling was torn down and replaced in the fall of 1771 with what was known as Crafts' Tavern, later the Publick House Inn. The thirteen bedrooms each piled as many as four to a bed for 3 shillings. The tavern included a men's-only smoking room, a ladies'-only parlor, a taproom (today's Pineapple Room), and a kitchen. In addition to food and beverage service, Crafts' retailed everyday

ABOVE *Giant hearth inside the Publick House Inn dining room.*

items such as sugar, nails, and tea, and it provided postal service and lodging accommodations. According to the inn's official history, Crafts' would courier mail weekly to and from Boston, bringing news of escalating hostility toward the Crown.

As a colonel in the local militia, Crafts drilled and outfitted soldiers on Sturbridge Common. When news of the Battles of Lexington and Concord reached Sturbridge on April 20, 1775, Crafts captained a company of cavalrymen from Sturbridge and the nearby towns of Charlton, Dudley, and Oxford to serve in the siege of Boston. Following the war, he raised another cavalry regiment in Worcester County to confront the rebellion under Daniel Shays in western Massachusetts.

Crafts suffered financially after the war as runaway inflation devalued colonial currency and a severe depression set in. He sold the tavern and eventually relocated to Vermont, where he and extended family established the town of Craftsbury, which still exists.

Sturbridge was bypassed by the railroads in the 1850s, and its economic fortunes took a turn for the worse. The tavern eventually became a boardinghouse for women, known as The Elms, in honor of the elm trees in front thought to have been planted by Colonel Crafts or his son Samuel. The building became a transfer station for the U.S. military during World War II, before finally being restored to a tavern and inn.

Today, the historic portion of the inn contains seventeen rooms and suites, with additional newer rooms located elsewhere on the property. From the narrow hallways, creaky floorboards, and very low doorknobs (as if measured for a hobbit), guests are everywhere presented with subtle reminders of the inn's age. A massive six-foot hearth fireplace dominates the taproom, and the historic atmosphere is completed by low-beam ceilings and traditional tavern fare—including lobster pie, pot roast, and roasted turkey, each served in continental proportions.

Colonial Cocktails

PHILADELPHIA FISH HOUSE PUNCH

RUM WAS THE MOST POPULAR SPIRIT in colonial America, enjoyed by commoners and elite alike. Americans drank rum straight or blended it with water, beer, or, most popular, punch. This recipe, from David Wondrich's adaptation in *Imbibe!* is meant for a party of 12 to 15 people.

INGREDIENTS

1 lb. demerara sugar

3 qt. water

1 pt. lemon juice

Peel of 3 lemons

Mixture of 3 oz. sweet peach brandy, 27 oz. brandy, and 18 oz. rum

DIRECTIONS

Pour the sugar into a large punch bowl.

Peel three lemons, avoiding the pith, and place in the sugar to enable extraction for about 30 minutes. Juice the lemons, setting juice aside.

Boil 1 pint of water, combine with the sugar in bowl, and stir to dissolve the sugar.

Remove the lemon peel from bowl and add to the punch bowl with all lemon juice and brandy/rum mixture.

Place the punch bowl in the refrigerator to cool for at least 1 hour.

Add block of ice and serve.

*Ice blocks can easily be made by freezing water in a plastic vessel, appropriately sized to your punch bowl. The larger the block, the longer it will stay frozen and the slower the punch will be diluted with water.

ABOVE *Portrait of Daniel Shays (left) and Job Shattuck as seen on the cover of Bickerstaff's Boston Almanac, 1787. Shays and Shattuck headed Shays' Rebellion.*

Washington continued on a prescient note: "Without some alteration in our political creed, the superstructure we have been seven years raising at the expence of much blood and treasure, must fall. We are fast verging to anarchy & confusion!"[9]

Amid deserting state militia and an impotent federal government, Boston merchants were forced to act. The merchants pooled £6,000 to raise a force of four thousand men under Revolutionary War General Benjamin Lincoln. Lincoln first marched on Springfield where, on January 25, 1787, he defended the federal arsenal there from a skittish rebel attack from which most rebel officers escaped. Shays and his men retreated to Petersham, separated from Lincoln by 30 miles and the harsh Massachusetts winter. This proved insufficient. On February 4, 1787, upon learning of Shays's position, Lincoln marched his men at night through a blizzard and mostly crushed the rebellion the following morning. A final battle on February 27, in Sheffield, Connecticut, put an end to the uprising with four dead, thirty wounded, and 150 captured. In addition to swearing an oath to state authority, surrendering rebels faced restrictions on voting and jury rights. In a sign of how destabilizing, dangerous, and politicized the business of tavern keeping had become, the rebels also faced a three-year prohibition from all tavern work and alcohol sales.[10]

CONSTITUTIONAL CONVENTION

Shays' Rebellion sent a shock through the American political system, convincing Washington, Madison, and other leading men to call on the states to reform the national charter. But before the famous Philadelphia Convention of 1787, a dress rehearsal of sorts took place in Annapolis, Maryland. In fact, delegates from several states were already meeting at Mann's Tavern in Annapolis to discuss reforming the federal government when Shays' Rebellion broke out. With only five participating states, however, a quorum could not be reached. New York delegate Alexander Hamilton recommended, with "an anxiety for the welfare of the United States" that "speedy measures may be taken, to effect a general meeting, of the States, in a future Convention."[11] While Mann's Tavern was destroyed long ago, the Middleton Tavern, established in 1750, still stands two blocks from where Mann's once stood. The Middleton has its own impressive history because Annapolis was the seat of the Continental Congress for a time. It was in Annapolis where Washington resigned his military commission and Congress ratified the Treaty of Paris, officially ending the Revolutionary War.

ABOVE *Portrait of Alexander Hamilton.*

OPPOSITE *Page one of the original U.S. Constitution.*

Once the call for a convention went out, it found broad, if anxious, support. In a letter to John Adams, Samuel Osgood wrote of the prevailing sentiment, expressing hope for a new republic while also hinting at the specter of monarchy and military rule:

> The Idea of a special Convention appointed by the States, to agree upon, & propose such Alterations as may appear necessary, seems to gain Ground—But the Danger is that neither Congress nor a Convention will do the Business. . . . And the Probability is at present, that, that Army, will be seriously employed—And in Case of a civil War—The Men of Property will certainly attach themselves very closely to that Army; the final issue of which, it is feared, will be, *that the Army will make the Government of the united States* [emphasis added].[12]

In the *Federalist Papers*, Alexander Hamilton and James Madison argued, "Liberty may be endangered by the abuses of liberty, as well as by the abuses of power." Hamilton's assessment was soon validated on the streets of Paris during the French Revolution, making it little

We the People

of the United States, in Order to form a more perfect Union, establish Justice, insure domestic Tranquility, provide for the common defence, promote the general Welfare, and secure the Blessings of Liberty to ourselves and our Posterity, do ordain and establish this Constitution for the United States of America.

Article. I.

Section. 1. All legislative Powers herein granted shall be vested in a Congress of the United States, which shall consist of a Senate and House of Representatives.

Section. 2. The House of Representatives shall be composed of Members chosen every second Year by the People of the several States, and the Electors in each State shall have the Qualifications requisite for Electors of the most numerous Branch of the State Legislature.

No Person shall be a Representative who shall not have attained to the Age of twenty five Years, and been seven Years a Citizen of the United States, and who shall not, when elected, be an Inhabitant of that State in which he shall be chosen.

Representatives and direct Taxes shall be apportioned among the several States which may be included within this Union, according to their respective Numbers, which shall be determined by adding to the whole Number of free Persons, including those bound to Service for a Term of Years, and excluding Indians not taxed, three fifths of all other Persons. The actual Enumeration shall be made within three Years after the first Meeting of the Congress of the United States, and within every subsequent Term of ten Years, in such Manner as they shall by Law direct. The Number of Representatives shall not exceed one for every thirty Thousand, but each State shall have at Least one Representative; and until such enumeration shall be made, the State of New Hampshire shall be entitled to chuse three, Massachusetts eight, Rhode-Island and Providence Plantations one, Connecticut five, New-York six, New Jersey four, Pennsylvania eight, Delaware one, Maryland six, Virginia ten, North Carolina five, South Carolina five, and Georgia three.

When vacancies happen in the Representation from any State, the Executive Authority thereof shall issue Writs of Election to fill such Vacancies.

The House of Representatives shall chuse their Speaker and other Officers; and shall have the sole Power of Impeachment.

Section. 3. The Senate of the United States shall be composed of two Senators from each State, chosen by the Legislature thereof for six Years; and each Senator shall have one Vote.

Immediately after they shall be assembled in Consequence of the first Election, they shall be divided as equally as may be into three Classes. The Seats of the Senators of the first Class shall be vacated at the Expiration of the second Year, of the second Class at the Expiration of the fourth Year, and of the third Class at the Expiration of the sixth Year, so that one third may be chosen every second Year; and if Vacancies happen by Resignation, or otherwise, during the Recess of the Legislature of any State, the Executive thereof may make temporary Appointments until the next Meeting of the Legislature, which shall then fill such Vacancies.

No Person shall be a Senator who shall not have attained to the Age of thirty Years, and been nine Years a Citizen of the United States, and who shall not, when elected, be an Inhabitant of that State for which he shall be chosen.

The Vice President of the United States shall be President of the Senate, but shall have no Vote, unless they be equally divided.

The Senate shall chuse their other Officers, and also a President pro tempore, in the Absence of the Vice President, or when he shall exercise the Office of President of the United States.

The Senate shall have the sole Power to try all Impeachments. When sitting for that Purpose, they shall be on Oath or Affirmation. When the President of the United States is tried, the Chief Justice shall preside: And no Person shall be convicted without the Concurrence of two thirds of the Members present.

Judgment in Cases of Impeachment shall not extend further than to removal from Office, and disqualification to hold and enjoy any Office of honor, Trust or Profit under the United States: but the Party convicted shall nevertheless be liable and subject to Indictment, Trial, Judgment and Punishment, according to Law.

Section. 4. The Times, Places and Manner of holding Elections for Senators and Representatives, shall be prescribed in each State by the Legislature thereof; but the Congress may at any time by Law make or alter such Regulations, except as to the Places of chusing Senators.

The Congress shall assemble at least once in every Year, and such Meeting shall be on the first Monday in December, unless they shall by Law appoint a different Day.

Section. 5. Each House shall be the Judge of the Elections, Returns and Qualifications of its own Members, and a Majority of each shall constitute a Quorum to do Business; but a smaller Number may adjourn from day to day, and may be authorized to compel the Attendance of absent Members, in such Manner, and under such Penalties as each House may provide.

Each House may determine the Rules of its Proceedings, punish its Members for disorderly Behaviour, and, with the Concurrence of two thirds, expel a Member.

Each House shall keep a Journal of its Proceedings, and from time to time publish the same, excepting such Parts as may in their Judgment require Secrecy; and the Yeas and Nays of the Members of either House on any question shall, at the Desire of one fifth of those Present, be entered on the Journal.

Neither House, during the Session of Congress, shall, without the Consent of the other, adjourn for more than three days, nor to any other Place than that in which the two Houses shall be sitting.

Section. 6. The Senators and Representatives shall receive a Compensation for their Services, to be ascertained by Law, and paid out of the Treasury of the United States. They shall in all Cases, except Treason, Felony and Breach of the Peace, be privileged from Arrest during their Attendance at the Session of their respective Houses, and in going to and returning from the same; and for any Speech or Debate in either House, they shall not be questioned in any other Place.

No Senator or Representative shall, during the Time for which he was elected, be appointed to any civil Office under the Authority of the United States, which shall have been created, or the Emoluments whereof shall have been encreased during such time; and no Person holding any Office under the United States, shall be a Member of either House during his Continuance in Office.

Section. 7. All Bills for raising Revenue shall originate in the House of Representatives; but the Senate may propose or concur with Amendments as on other Bills.

Every Bill which shall have passed the House of Representatives and the Senate, shall, before it become a Law, be presented to the President of the wonder that his opinion carried great weight with General Washington. And on America's current position Hamilton was clear: "the former" he wrote, is "most to be apprehended by the United States."[13]

Lest the establishment of an American monarchy be dismissed by modern readers as an unlikely or even unserious potential outcome of the Revolution, one need only review the sentiment of the commander in chief himself. Washington made clear his belief that the greatest danger facing the United States was not the abuse of power but the abuses resulting from the absence of power. In a remarkably candid letter to James Madison prior to the Constitutional Convention, a somber Washington confessed that his "opinion of public virtue" had been "so far changed" by recent events that he was readily "admitting the utility;—nay necessity" of monarchy. The only thing that held him back, it seems, apart from personal humility, was the belief that the public would rebel. "I am fully of [the] opinion that those who lean to a Monarchical governmt. have . . . not consulted the public mind," he wrote, adding that such a move would shake "the Peace of this Country to its foundation."[14] All the more reason, he wrote, that the convention must succeed: "If the system proves inefficient . . . then, and not till then, in my opinion can [monarchy] be attempted without involving all the evils of civil discord."[15] That Washington had the power, opportunity, and inclination to support establishing an American monarchy and yet still refused power makes his character and leadership style all the more impressive.

This was the backdrop against which delegates convened at Independence Hall in Philadelphia from May through September 1787. Delegates were sworn to secrecy for the five-month convention, with Washington presiding. Given the gravity of these affairs, it's little wonder that on signing the finished draft of the Constitution, Philadelphia threw the departing Washington and the other delegates a huge bash at the City Tavern. Sponsored by the First Troop Philadelphia City Cavalry, Washington and fifty-four other gentlemen conquered seven bowls of rum punch, eight bottles of cider, thirty-four bottles of beer, fifty-four bottles of madeira, and sixty bottles of French bordeaux. The total cost has been estimated to have equaled $15,400 in today's dollars.[16]

ABOVE *"Washington taking leave of the officers of his army: at Francis's Tavern, Broad Street, New York, Dec. 4th. 1783." by N. Currier, c. 1848.*

On July 21, 1788, New Hampshire became the ninth and decisive state to ratify the U.S. Constitution, establishing it as the law of the land and putting in motion the first presidential election, to be held in December. George Washington agreed to lend his immense popularity to the new office of the presidency and had hoped to unify the nation with a series of tours designed to visit each state that had ratified the Constitution. Six months after he was sworn in, Washington began this tour by leaving New York (then the national capital) to take a

four-week presidential tour of New England. Washington and his staff stayed in many private homes and several taverns across New England, leading to the many dubious claims that "Washington slept here." With the brevity of a military man, Washington did keep a journal on this excursion, during which time he mentions several taverns:

ABOVE *"The dawn of peace. Morning of the surrender of Yorktown," by Gilchrist A. Campbell, c. 1881.*

> **October 10, 1789:** "Dined at the tavern [on Ward's Island, New York] kept by a Captain Mariner, and came home in the evening."
>
> **October 11, 1789:** "Commenced my Journey about 9 o'clock for Boston and a tour through the Eastern States. About 10 o'clock we arrived at the house of one Hoyatt, who keeps a Tavern at Kingsbridge, where we dined . . . we proceeded to the Tavern of a Mrs. Haviland at Rye [New York]; who keeps a very neat and decent Inn."

October 18, 1789: "The Governor, the Lieut. Governor, the Mayor, and Speaker . . . all dined with me, (by invitation,) as did Genl. Huntington, at the House of Mr. Brown, where I lodged, and who keeps a good Tavern."

October 19, 1789: "The ride is very pleasant, but the Road is sandy, which it continues to be within a mile of the Tavern (Carrington's, which is but an ordinary house,) at Wallingford [Connecticut]. At Weathersfield we were met by a party of the Hartford light horse, and a number of Gentlemen from the same place with Col. Wadsworth at their head, and escorted to Bull's Tavern [in Hartford], where we lodged."

October 21, 1789: "Parson's Tavern, where I lodged." [Connecticut]

October 22, 1789: "Lodged at the House of one Jenks, who keeps a pretty good Tavern." [Massachusetts]

November 5, 1789: "Breakfasted at Abbot's tavern, in Andover [Massachusetts]."

November 6, 1789: "The house in Uxbridge [Massachusetts] had a good external appearance, (for a tavern) but the owner of it being from home, and the wife sick, we could not gain admittance; which was the reason of my coming on to Taft's, where though the people were obliging, the entertainment was not very inviting."

November 8, 1789: "It being contrary to law and disagreeable to the People of this State (Connecticut) to travel on the Sabbath day—and my horses, after passing through such intolerable roads, wanting rest, I stayed at Perkins' tavern (which, by the by, is not a good one,) all day—and a meeting-house being within a few rods of the door, I attended morning and evening service, and heard very lame discourses from a Mr. Pond."

November 12, 1789: "A little before sunrise we left Marvin's, and breakfasting at Stamford, 13 miles distant, reached the Widow Haviland's [tavern], 12 miles further . . ." [New York]

November 13, 1789: "Breakfasted at Hoyet's tavern, this side of King's-bridge."[17] [New York]

Gadsby's Tavern

EST. 1785 ✱ TODAY OPERATES AS A RESTAURANT, TAPROOM, AND MUSEUM ✱ ALEXANDRIA, VIRGINIA

In 1785, John Wise erected an elegant tavern in the middle of downtown Alexandria, Virginia, a bustling port city along the Potomac and an epicenter of the American tobacco trade. The spacious tavern boasted a public taproom, multiple private dining rooms, and spacious accommodations. Wise was an ambitious man and business was booming. In 1792, he expanded the tavern on the adjacent lot, naming it the City Tavern and Hotel. Now with twenty rooms in total, Wise rented the building to Englishman John Gadsby, whose name it soon informally took.

As the fancy "hotel" label implied, the new space boasted the finest amenities and used some of the most advanced technology of the day. During the winter, carriages towed ice from the Potomac and lowered it into the tavern's subterranean ice well. When packed in

Gadsby's Tavern is today divided into a museum (bottom left and opposite) and a restaurant and dining room (above).

and covered with straw, the well was capable of keeping ice frozen through even Virginia's sweltering summers. Another oddity can be seen from the second-story hall: a doorway seemingly floats in the wall a good 8 feet above the floor—without any stairs in sight. The opening is accessible only by ladder, which musicians used to climb to access the ballroom balcony opposite the hall.

The Gadsby's ballroom is by far the largest and most impressive such space of the taverns featured in this book, and probably of any other tavern surviving from the era. Judging from Gadsby's clientele, it was likely considered equally impressive by its contemporaries. On March 22, 1797, George Washington was feted there with what was then estimated to have been the largest banquet ever held in Alexandria. Sixteen toasts were given, and a painting of Mount Vernon was hung from the ceiling in Washington's honor.

In fact, Washington became a regular customer. He dined there again on May 5, 1797, and may have attended a Freemason dinner on December 27 later that year. In 1798, he celebrated his birthday at

Gadsby's, had a business lunch on August 6, and received a sixteen-round salute from the steps of the tavern from "Captain Young's troops of cavalry and the company of Alexandria blues" on November 5. On February 11, 1799, he "went up to Alexandria to the celebration of my birth day . . . an elegant Ball & Supper at Night." Barely a month before he died, Washington politely declined an invitation for himself and Martha to a dance party at Gadsby's, explaining that "our dancing days are no more."

The outcome of the vicious presidential election between Thomas Jefferson and John Adams was still unknown when Jefferson stayed overnight at the Gadsby's on January 3, 1801. After Jefferson emerged victorious on February 17, he returned to Gadsby's for an inaugural banquet during which he toasted "Prosperity to the town of Alexandria." John Adams, the marquis de Lafayette, and John Quincy Adams are all believed to have also visited the tavern.

Gadsby's splendor kept it competitive througout the nineteenth century. By the early twentieth century, however, the Gadsby's old age had caught up. The New York Metropolitan Museum of Art culled the ballroom's original woodwork and other fixtures in 1917 for an American history exhibit (the originals are still in New York, and the ballroom has been restored with replica furnishings). The American Legion began restoring both buildings in the 1920s, and eventually sold them to the City of Alexandria for a more complete restoration in time for the 1976 bicentennial.

Today, the 1785 structure of Gadsby's Tavern functions as a museum and is available for tours. The 1792 structure, which still uses its original door, is a restaurant and taproom specializing in colonial fare, complete with period clothing for the servers and the odd period actor and musician milling about. The expertly restored ballroom is rented out for major events, including cider and beer tastings, and even the ice well has been restored for public viewing from the sidewalk.

WHISKEY REBELLION

With independence secured, Shays' Rebellion suppressed, the Constitution ratified, and Washington elected president, the United States began its experiment of national union in earnest. But the rebellions weren't over. Treasury Secretary Alexander Hamilton had successfully urged Congress to establish national credit by assuming the debts incurred by the states during the Revolutionary War. "Assumption," as the policy was known, had an unintended impact on whiskey production, resulting in the first major challenge to President Washington and, by extension, American constitutional authority.

Although Americans had been making whiskey since the earliest days of settlement, rum had always remained king. In his excellent history on rum and the American Revolution, Ian Williams points out that before the war, the American colonies were essentially sustenance economies, and grain was simply too essential a foodstuff to be used for spirits. In 1676, New York Governor Edmund Andros even outlawed distilling grain. Of whatever surplus grain there was, merchants fared better by trading it to the West Indies for molasses to fuel domestic rum stills. The Revolutionary War, however, disrupted the import of West Indies molasses, creating an opening for whiskey. This crack in the market was pried open further after the war, when American colonists began settling western lands previously restricted by Great Britain.[18] The explosion in rye and corn cultivation that followed created a domestic whiskey boom that would in some ways define nineteenth-century America, particularly in the saloons of the west. By the time Washington had assumed the presidency, whiskey was closing in on rum as America's spirit of choice.

After Hamilton's debt assumption policy took effect, the new federal government sought revenue sources to pay off the debt. On January 27, 1791, Congress approved a tax on distilled spirits on a 35-to-21 vote. Western grain farmers, particularly in Pennsylvania, heavily criticized the law. At issue was basic fairness. The law allowed distillers to lower their effective tax rate by producing more whiskey, effectively creating a regressive tax on small whiskey outfits. In an era when paper money was still unreliable and specie was rare,

ABOVE *Painting, attributed to Frederick Kemmelmeyer, shows Washington reviewing his troops near Fort Cumberland, Maryland, before marching to quash the Whiskey Rebellion in Pennsylvania.*

many laborers were paid in whiskey. To them, the whiskey tax was an income tax.

As during the American Revolution and Shays' Rebellion, opponents of the distilled spirits tax organized into tavern assemblies, formed Committees of Correspondence, submitted petitions, and even resorted to terror. Tax collectors were tarred and feathered, whipped, burned in effigy, and their property destroyed. In western Pennsylvania, radicalized farmers seized control of the local militia and, by default, local government. Several rebel taverns still stand, including Jean Bonnet's in Bedford, Pennsylvania.

As with Shays' Rebellion, Washington was appalled. "A small portion of the United States," he wrote, cannot "dictate to the whole union." In what we would now call his State of the Union address to Congress in 1794, Washington described the situation as he saw it:

Colonial Cocktails

CHOWNING'S RATTLE SKULL

INGREDIENTS

5 oz. dark beer (preferably porter)

¾ oz. dark rum

½ tsp. lime juice

Ground nutmeg

DIRECTIONS

Combine rum, beer, and lime juice in a chilled tumbler.

Stir gently.

Garnish with the nutmeg.

COLONIAL AMERICANS WERE a hardy people whose isolation on the American frontier left little choice but to embrace the virtues of simplicity and frugality. This attitude extended to beverages, which were blends of the limited ingredients at hand. A case in point is the Rattle Skull, a spicy, and intimidating, concoction of beer, rum, and lime that works surprisingly well. Like many other colonial cocktails, the drink seems to be specifically engineered for sipping by a fire during the peak autumn leaf season. This recipe comes from Chowning's Tavern in Colonial Williamsburg.

> While the greater part of Pennsylvania itself were conforming themselves to the acts of excise; a few Counties were resolved to frustrate them. . . . Legal process was therefore delivered to the Marshal, against the Rioters and delinquent distillers. No sooner was he understood to be engaged in this duty, than the vengeance of armed men was aimed at his person, and the person and property of the Inspector of the Revenue. They fired upon the marshal, arrested him—and detained him, for some time, as a prisoner. He was obliged by the jeopardy of his life, to renounce the service of other process, on the west side of the Alleghany mountain; and a deputation was afterwards sent to him to demand a surrender of that which he had served. A numerous body repeatedly attacked the house of the Inspector, seized his papers of Office—and finally destroyed by fire, his buildings and whatsoever they contained. Both of these Officers, from a just regard to their safety, fled to the Seat of Government; it being avowed, that the motives to such outrages were to compel the resignation of the Inspector—to withstand by force of arms the authority of the United States, and thereby to extort a repeal of the laws of excise, and an alteration in the conduct of Government.

Washington eventually raised thirteen thousand troops and marched them into rebel Pennsylvania territory, becoming the first and only sitting president to physically lead an army into conflict. The rebellion fell apart during the foray, resulting in the arrest of a couple of dozen of its leaders, all of whom were pardoned. Washington remained deeply unpopular in the western counties of Pennsylvania, and tavern signs bearing his likeness, such the President's Head Tavern, were shot at repeatedly by embittered rebels.[19] Even a culture war–style politics emerged, with whiskey drinking touted as rustic and independent, while wine was associated with East Coast snobbery. Hugh Henry Brackenridge, a rebel leader, polemicist, publisher, and author of what many consider America's first novel (*Father Bombo's Pilgrimage to Mecca*), wrote of whiskey that it was "far better than the drink ca'd wine: Wi' me compar'd tis wash for swine."[20] Just five years later, in 1799, George Washington made his last military appearancs on the steps of Alexandria's Gadsby's Tavern in Virginia, while reviewing the Alexandria Militia.[21]

RISE OF WHISKEY

A peculiar set of factors converged in early America that resulted in a social tolerance for day-long consumption of low-to-moderately alcoholic beverages like spruce beer, hard cider, and watered-down rum. First, freshwater was considered unsafe to drink. Second, alcohol was a valuable calorie supplement for isolated settlers on a cold continent. Finally, poor infrastructure made transporting grain and fruit extremely difficult, leading farmers to preserve the value of excess crops by distilling them into ardent spirits that were storable and easier to transport. While hangovers are bad, cholera, dysentery, and pauperism were much worse.

Provided the drinks are both moderately alcoholic and moderately priced, a society might be able to pull off a habit of constant drinking without too much abuse. Colonial America seems to have had some success on this front. "Drunkenness" wrote Thomas Jefferson, may have been "more common in all the American States than in France, but it is less common there than in England."[22] Washington wrote proudly of post-Revolutionary Virginia as a place where "there was less drunkenness, [and] that people no longer forced drinks on their guests or made it a point of honor to send them home drunk."[23] The founders may have disdained drunkenness, but they weren't teetotalers: John Adams began each day with a mug of hard cider, George Washington developed his own beer recipe, and Thomas Jefferson carefully introduced French vines to Monticello. In short, colonial and post-Revolutionary America was like a functioning alcoholic—marginally self-destructive yet still capable of getting to work in the morning. But when cheap and plentiful whiskey is grafted atop such a libatious culture, one mustn't be surprised if the wheels suddenly come off.

In 1795, Dr. Benjamin Rush, a signer of the Declaration of Independence and the U.S. Army's first surgeon general, published what could be considered the opening shot of the temperance movement. In his essay, "An Inquiry into the Effects of Ardent Spirits upon the Human Body and Mind," Rush estimated that four thosuand

ABOVE *Exterior of Washington's whiskey stills at Mount Vernon.*

Americans were being killed by alcohol poisoning annually, or about one thousand deaths per 1 million people.[24] This estimate, if accurate, represents nightmarish alcoholism and depravity on a Boschian scale. For context, the Centers for Disease Control estimated that alcohol poisoning killed about twenty-two hundred Americans in 2012, or about 8.8 for every 1 million people.[25] One colorful anecdote that Rush provided includes a case of animal abuse followed by redemption:

". . . men of every class unite and besiege the general and state governments, with petitions to limit the number of taverns . . ."
—Dr. Benjamin Rush

ABOVE *Portrait of Dr. Benjamin Rush.*

> A noted drunkard was once followed by a favourite goat, to a tavern, into which he was invited by his master, and drenched with some of his liquor. The poor animal staggered home with his master, a good deal intoxicated. The next day he followed him to his accustomed tavern. When the goat came to the door, he paused: his master made signs to him to follow him into the house. The goat stood still. An attempt was made to thrust him into the tavern. He resisted, as if struck with the recollection of what he suffered from being intoxicated the night before. His master was so much affected by a sense of shame, in observing the conduct of his goat to be so much more rational than his own, that he ceased from that time to drink spiritous liquors.[26]

In addition to being a doctor, Rush was a political actor at a time when rebellion was perceived to be closely associated with alcohol—likely because it often was. As such, "An Inquiry into the Effects of Ardent Spirits" crescendos with a feverish admonishment for temperance and even tilts toward theocracy:

> The loss of 4000 American citizens, by the yellow fever, in a single year, awakened general sympathy and terror. . . . Why is not the same zeal manifested in protecting our citizens from the more general and consuming ravages of distilled spirits? Should the customs of civilized life, preserve our nation from extinction . . . by those liquors; they cannot prevent our country being governed by men, chosen by intemperate and corrupted voters. From such legislators, the republic would soon be in danger. To avert this evil—men of every class unite and besiege the general and state governments, with petitions to limit the number of taverns—to impose heavy duties upon ardent spirits—to inflict a mark of disgrace, or a temporary abridgment of some civil right, upon every man, convicted of drunkenness; and finally, to secure the property of habitual drunkards, for the benefit of their families, by placing it in the hands of trustees, appointed for that purpose, by a court of justice. To aid the operation of these laws, would it not be extremely useful for the rulers of the different denominations of Christian churches to unite, and *render the sale and consumption of ardent spirits a subject of ecclesiastical jurisdiction* [italics added]?[27]

Washington: Whiskey Kingpin

GEORGE WASHINGTON WAS BORN TO A NATION of rum drinkers and left it a nation firmly in the hands of whiskey. Whiskey's march to dominance started soon after the Revolution opened the western frontier to American settlement, and corn and rye cultivation quickly followed. But whiskey also got a big boost from Washington himself. In 1797, Washington agreed to build two whiskey stills adjacent to his gristmill and produced 600 gallons by the end of the year. The whiskey business was brisk, and Washington added three more stills the following year at a time when the typical whiskey operation consisted of a single still producing a couple of hundred gallons annually. The Washington whiskey leviathan blasted out 10,500 gallons in 1798, contributing to both America's nineteenth-century whiskey boom and the temperance movement that followed it.

ABOVE *Rebuilt functioning whiskey stills at Mount Vernon. Washington's whiskey went straight from the still to the bottle, without any barrel aging, a tradition continued today.*

SOURCE

Dennis Pogue and Esther White, *George Washington's Gristmill at Mount Vernon* (Mount Vernon: George Washington's Mount Vernon Estate & Gardens, 2005).

Captain Daniel Packer Inne

EST. 1756 ✶ TODAY OPERATES AS A RESTAURANT AND BAR ✶ MYSTIC, CONNECTICUT

Retired square-rigger captain Daniel Packer purchased a plot of land adjacent to Connecticut's Mystic River in 1754, and two years later he opened the inn that still bears his name. The inn's location midway between New York and Boston, and its rope ferry service across the Mystic River, guaranteed brisk business. Incredibly, the inn remained in the Packer family until purchased by the Keeler family in 1979, which undertook a major restoration using traditional colonial building methods. The Packer's dark post-and-beam downstairs tavern is heated by the original fireplace, while the original lodging space has long

since been converted into several large dining rooms. Other ingredients complete the inn's authentic atmosphere, including views overlooking the Mystic Seaport, nightly live music, highly rated seafood, and a wooden pillar over the bar carved with the names of years' worth of patrons.

Ye Olde Tavern

EST. 1760 AS HITCHCOCK TAVERN ✱ TODAY OPERATES AS RESTAURANT, BAR, AND INN ✱ FREQUENTED BY GEORGE WASHINGTON, JOHN ADAMS, MARQUIS DE LAFAYETTE ✱ WEST BROOKFIELD, MASSACHUSETTS

David Hitchcock was about twenty years old when he built a two-story gambrel-roofed tavern in West Brookfield, Massachusetts. Hitchcock became a leading local patriot during the Revolution and was appointed a captain by Governor John Hancock. Known today as Ye Old Tavern, Hitchcock's Tavern still provides food, drink, and lodging, making it one of the—if not the—oldest continuously operating taverns in the United States. The tavern's location along the Olde Bay Road between Boston and Albany secured for it an impressive guest list and a key role in the history of the surrounding area. George Washington's diary confirms he dined at the tavern on October 22, 1789, during his presidential tour of New England, and John Adams mentions his stay in a November 27, 1796, letter to Abigail. Daniel Shays stayed at the tavern before he infamously helped launch Shays' Rebellion, and the marquis de Lafayette is believed to have visited during his American tour of 1824.

The tavern has seen many different owners over its 250-year history and has recently undergone an extensive renovation. The restaurant and bar space, though still featuring the original fireplace, has a modern look, and the twenty-one guest rooms have also recently been renovated to modern standards. The tavern's exterior is beautifully preserved, and a framed collection of photos and illustrations of the building kept near the entrance provides an interesting glimpse at the changes made over the centuries. The restaurant and bar serve lunch and dinner and are popular with local residents for hosting major events.

SOURCES

Captain David Hitchcock Genealogy Pages, West Brookfield, MA, retrieved November 15, 2015, from http://westbrookfieldgenealogy.org.

The Diaries of George Washington. Donald Jackson and Dorothy Twohig, eds. *The Papers of George Washington*, Vol. 5 (Charlottesville: University Press of Virginia, 1979), 471.

"John Adams to Abigail Adams, 27 November 1796," in *The Adams Paper: Adams Family Correspondence*, vol. 11: *July 1795–February 1797*, ed. Margaret A. Hogan, C. James Taylor, Sara Martin, Neal E. Millikan, Hobson Woodward, Sara B. Sikes, and Gregg L. Lint (Cambridge, MA: Harvard University Press, 2013), 419–20.

Rush's findings were lamented, though the problem continued to get worse, fueled by cheap whiskey. Washington himself even got into the business. In 1797, Washington built two whiskey stills adjacent to his gristmill at Mount Vernon, which began producing 600 gallons that year. Washington added three more stills the following year, creating 10,500 gallons in 1798.[28] Business was so brisk that Washington didn't even bother barrel aging and instead sold his clear firewater fresh out of the still. Not everyone jumped into the whiskey business. Jimmy Wilson, for fifty years Boston's town crier, would stand and shout, bell in hand, the news of the day to the town. Upon retirement in 1795, Wilson opened the Bell-in-Hand Tavern on Boston's North End. And while the Bell-in-Hand grew famous for serving ale in two mugs (one for the spillover froth), he refused to serve ardent spirits.

Fueled by an abundance of cheap whiskey, the alcohol habit of Americans careened toward epidemic during the first decades of the nineteenth century. An embarrassed and disgusted John Adams wrote in 1819:

> Is it not humiliating that Mahometans [Muslims] and Hindoes [sic] should put to shame the whole Christian world by their superior examples of Temperance? Is it not degrading to Englishmen & Americans that they are so infinitely exceeded by the French in this cardinal virtue & is it not mortifying beyond all expression that we Americans should exceed all other & millions of people in the world in this degrading beastly vise of Intemperance.[29]

American alcohol consumption eventually peaked in 1830 at a liver-busting 7.1 gallons of pure alcohol consumed per adult per year, crushing contemporary leader Lithuania's 4.27 gallons a day by 66 percent.[30] Such widespread abuse led to the creation of the American Temperance Society in 1826 and the flood of temperance propaganda that followed. One of the most famous images from the era is *The Drunkard's Progress*, an 1846 illustration that depicts nine stages of alcoholism beginning with "a drink with a friend" and culminating with "death by suicide." A mid-twentieth-century reproduction of *The Drunkard's Progress* can be found on the taproom wall of the Bull Run Tavern in Shirley, Massachusetts. However, Rush's conclusion

ABOVE *"The Drunkards Progress. From the first glass to the grave," by an unknown artist, New York, c. 1846.*

that alcoholism was a disease rather than the sole result of bad choices and sin was revolutionary. He even realized that alcoholism could be hereditary and recommended complete abstinence as treatment. For this and other advances in mental health, Rush's image is used on the seal of the American Psychiatric Association. That such a statement could come from a Revolutionary whose cause would have been impossible without taverns speaks to how repeated rebellion and the whiskey boom changed the scene.

With the deaths of Thomas Jefferson and John Adams occurring on the same day, July 4, 1826, the Revolutionary generation finally passed. America's colonial taverns were also facing their demise at the hands of changing tastes and economic development. The United States of the mid–nineteenth century was becoming increasingly wealthy and increasingly urban. Tastes grew more refined and luxurious, and French-sounding *hôtels* began to gain popularity. Even the most elegant taverns became seen as cramped and obsolete. The trend was particularly devastating for urban taverns, where limited land resulted in a wave of demolitions. Philadelphia, once famous for scores of taverns, today has only one original tavern building, which has long since been converted into apartments. Wealth and trade migrated from old post roads to the new boomtowns along railroad lines. Taverns lost their customers and fell into disrepair. Many of those that didn't become private residences were converted into boardinghouses and suffered long periods of neglect. Many burned. Both the City Tavern in Philadelphia and Boston's Green Dragon Tavern were destroyed in 1854, and the Raleigh burned to the ground in 1859. Some deprecated the tavern's decline even then. James Blaine, secretary of state under President Harrison, once dined with friends at Pennsylvania's Caldwell's Tavern writing, "We did not use the high sounding hotel, but the good old Anglo-Saxon tavern."[31]

And yet, many taverns built prior to 1800 did survive, about 310 by my count. Of these, about 140 are today private residences, seventy-two are restaurants or bars, forty-nine museums, thirty-six inns, twelve community buildings, and a smattering of cafés and offices. Some are remarkably well preserved, while others are barely recognizable as historically relevant. Of those still pouring drinks, some cater to blue-collar workers, while others provide polished backdrops to weddings, corporate events, and other formal gatherings.

America's taverns were the indispensable institution of independence. These were the places where the movement began, the soldiers were recruited, and the battles were planned; where victories were celebrated, the dead were mourned, and enemies met their fate.

In the twenty-first century, we are fortunate to have a bottomless variety of businesses providing what was once available only in a tavern. Today alcohol is much safer, the hotel bed far more comfortable, there is indoor plumbing, and communicating is unimaginably more efficient. And yet for all these gains, we'll never know the profound sense of community that such interdependence creates. Even the most authentic surviving colonial tavern provides only a shadow of its former social function today. Our century has no equivalent to the tavern as an institution. To huddle beneath the posts and beams of the tavern ceiling, ale in hand, beside the same fire that sustained a Washington, or a Lafayette, or a Franklin, or Adams, or Jefferson, is to engage with history in a way that no book or museum can match.

BELOW *"Village Tavern," by John Lewis Krimmel, c. 1813, shows an American tavern scene after the Revolutionary War.*

BEN FRANKLIN'S DRINKER'S DICTIONARY

ON JANUARY 6, 1737, the thirty-one-year-old Benjamin Franklin published "The Drinker's Dictionary," with 228 different expressions for "drunk." Franklin promised that the words weren't "borrow'd from Foreign Languages . . . but gather'd wholly from the modern Tavern-Conversation of Tiplers."

A CUP TOO MUCH
AS DIZZY AS A GOOSE
AS DRUNK AS A BEGGAR
AS DRUNK AS DAVID'S SOW
AS GOOD CONDITIONED AS A PUPPY
AS STIFF AS A RING-BOLT
BEEN AMONG THE PHILISTINES
BEEN AT AN INDIAN FEAST
BEEN AT BARBADOES
BEEN AT GENEVA
BEEN BEFORE GEORGE
BEEN IN THE SUN
BEEN TO A FUNERAL
BEEN TO FRANCE
BEEN TO JERICO
BEEN WITH SIR JOHN GOA
BEWITCH'D
BLED
BLOCK AND BLOCK
BOOZ'D THE GAGE
BOOZY
BOWZ'D
BREAKFAST
BURDOCK'D
BUSKEY
BUZZEY

CAGRIN'D
CAPABLE
CATCH'D
CHERRY MERRY
CHERUBIMICAL
CHICKERY
CHIPPER
CLIPS THE KING'S ENGLISH
COCK'D
COCK EY'D
COGUY
CONCERN'D
CONSIDERING CAP
COPEY
CRACK'D
CRAMP'D
CREATURE
CRUMP FOOTED
CURV'D
CUT
DOUBLE TONGU'D
DRUNK AS A WHEEL-BARROW
EAT A PUDDING BAGG
EAT OPIUM
ENTER'D
FEARS NO MAN

FETTER'D
FLUSH'D
FOX'D
FROZE HIS MOUTH
FROZEN
FUDDLED
FUZL'D
GENEROUS
GLAIZ'D
GLOBULAR
GOING TO JERUSALEM
GOLD-HEADED
GOT A BRASS EYE
GOT CORNS IN HIS HEAD
GOT KIB'D HEELS
GOT THE GLANDERS
GOT THE GOUT
GOT THE INDIAN VAPOURS
GOT THE NIGHT MARE
GOT THE POLE EVIL
GRAND ELIXIR
GROATABLE
HAD A KICK IN THE GUTS
HALF-PENNY
HALF SEAS OVER
HALF WAY TO CONCORD

HE CARRIES TOO MUCH SAIL

HE MAKES INDENTURES

HE'S HAD A THUMP OVER THE HEAD WITH SAMPSON'S JAWBONE

HE'S OIL'D

HET HIS KETTLE

HIS FLAG IS OUT

HIS SHOE PINCHES HIM

HOME

IN HIS PROSPERITY

IN THE SUDDS

IT IS STAR-LIGHT WITH HIM

JAGG'D

JAMBLED

JOCULAR

JOLLY

JUICY

KILL'D HIS DOG

KNAPT

LAPPY

LIGHT

LIMBER

LOADED HIS CART

LORDLY

LOST HIS RUDDER

MADE AN EXAMPLE

MAUDLIN

MELLOW

MERRY

MIDDLING

MOON-EY'D

MOUNTOUS

MUDDLED

MUDDY

NIMPTOPSICAL

NON COMPOS

OUT OF THE WAY

OVERSET

OWES NO MAN A FARTHING

OXYCROCIUM

PHARAOH

PHILIPPIANS

PIDGEON EY'D

PISS'D IN THE BROOK

PRIDDY

PUNGEY

RADDLED

RAGGED

RAIS'D

RAIS'D HIS MONUMENTS

RELIGIOUS

RICH

RICHARD

SAILS OUT

SEAFARING

SEEN A FLOCK OF MOONS

SEEN THE FRENCH KING

SEEN THE YELLOW STAR

SIR JOHN STRAWBERRY

SMELT OF AN ONION

SOAK'D

SOFT

SORE FOOTED

SPIRITS

SPOKE WITH HIS FRIEND

STAGGERISH

STEW'D

STRONG

STUBB'D

SWAMPT

TANN'D

THE BREWER'S BASKET

THE KING IS HIS COUSIN

TIPIUM GROVE

TIPSEY

TOKEN

TONGUE-TY'D

TOOK HIS DROPS

TOPSY TURVEY

VALIANT

WAMBLE CROP'D

WASTED HIS PAUNCH

WELL IN FOR 'T

WELL TO LIVE

WET BOTH EYES

WITH ALL HIS STUDDING SAILS OUT

WITH HIS LEGGS

SOURCE
The Drinker's Dictionary. *The Pennsylvania Gazette*, January 13, 1736, retrieved from the FranklinPapers.org.

INDEX OF SURVIVING COLONIAL TAVERNS

Note: Unless otherwise specified, dates given indicate estimated year the property first began operating as tavern (as opposed to date of construction). "Taproom" is used when the bar in question is of the eighteenth century–style typified by a corner countertop occupying a small room with low ceilings.

CONNECTICUT

Bee and Thistle Inn
Est. 1756
Today operates as a restaurant and inn
100 Lyme St.
Old Lyme, CT 06371

Breed's Tavern
Est. 1777
Today operates as office space
3-15 Tavern Lane
Colchester, CT 06415

Captain Daniel Packer Inne
Est. 1756
Today operates as a restaurant and bar
32 Water St.
Groton, CT 06355

Captain William Bull Tavern
Est. 1745
Today operates as a restaurant and inn
571 Torrington Rd.
Litchfield, CT 06759

Curtis House Inn
Est. 1754
Today operates as a restaurant and inn
506 Main Street South
South Woodbury, CT 06798

Deacon Timothy Pratt
Est. 1746
Today operates as a bed and breakfast
325 Main St.
Old Saybrook, CT 06475

Griswold Inn
Est. 1776
Today operates as an inn, restaurant, bar, and wine bar
36 Main St.
Essex, CT 06426

Hanford-Silliman House
Est. 1764
Today operates as a museum
13 Oenoke Ridge
New Canaan, CT 06840

Keeler Tavern
Est. 1772
Today operates as a museum
132 Main St.
Ridgefield, CT 06877

Meigs-Bishop House
Est. c. 1690
Today operates as a tea house
45 Wall St.
Madison, CT 06443

Phelps Tavern
Est. c. 1771
Today functions as a community building
800 Hopmeadow St.
Simsbury, CT 06070

Putnam Cottage
Est. c. 1690
Today operates as a museum
243 East Putnam Ave.
Greenwich, CT 06830

Sun Tavern
Est. 1780
Today operates as a museum
1 Town Hall Green
Fairfield, CT 06824

3 Liberty Green Bed and Breakfast
Est. 1734
Today operates as a bed and breakfast
3 Liberty St.
Clinton, CT 06413

Tracey-Watson House
Est. 1760
Today operates as a publishing house
3 Devotion Rd.
Scotland, CT 06264

DELAWARE

Jessop's Tavern
Est. c. 1724
Today operates as a restaurant and bar
114 Delaware St.
New Castle, DE 19720

Gilpin House/McCullough Tavern
Est. 1797
Today operates as a bank
210 Delaware St.
New Castle, DE 19720

Robinson House
Est. 1723
Today functions as a community building
1 Naamans Rd.
Claymont, DE 19703

GEORGIA

Pirates' House
Est. 1753
Today operates as a restaurant
20 East Broad St.
Savannah, GA 31401

MASSACHUSETTS

Baird Tavern
Est. 1768
Today operates as a bed and breakfast
2 Old Chester Rd.
Blandford, MA 01008

Barker Tavern
Est. 1634
Today operates as a restaurant
21 Barker Rd.
Scituate Harbor, MA 02066

Bell in Hand Tavern
Est. 1795
Today operates as a restaurant
45 Union St.
Boston, MA 02108

Blanchard's Tavern
Est. 1784
Today operates as a museum
98 North Main St.
Avon, MA 02322

Brookfield Inn
Est. 1768
Today operates as a bed and breakfast
8 West Main St.
Brookfield, MA 01506

Buckman Tavern
Est. 1713
Today operates as a museum
1 Bedford St.
Lexington, MA 02420

Bull Run
Est. c. 1740* as Sawtell's Tavern
Today operates as a restaurant, bar, and music venue
215 Great Rd.
Shirley, MA 01464
*Original building destroyed, current tavern is from c. 1800.

Candleberry Inn
Est. c. 1790
Today operates as a bed and breakfast
1882 Main St.
Brewster, MA 02631

Colonial Inn
Built 1716, Est. 1889*
Today operates as an inn, restaurant and taproom.
48 Monument Square
Concord, MA 01742
*Originally private residence. Listed for role in Battles of Lexington and Concord.

Dan'l Webster Inn
Est. c. 1750, Rebuilt 1971*
Today operates as a restaurant and inn
149 Main St.
Sandwich, MA 02563
*Original building destroyed by fire in 1971

Duston-Garrison House
Est. c. 1697
Today operates as a museum
665 Hilldale Ave.
Haverhill, MA 01832

Frary House
Est. c. 1750
Today operates as a museum
84B Old Main Street
Deerfield, MA 01342

Golden Ball Tavern
Est. 1768
Today operates as a museum
662 Boston Post Rd.
Weston, MA 02493

Hale-Boynton House
Est. 1764
Today operates as a private school
1 Elm Street*
Newbury, MA 01922
*Actual tavern located on Middle Street across from Gymnasium

Hartwell Tavern
Est. 1756
Today operates as a museum
Virginia Rd.
Lincoln, MA 01742

Historic Merrell Inn
Est. 1794
Today operates as an inn
1565 Pleasant St.
South Lee, MA 01260

Jabez Howland House
Est. 1667
Today operates as a museum
33 Sandwich St.
Plymouth, MA 02360

John Whipple House
Est. 1677
Today functions as a community building
53 South Main St.
Ipswich, MA 01938

Jones Tavern
Est. 1750
Today operates as a museum
128 Main St.
Acton, MA 01720

Josiah Smith Tavern
Est. 1757
Today functions as a community building
358 Boston Post Rd.
Weston, MA 02493

Kimball Tavern
Est. 1690
Today operates as an antique shop
2 Salem St.
Bradford, MA 01835

Longfellow's Wayside Inn
Est. 1716
Today operates as a restaurant, taproom, gristmill, and inn
72 Wayside Inn Rd.
Sudbury, MA 01776

Munroe Tavern
Est. 1735
Today operates as a museum
1332 Massachusetts Ave.
Lexington, MA 02420

New Boston Inn
Est. c. 1743
Today operates as a restaurant, taproom, and inn
101 North Main St.
Sandisfield, MA 01255

Old Inn on the Green
Est. c. 1760
Today operates as a restaurant and inn
134 Hartsville-New Marlborough Road
New Marlborough, MA 01230

Old Ordinary
Est. c. 1688
Today operates as a museum
34 Main St.
Hingham, MA 02043

Old Tavern Farm
Est. c. 1740
Today operates as a bed and breakfast
817 Colrain Rd.
Greenfield, MA 01301

Old Yarmouth Inn
Est. c. 1696
Today operates as a restaurant
223 Route 6A
Yarmouth Port, MA 02675

Parker Tavern
Est. c. 1694
Today operates as a museum
103 Washington St.
Reading, MA 01867

Peletiah Morse's Tavern
Est. 1748
Today operates as a government building
33 Eliot St.
South Natick, MA 01760

Publick House Historic Inn
Est. 1771
Today operates as an inn, restaurant, taproom, bar, and bakery
277 Main St.
Sturbridge, MA 01566

Red Lion Inn
Est. 1773
Today operates as a restaurant and inn
30 Main St.
Stockbridge, MA 01262

Swet-Ilsley House
Est. 1670
Today operates as a museum
4 High St.
Newbury, MA 01951

Village Inn
Est. 1771
Today operates as a restaurant, bar, and inn
16 Church St.
Lenox, MA 01240

Warren Tavern
Est. c. 1780
Today operates as a restaurant and bar
2 Pleasant Street
Charlestown, MA 02129

White-Ellery House
Est. 1735
Today operates as a museum
247 Washington St.
Gloucester, MA 01930

Wiggins Tavern
Est. 1786
Today operates as a restaurant and inn
36 King St.
Northampton, MA 01060

Wright Tavern
Est. 1747
Today operates as various offices
2 Lexington Rd.
Concord, MA 01742

Ye Olde Tavern
Est. 1760
Today operates as a restaurant, bar, and inn
7 East Main St.
West Brookfield, MA 01585

MARYLAND

George Washington House
Est. 1752 as the Indian Queen Tavern
Today functions as a community building
4302 Baltimore Ave.
Bladensburg, MD 20710

Horse You Came In On Saloon
Est. 1775
Today operates as a restaurant and bar
1626 Thames St.
Baltimore, MD 21231

Maryland Inn
Est. 1784
Today operates as a restaurant and inn
16 Church Circle
Annapolis, MD 21401

Middleton Tavern
Est. 1750
Today operates as a restaurant and bar
2 Market Space
Annapolis, MD 21401

Old South Mountain Inn
Est. 1732
Today operates as a restaurant
6132 Old National Pike
Boonsboro, MD 21713

Reynolds Tavern
Est. 1747
Today operates as a restaurant and bar
7 Church Circle
Annapolis, MD 21401

Rising Sun Inn
Est. 1753
Today operates as a museum
1090 Generals Highway
Millersville, MD 21032

White Swan Tavern
Est. 1793
Today operates as a bed and breakfast
231 High St.
Chestertown, MD 21620

MAINE

Burnham Tavern
Est. 1770
Today operates as a museum
14 Colonial Way
Machias, ME 04654

Jameson Tavern
Est. 1779
Today operates as a restaurant
115 Main St.
Freeport, ME 04032

Jefford Tavern
Est. 1750
Today functions as a community building
207 York St.
York, ME 03909

Royalsborough Inn
Est. 1772
Today operates as a bed and breakfast
1290 Royalsborough Rd.
Durham, ME 04222

NEW HAMPSHIRE

Chesterfield Inn
Est. c. 1787
Today operates as a restaurant and inn
20 Cross Road
West Chesterfield, NH 03466

Fitzwilliam Inn
Est. 1796
Today operates as a restaurant and inn
62 New Hampshire 119 W
Fitzwilliam, NH 03447

Hancock Inn
Est. 1789
Today operates as a restaurant, bar, and inn
33 Main St.
Hancock, NH 03449

Inn at Valley Farms
Est. 1774
Today operates as a bed and breakfast
633 Wentworth Rd.
Walpole, NH 03608

John Paul Jones House
Est. 1776
Today operates as a museum
43 Middle St.
Portsmouth, NH 03801

William Pitt Tavern
Est. c. 1766 as Earl of Halifax Tavern
Today operates as a museum
14 Hancock St.
Portsmouth, NH 03801

Wyman Tavern
Est. 1762
Today operates as a museum
339 Main St.
Keene, NH 03431

NEW JERSEY

Barnsboro Inn
Est. c. 1776
Today operates as a restaurant and bar
699 Main St.
Sewell, NJ 08080

Black Horse Tavern
Est. 1754
Today operates as a restaurant and bar
1 West Main St.
Mendham, NJ 07945

Colt's Neck Inn
Est. 1717
Today operates as a restaurant
6 County Road, Route 537 West
Colt Neck, NJ 07722

Fleming Castle
Est. 1756
Today operates as a museum
5 Bonnell St.
Flemington, NJ 08822

Ford Mansion and Washington's Headquarters Museum
Est. c. 1774
Today operates as a museum
30 Washington Pl.
Morristown, NJ 07960

Gabreil Daveis Tavern House
Est. 1756
Today operates as a museum
Third Ave.
Glendora, NJ 08029

Hancock House
Est. 1734
Today operates as a museum
3 Front St.
Hancock's Bridge, NJ 08038

Indian King Tavern
Est. 1750
Today operates as a museum
233 Kings Highway East
Haddonfield, NJ 08033

Jones Tavern
Est. 1760
Today operates as miscellaneous offices
90 Beaver Ave.
Annandale, NJ 08801

Merchants and Drovers Tavern
Est. 1798
Today operates as a museum
1623 St. Georges Ave.
Rahway, NJ 07065

Mill Street Hotel & Tavern
Est. 1723
Today operates as a bar and inn offering medium- and long-term rentals
67 Mill St.
Mount Holly, NJ 08060

Pittstown Inn
Est. 1760
Today operates as a restaurant and bar
350 Pittstown Road
Pittstown, NJ 08867

Proprietary House
Est. 1764
Today operates as a museum
149 Kearny Ave.
Perth Amboy, NJ 08861

Smithville Inn
Est. 1787
Today operates as a restaurant
1 North New York Rd.
Galloway, NJ 08205

Stage House Tavern
Est. 1737
Today operates as a restaurant and bar
366 Park Ave.
Scotch Plains, NJ 07076

Steuben House
Est. 1752
Today operates as a museum
1209 Main St.
River Edge, NJ 07661

Tavro 13
Est. 1771
Today operates as a restaurant
1301 Kings Highway
Swedesboro, NJ 08085

Terrill Tavern
Est. c. 1765
Today operates as a museum
1623 St. Georges Ave.
Rahway, NJ 07065

Village Inn
Est. 1726
Today functions as a community building
2 Water St.
Englishtown, NJ 07726

NEW YORK

Baird's Tavern
Est. 1766
Today operates as a museum
105 Main St.
Warwick, NY 10990

Beekman Arms
Est. 1766
Today operates as a restaurant and inn
6387 Mill St.
Rhinebeck, NY 12572

Fraunces Tavern
Est. 1762
Today operates as a restaurant, bar, and museum
54 Pearl St.
New York, NY 10004

Morris-Jumel Mansion
Est. 1765
Today operates as a museum
65 Jumel Terrace
New York, NY 10032

Old '76 House
Est. c. 1755
Today operates as a bar and restaurant
110 Main St.
Tappan, NY 10983

Union Hall Inn
Est. 1798
Today operates as a restaurant
2 Union Pl.
Johnstown, NY 12095

Wayside Inn
Est. 1729
Today functions as a community building
1039 Post Rd.
Scarsdale, NY 10583

Weigand Tavern
Est. 1780
Not open to the public
326 Liberty Street
Newburgh, NY 12550

Widow Haviland's Tavern (or Square House)
Est. 1730
Today operates as a museum
1 Purchase St.
Rye, NY 10580

PENNSYLVANIA

Black Horse Inn
Est. 1744
Today functions as a community building
1432 Bethlehem Pike
Flourtown, PA 19031

Blue Bell Inn
Est. 1743
Today operates as a restaurant
601 Skippack Pike
Blue Bell, PA 19422

Broad Axe Tavern
Est. c. 1681
Today operates as a restaurant and bar
901 West Butler Pike
Ambler, PA 19002

City Tavern
Est. 1773, rebuilt in 1976
Today operates as a restaurant and taproom
188 South Second St.
Philadelphia, PA 19106

Compass Inn
Est. 1799
Today operates as a museum
1382 Route 30 East
Laughlintown, PA 15655

Conestoga Inn
Est. 1789
Today operates as a restaurant
1501 East King St.
Lancaster, PA 17602

Fountain House
Est. 1758
Today operates as a coffee shop
10 North Main St.
Doylestown, PA 18901

Franklin House
Est. 1746
Today operates as a restaurant
101 North Market St.
Schaefferstown, PA 17088

Fulton House
Est. 1793
Today functions as a community building
112-116 Lincoln Way East
McConnellsburg, PA 17233

General Greene Inn
Est. 1763
Today operates as an antique shop
4705 York Rd.
Buckingham, PA 18912

General Warren Inne
Est. 1745
Today operates as an inn, restaurant, taproom, bar, and bakery
9 Old Lancaster Road
Malvern, PA 19355

General Washington Inn
Est. 1761 as the King of Arms Tavern
Today operates as offices
463 East Lancaster Ave.
Downington, PA 19335

General Wayne Inn
Est. 1704
Today functions as a community building
625 Montgomery Ave.
Merion Station, PA 19066

Golden Plough Tavern
Est. 1741
Today operates as a museum
157 West Market St.
York, PA 17401

Green Tree Tavern
Est. 1748
Today functions as a church
6023 Germantown Ave.
Philadelphia, PA 19144

Green Tree Tavern
Est. 1799
Today operates as an insurance brokerage
7944 Frankford Ave.
Holmesburg, PA 19136

Horse Tavern and Grill
Est. 1757
Today operates as a restaurant and bar
1000 Old Bethlehem Pike
Sellersville, PA 18960

Jean Bonnet Tavern
Est. 1780
Today operates as a restaurant and inn
6048 US 30
Bedford, PA 15522

Kemp's Hotel
Est. 1740
Today operates as a yoga studio
15305 Kutztown Rd.
Maxatawny Township, PA 19530

King George II Inn
Est. 1681
Today operates as a restaurant, bar, and inn offering medium- and long-term rentals
102 Radcliffe St.
Bristol, PA 19007

King of Prussia Inn
Est. 1769
Today functions as a community building
101 Bill Smith Blvd.
King of Prussia, PA 19406

Lady Washington Inn
Est. 1761
Today operates as a hair salon
2550 Huntingdon Pike
Huntingdon Valley, PA 19006

McCoole's at the Historic Red Lion Inn
Est. 1747
Today operates as a restaurant and bar
4 South Main St.
Quakertown, PA 18951

Revere Tavern
Est. 1740
Today operates as a restaurant and inn
3063 Lincoln Highway
Paradise, PA 17562

Rising Sun Inn
Est. 1739
Today operates as a restaurant
898 Allentown Rd.
Franconia, PA 18969

Seven Stars Tavern
Est. 1736
Today operates as a restaurant
263 Hoffecker Rd.
Phoenixville, PA 19460

Ship Inn
Est. 1796
Today operates as a restaurant and bar
693 East Lincoln Hwy.
Exton, PA 19341

Spring House Tavern
Est. 1719
Today operates as a restaurant
1032 North Bethlehem Pike
Spring House, PA 19477

Square Tavern
Est. 1742
Today operates as a museum
2 Paper Mill Rd.
Newton Square, PA 19073

Sun Inn
Est. 1758
Today operates as a museum
556 Main St. #2
Bethlehem, PA 18018

Trappe Tavern
Est. c. 1750
Today operates as a restaurant and bar
416 West Main St.
Trappe, PA 19426

Uhler's Hotel
Est. 1789
Today building is closed
4901 Kesslersville Road
Easton, PA 18040

Wheel Pump Inn
Est. 1742
Today operates as a lighting store
529 Bethlehem Pike
Glenside, PA, 19038

White Horse Tavern
Est. 1715
Today operates as a restaurant and bar
707 East Lancaster Ave.
Frazer, PA 19355

White Swan
Est. c. 1793
Today operates as a restaurant and bar
1264 East Newport Rd.
Lititz, PA 17543

William Penn Inn
Est. 1714
Today operates as a restaurant and inn
1017 DeKalb Pike
Ambler, PA 19002

RHODE ISLAND

Eleazer Arnold House
Est. 1693
Today operates as a museum
487 Great Rd.
Lincoln, RI 02865

Francis Malbone House
Est. 1760
Today operates as a bed and breakfast
392 Thames St.
Newport, RI 02840

White Horse Tavern
Est. 1673
Today operates as a restaurant and taproom
26 Marlborough St.
Newport, RI 02840

SOUTH CAROLINA

Kershaw-Cornwalis House
Est. 1794
Today operates as a museum
222 Broad St.
Camden, SC 29020

McCrady's
Est. 1778
Today operates as a restaurant
2 Unity Alley
Charleston, SC 29401

Tavern in Old Salem
Est. 1784
Today operates as a restaurant
736 South Main St.
Winston-Salem, SC 27101

VIRGINIA

Boyd Tavern
Est. 1785
Today functions as a community building
449 Washington St.
Boydton, VA 23917

Carlyle House
Est. 1753
Today operates as a museum
121 North Fairfax St.
Alexandria, VA 22314

Gadsby's Tavern
Est. 1785
Today operates as a restaurant, taproom, and museum
138 North Royal St.
Alexandria, VA 22314

Michie Tavern
Est. 1784
Today operates as a restaurant
683 Thomas Jefferson Parkway
Charlottesville, VA 22902

Raleigh Tavern
Est. 1717, rebuilt in 1932
Today operates as a bakery and museum
413 East Duke of Gloucester St.
Williamsburg, VA, 23185

Red Fox Inn and Tavern
Est. 1728
Today operates as a restaurant and inn
2 E. Washington St.
Middleburg, VA, 20117

Rising Sun
Est. 1760
Today operates as a museum
1304 Caroline St.
Fredericksburg, VA, 22401

The Tavern
Est. 1779
Today operates as a restaurant
222 East Main St.
Abingdon, VA 24210

VERMONT

Chimney Point Tavern
Est. 1785
Today operates as a museum
7305 VT-125
Vergennes, VT 05491

Dorset Inn
Est. 1796
Today operates as a restaurant and inn
8 Church St.
Dorset, VT 05251

Elijah West's Windsor Tavern
Est. 1760
Today operates as a museum
16 North Main St.
Windsor, VT 05089

Henry Farm Inn
Est. 1790
Today operates as a bed and breakfast
2206 Green Mountain Turnpike
Chester, VT 05143

Henry House Inn
Est. 1769
Today operates as a bed and breakfast
1338 Murphy Rd.
North Bennington, VT 05257

The Inn at Weathersfield
Est. 1792
Today operates as a restaurant and inn
1342 Route 106
Perkinsville, VT 05151

Old Constitution House
Est. c. 1777 as the Windsor Tavern
Today operates as a museum
16 Main St.
Windsor, VT 05089

Three Mountain Inn
Est. 1790
Today operates as a restaurant, taproom, and inn
30 Depot St.
Jamaica, VT 05343

Ye Olde Tavern
Est. 1790
Today operates as a restaurant
5183 Main St.
Manchester Center, VT 05255

ACKNOWLEDGMENTS

This book wouldn't have been possible without the help and support of friends, colleagues, and tavern keepers on both sides of the country. I owe enormous thanks to my friend Dustin Jones for convincing me this idea wasn't crazy and for guiding me through the publishing universe; to my wife, Rachel, for being patient with my long hours away from home at San Francisco's Cafe La Boheme, where I wrote most of this book, and for joining me on an incredible two-week tavern road trip; to Awad and Jackie, owners of Cafe La Boheme, for letting me collect dust in the corner of their cafe; to Jim Moore for letting me borrow his camera, and to Scott Enberg for showing me how to use Jim Moore's camera; to my sister, Molly, for showcasing Colonial Williamsburg, and to my dad, Ron, and step-mom, Jennifer, for meeting up with Rachel and me in Boston on the first leg of our trip and properly stocking us with pumpkin beer and homemade trail mix.

Perhaps most important, I owe a tremendous debt of gratitude to the tavern keepers who graciously lent me their time and their beer. Thanks are due to John Harnett at the Warren Tavern, the first on my tour, for showing me what a spiced rim can do to pumpkin beer; to Susan Bennett, for meeting me after hours to walk me through both the Buckman and Munroe Taverns and for fact-checking my copy; to Bill at the National Park Service, for walking me through Hartwell Tavern at the crack of dawn; and to Alison, for telling me all the great family stories behind the Bull Run Tavern in Shirley, Massachusetts. From Longfellow's Wayside Inn, big thanks are due to general manager Steve for walking me through the inn's history, to bartender Marvin for pouring me my first coow-woow, and archivist Roberta for answering my unusual questions and granting me access to the archives. I owe thanks to Michael at the Publick House Inn for his generosity, history lesson, and tip to check out Old Sturbridge Village; and to Nicholas for the late-night pirate stories at the White Horse Tavern in Newport; to Joan at the Griswold Inn, for her extraordinary generosity and for showing us some of the coolest prohibition era posters I've ever seen; to Robert at the Old '76 House in Tappan, New York, for pouring me a noon pint and letting me hold one of his colonial muskets; to Jessica at New York City's Fraunces Tavern for arranging in advance for me to take photos after closing hours; to Lisa at the Captain Daniel Packer Inne, for letting me snap photos before the inn opened; to Darlene at the Mill Street Hotel & Tavern, for showing us local hospitality and for pulling out the old liquor licenses; to Robert at Bristol's King George II Inn for taking me into the cellar and showing me the old prison window; to the generous Patrick at Malvern's lovely General Warren Inne, for showcasing the improvements made to the tavern over the years (nicely done on the springhouse and patio); and to Elizabeth at Gadsby's Tavern museum, for the personal tour and for enlightening me about George Washington's dogs.

Finally, I must acknowledge the work of Kym Rice, Helene Smith, Ian Williams, Christine Sismondo, Elise Lathrop, and many others on whose shoulders this book stands, and to the National Archives, the Library of Congress, Massachusetts Historical Society, and the Franklin Papers archived by Yale University. Your archives make it possible for authors like me to attempt to bring the founding fathers alive.

NOTES

CHAPTER ONE

1. John Adams, diary, May 29, 1760, Massachusetts Historical Society, http://www.masshist.org/digitaladams/archive/doc?id=D5&hi=1&query=Nurseries%20 Legislators&tag=text&archive=all&rec=2&start=0&numRecs=32.

2. Howard Zinn and Anthony Arnove, *Voices of a People's History of the United States* (New York: Seven Stories Press, 2004), 79.

3. Thomas Jefferson to Thomas Jefferson Randolph, November 24, 1808, in *The Works of Thomas Jefferson in Twelve Volumes*, collected and ed. Paul Leicester Ford (New York: G.P. Putnam's Sons), 1905.

4. Thomas Jefferson to James Monroe, February 21, 1823, in *Thomas Jefferson and James Monroe Correspondence*, transcribed and ed. Gerard W. Gawalt (Washington, DC: Library of Congress, Manuscript Division).

5. Broadside: Library Company of Philadelphia [March 29, 1764], "Explanatory REMARKS on the ASSEMBLY'S RESOLVES," *Pennsylvania Gazette*, no. 1840, March 29, 1764. http://franklinpapers.org/franklin//framedVolumes.jsp.

6. Pennsylvania Assembly, Resolves upon the Present Circumstances, March 24, 1764, http://founders.archives.gov/documents/Franklin/01-11-02-0030.

7. Rice, Kym. *Early American Taverns: For the Entertainment of Friends and Strangers* (Chicago: Regnery Gateway, 1983), 94.

8. *OECD.Stat*, "Non-Medical Determinants of Health: Alcohol Consumption," retrieved August 6, 2015, from http://stats.oecd.org/index.aspx?queryid=30126.

9. Helene Smith, *Tavern Signs of America* (Greensburg, PA: MacDonald/Swärd Publishing Company, 1989), 36.

10. Ibid., 35.

11. Rice, *Early American Taverns*, 64.

12. Ibid., 64.

13. Ibid., 26.

14. Ibid., 26.

15. Christine Sismondo, *America Walks into a Bar* (New York: Oxford University Press, 2006), 5.

16. Rice, *Early American Taverns*, 29.

17. John F. Watson, *The Annals of Philadelphia* (Philadelphia: J. M. Stoddart & Co., 1881), 306.

18. *Poor Richard, 1734. An Almanack For the Year of Christ 1734 . . . By Richard Saunders, Philom* (Philadelphia: Printed and sold by B. Franklin, at the New Printing-Office near the Market, 1734).

19. Smith, *Tavern Signs of America*, 59.

20. Ibid., 44.

21. Rice, *Early American Taverns*, 101.

22. Smith, *Tavern Signs of America*, 71.

23. Sismondo, *America Walks into a Bar*, 63.

24. Catlett Lowell, *Thomas Jefferson: A Free Mind* (Bloomington, IN: Trafford, 2006), 12.

25. Lisa Bramen, "Swilling the Planters with Bumbo: When Booze Bought Elections," *Smithsonian Magazine*, October 20, 2010, http://www.smithsonianmag.com/arts-culture /swilling-the-planters-with-bumbo-when-booze-bought-elections-102758236/?no-ist.

26. Gordon Lloyd, "The Constitutional Convention," Teaching American History.org, http://teachingamericanhistory.org/convention/citytavern/.

27. "George Washington's Distillery," http://www.mountvernon.org/the-estate-gardens /distillery/.

28. R. S. O'Loughlin, ed., *The Delineator*, vol. 65, edited by H. F. Montgomery, Charles Dwyer (New York: Butterick Publishing Co., 1905), 1039.

29. "Misquote Ben Franklin Day," Beer PHXation Blob, March 29, 2012, http://www.beerphxation.com/2012/03/march-30-misquote-ben-franklin-day.html.

30. Walter Isaacson, *Benjamin Franklin: An American Life* (New York: Simon & Schuster, 2003), 374.

31. Smith, *Tavern Signs of America*, 56

32. Rice, *Early American Taverns*, 51.

33. Ibid., 55.

34. "Life in Port: Working Women," *Women and the Sea*, https://www.marinersmuseum .org/sites/micro/women/lifeinport/keepers.htm.

35. Rice, *Early American Taverns*, 55.

36. Salinger, Sharon V. "Taverns and Drinking in Early America" (Baltimore: John Hopkins University Press, 2004), 114.

37. Rice, *Early American Taverns*, 74.

38. Ibid., 81.

39. Ibid., 102.

40. Smith, *Tavern Signs of America*, 69.

41. Ibid., 7.

42. Rice, *Early American Taverns*, 24.

43. Sismondo, *America Walks into a Bar*, 75.

44. Smith, *Tavern Signs of America*, 27.

45. Ibid., 14.

46. Watson, *Annals of Philadelphia*, 467.

47. Smith, *Tavern Signs of America*, 91.

48. William West, *Tavern Anecdotes and Reminiscences of the Origins of Signs, Clubs, Coffeehouses, Streets, City Companies, Wards, &c.* (London: G. H. Davidson, Ireland Yard, Doctors' Commons), B.

49. Smith, *Tavern Signs of America*, 3.

50. Ibid., 59.

51. Ibid., 4.

52. Ibid., 92.

53. West, *Tavern Anecdotes and Reminiscences . . .*, vi.

54. Smith, *Tavern Signs of America*, 5.

55. Complied by the author from various sources, primarily the index provided by Elise Lathrop.

56. Smith, *Tavern Signs of America*, 58.

CHAPTER TWO

1. Ian Williams, *Rum: A Social and Sociable History of the Real Spirit of 1776* (New York: Nation Books, 2006), 126.

2. Ibid., 135.

3. Chuck Springston, "Population of the Thirteen Colonies, 1610–1790," October 28, 2013, http://www.yttwebzine.com/yesterday/2013/10/28/75757/population_13_colonies_chart.

4. National Archives, "Benjamin Franklin's Contributions to a History of the British Colonies in America [Before 20 May 1773]," http://founders.archives.gov/documents/Franklin/01-20-02-0120.

5. Alice Morse Earle, *Stage-coach and Tavern Days* (New York: The MacMillan Company, 1900), 189.

6. Sismondo, *America Walks into a Bar*, 1333.

7. Williams, *Rum*, 148.

8. "Benjamin Franklin to Peter Collinson, 30 April 1764," in *The Papers of Benjamin Franklin*, vol. 11: *January 1, through December 31, 1764*, ed. Leonard W. Labaree (New Haven, CT: Yale University Press, 1967), 180–84, http://founders.archives.gov/documents/Franklin/01-11-02-0044.

9. Samuel Adams to Royal Tyler, James Otis, Thomas Cushing, and Oxenbridge Thatcher, May 24, 1764, "Protest against Taxation," in Benson John Lossing, *Harper's Encyclopedia of United States History from 458 A.D. to 1905* (New York: Harpers, 1905).

10. Williams, *Rum*, 157.

11. A. D. Jones, *The Illustrated American Biography*, vol. 3 (New York: I. Milton Emerson & Co., 1855), 92.

12. Ibid., 92

13. Zinn and Anthony, *Voices of a People's History of the United States*, 79.

14. "The Stamp Act Riot of 1765," *NewportHistory*, http://www.revolutionarynewport.com/the-1765-stamp-act-riot.html.

15. David Lee Russel, *The American Revolution in the Southern Colonies* (Jefferson, NC: McFarland , 2000), 27.

16. James Nelson, *With Fire and Sword* (New York: St. Martin's Press, 2011), 43.

17. Rice, *Early American Taverns*, 122.

18. "William Smith to J. Morgan Esq. Letters of Governor Francis Fauquier," *William and Mary Quarterly* 21 (1913): 163–71, http://www.jstor.org/stable/1914695.

19. Frank Moore, *Diary of the American Revolution: From Newspapers and Original Documents*, vol. 1 (New York: Scribner 1860), 359.

20. Benjamin Irvin, "Tar and Feathers in Revolutionary America," blog, retrieved September 1, 2015, from http://revolution.h-net.msu.edu/essays/irvin.feathers.html.

21. Gordon S. Wood, "A Note on Mobs in the American Revolution," *William and Mary Quarterly*, 3rd ser., 23 (1966): 635–42. Omohundro Institute of Early American History and Culture. Retrieved August 25, 2015, from http://www.jstor.org/stable/1919130.

22. Smith, *Tavern Signs of America*, 13.

23. Edward M. Gair, "The Mystery of the Green Dragon Tavern and Boston Tea Party," *Masonic Trowel*, retrieved August 29, 2015, from http://www.themasonictrowel.com/Articles/History/united_states_files/the_mystery_green_dragon_cavern_and_boston_tea_party.htm.

24. Rice, *Early American Taverns*, 124.

25. "New York Merchants Non-Importation Agreement, October 31, 1765," *New York Mercury*, November 7, 1765, http://avalon.law.yale.edu/18th_century/newyork_non_importation_1765.asp.

26. "Thomas Jefferson's Notes on Patrick Henry [before 12 April 1812]," in *The Papers of Thomas Jefferson, Retirement Series*, vol. 4: *18 June 1811 to 30 April 1812*, ed. J. Jefferson Looney (Princeton: Princeton University Press, 2007), 598–605, http://founders.archives.gov/documents/Jefferson/03-04-02-0496-0003.

27. "Enclosure: Patrick Henry's Stamp Act Resolves, 30 May 1765," in *The Papers of Thomas Jefferson, Retirement Series*, vol. 7: *28 November 1813 to 30 September 1814*, ed. J. Jefferson Looney (Princeton: Princeton University Press, 2010), 496–97, http://founders.archives.gov/documents/Jefferson/03-07-02-0369-0002.

28. "Thomas Jefferson's Notes on Patrick Henry."

29. Resolutions of the Continental Congress October 19, 1765, Avalon Project, Yale Law School, http://avalon.law.yale.edu/18th_century/resolu65.asp.

30. Nelson, *With Fire and Sword*, 65.

31. "His Examination before the House of Commons: Benjamin Franklin (1706–1837)," 1766, Bartleby.com, http://www.bartleby.com/268/8/10.html.

32. C. James Taylor, ed., *Founding Families: Digital Editions of the Papers of the Winthrops and the Adamses* (Boston: Massachusetts Historical Society, 2015), http://www.masshist.org/publications/apde2/view?id=ADMS-05-02-02-0006-0004-0001.

33. Lawrence A. Kocher and Howard Dearstyne, "Arcihabald Blair'd Storehouse (NB) Architectural Report, Block 18-1 Building 6A Lot 46" (Williamsburg, VA: Colonial Williamsburg Foundation Library, 1990), http://research.history.org/DigitalLibrary/View/index.cfm?doc=ResearchReports/RR1402.xml/.

34. William G. Stanard, ed. "Letters from William and Mary College, 1798–1901." *Virginia Magazine of History and Biography*. Virginia Historical Society, December 31, 1921, 162–64.

35. Raleigh Tavern," Colonial Williamsburg Foundation, http://www.history.org/almanack/places/hb/hbral.cfm.

36. Ibid.

37. Ibid.

38. Thomas Jefferson, *The Works of Thomas Jefferson, Federal Edition* (New York: Putnam, 1904–1905), http://oll.libertyfund.org/titles/800.

39. Americanus, "Open Letter to the Earl Hillsborough," *Boston Gazette*, March 5, 1770, no. 778, http://www.masshist.org/dorr/volume/3/sequence/96.

40. Sismondo, *America Walks into a Bar*, 65.

41. Smith, *Tavern Signs of America*, 70.

42. Robert Middlekauff, *The Glorious Cause: The American Revolution, 1763–1789* (New York: Oxford University Press, 2005).

43. Sismondo, *America Walks into a Bar*, 65–66.

44. Thomas Jefferson, *Autobiography of Thomas Jefferson, 1743–1790, Together with a Summary of the Chief Events on Jefferson's Life* (New York: Putnam, 1914), 7.

45. Ibid., 10.

CHAPTER THREE

1. "Three Ships Used in Boston Tea Party," Boston Tea Party Ships and Museum, retrieved September 5, 2015, from http://www.bostonteapartyship.com/article/three-ships-tea-party.

2. "To Capt. Ayres, of the Ship Polly, on a Voyage from London to Philadelphia. Philadelphia, 27 November 1773," retrieved September 5, 2015, from http://www.sothebys.com/en/auctions/ecatalogue/lot.14.html/2012/books-manuscripts-n08864?sort=lotnumm.

3. This notice from the "Chairman of the Committee for Tarring and Feathering" in Boston denounced the tea consignees as "traitors to their country." https://en.wikipedia.org/wiki/Boston_Tea_Party#/media/File:BostonTeaPartyJoyceNotice.jpg.

4. State of Maryland, "The Burning of the *Peggy Stewart*," Maryland Commission on Artistic Property, retrieved September 5, 2015, from http://msa.maryland.gov/msa/speccol/sc1500/sc1545/001100/001111/text/label.html.

5. David W. Conroy, *In Public Houses: Drink and the Revolution of Authority in Colonial Massachusetts* (Chapel Hill: University of North Carolina Press, 1995), 279.

6. Rice, *Early American Taverns*, 129.

7. John Buescher, "Are There Instances of Raids Similar to the Boston Tea Party?" TeachingHistory.org, http://teachinghistory.org/history-content/ask-a-historian/20657.

8. John Adams, diary, December 17, 1773, John Adams Family Papers, https://www.masshist.org/digitaladams/archive/doc?id=D19&bc=%2Fdigitaladams%2Farchive%2Fbrowse%2Fdiaries_by_date.php.

9. *The Parliamentary History of England, from the Earliest Period to the Year 1803*, vol. 17 (London: T. C. Hansard, 1813), 1281.

10. "The Colonies Move towards Open Rebellion, 1773–1774," Library of Congress, retrieved September 5, 2015, from http://www.loc.gov/teachers/classroommaterials/presentationsandactivities/presentations/timeline/amrev/rebelln/.

11. Jared Sparks, *The Writings of George Washington: Life of Washington* (Boston: American Stationers Company, 1837), 123.

12. "George Washington to George William Fairfax, 10–15 June 1774," in *The Papers of George Washington*, Colonial Series, vol. 10: *21 March 1774–15 June 1775*, ed. W. W. Abbot and Dorothy Twohig (Charlottesville: University Press of Virginia, 1995), 94–101.

13. John Adams to Benjamin Rush, May 21, 1807, retrieved from http://www.christies.com/lotfinder/paintings/adams-john-autograph-letter-signed-to-3886745-details.aspx?from=searchresults&intObjectID=3886745&sid=ca2cc058-4109-4c29-9aaf-ac5bf39ae557.

14. U.S. National Park Service, "The Hancock Returns," Minute Man National Park, retrieved September 5, 2015, from http://www.nps.gov/mima/planyourvisit/the-hancock.htm.

15. Rice, *Early American Taverns*, 37.

16. Watson, *Annals of Philadelphia*, 401.

17. Melvin Bernstein, "Concord's Best-Kept Secret: The Wright Tavern," *Concord Journal*, March 12, 2015, http://concord.wickedlocal.com/article/20150312/News/150319009.

18. George Bancroft, *History of the United States from the Discovery of the American Continent* (Boston: Little, Brown, 1858), 256.

19. Samuel Adams, "Letter to a Southern Friend," in *The Writings of Samuel Adams*, vol. 3, ed. Alonzo Cushing (New York: Putnam, 1907), 200.

20. Thomas Gage to Lieutenant Colonel Smith, April 18, 1775, retrieved September 6, 2015, from http://teachingamericanhistory.org/library/document/orders-from-general-thomas-gage-to-lieut-colonel-smith-10th-regiment-foot/.

21. Henry Wadsworth Longfellow, excerpt from "Paul Revere's Ride," http://memory.loc.gov/ammem/today/apr19.html.

22. Aruther Bernon Tourtellot, *Lexington and Concord: The Beginning of the War of the American Revolution* (New York: Norton, 2000).

23. United States, "Depositions Concerning Lexington and Concord, April 1775," in *Journals of the Continental Congress*, Library of Congress, retrieved September 6, 2015, from http://www.loc.gov/teachers/classroommaterials/presentationsandactivities/presentations/timeline/amrev/shots/concern.html.

24. Lt. William Sutherland to General Gage, April 27, in Allen French, *General Gage's Informers* (Ann Arbor: University of Michigan Press, 1932), 42 ff., 58 ff., 85 ff., 111 ff.

25. Walter Borneman, *American Spring* (New York: Little, Brown, 2014), 170.

26. Frederic Hudson, "The Concord Fight," *Harper's New Monthly Magazine* 50 (December 1874-May 1875), 794.

27. Alice Morse Earle, *Stage-coach and Tavern Days* (New York: The MacMillan Company, 1900), 183.

28. Nelson, *With Fire and Sword*, 28.

29. U.S. Department of the Interior, National Parks Service, *Boston and the American Revolution* (1998), 59.

30. Nelson, *With Fire and Sword*, 50.

31. "[Novanglus Papers, 1774–1775]," in *The Adams Papers, Diary and Autobiography of John Adams*, vol. 3: *Diary, 1782–1804*, ed. L. H. Butterfield (Cambridge, MA: Harvard University Press, 1961), 313–14, http://founders.archives.gov/documents/Adams/01-03-02-0016-0023.

32. "From Benjamin Franklin to David Hartley, 8 May 1775," in *The Papers of Benjamin Franklin*, vol. 22: *March 23, 1775, through October 27, 1776*, ed. William B. Willcox (New Haven, CT: Yale University Press, 1982), 34, http://founders.archives.gov/documents/Franklin/01-22-02-0018.

33. Massachusetts Historical Society, "The Battle of Bunker Hill," retrieved September 9, 2015, from http://www.masshist.org/revolution/bunkerhill.php.

34. Smith, *Tavern Signs of America*, 52.

35. "From John Adams to Moses Gill, 10 June 1775," in *The Adams Papers, Papers of John Adams*, vol. 3: *May 1775–January 1776*, 20–22.

36. Fraunces Tavern Museum, "54 Pearl Street History," http://frauncestavernmuseum.org/history-and-education/history-of-fraunces-tavern/.

37. "Marine Corps Marks Its Founding in Philly in 1775," Philly.com, retrieved September 9, 2015, from http://www.philly.com/philly/news/20141111_Marines_Corps_marks_its_founding_in_Philly_in_1775.html.

38. John Adams to Benjamin Rush, May 21, 1807.

39. Smith, *Tavern Signs of America*, 72.

40. Ibid., 19.

41. Ibid.

42. Ibid., 100.

43. "New York's Tories." *Chicago Tribune*. May 12, 1946, http://archives.chicagotribune.com/1946/05/12/page/129/article/new-yorks-tories.

44. George Washington, *The Writings of George Washington from the Original Manuscript Sources*, ed. John Fitzpatrick (Washington, DC: U.S. Government Printing Office, 1931), 399.

45. "New York's Tories." *Chicago Tribune*. May 12, 1946, http://archives.chicagotribune.com/1946/05/12/page/129/article/new-yorks-tories.

46. Michael Pollack, "Did George Washington Want to Burn New York City?" *New York Times*, January 31, 2014, http://www.nytimes.com/2014/02/02/nyregion/did-george-washington-want-to-burn-new-york-city.html?_r=0.

47. Henry Russel Drowne, "A Sketch of Fraunces Tavern and Those Connected with Its History" (New York, 1919), https://archive.org/stream/asketchfraunces00drowgoog#page/n2/mode/2up.

48. Fraunces Tavern Museum, "54 Pearl Street History," http://frauncestavernmuseum.org/history-and-education/history-of-fraunces-tavern/.

49. Drowne, "A Sketch of Fraunces Tavern."

50. George Washington to Continental Congress, December 27, 1776, in *The George Washington Papers at the Library of Congress, 1741–1799*, retrieved September 11, 2015, from http://memory.loc.gov/cgi-bin/query/r?ammem/mgw:@field(DOCID+@lit(gw060337)).

51. "From George Washington to John Hancock, 2 July 1777," in *The Papers of George Washington*, vol. 10: *11 June 1777–18 August 1777*, ed. Frank E. Grizzard Jr. (Charlottesville: University Press of Virginia, 2000), 168– 70, http://founders.archives.gov/documents/Washington/03-10-02-0169.

52. "George Washington to John Hancock, 5 September 1777," in *The Papers of George Washington, Revolutionary War Series*, vol. 11: *19 August 1777–25 October 1777*, ed. Philander D. Chase and Edward G. Lengel (Charlottesville: University Press of Virginia, 2001), 150. http://founders.archives.gov/documents/Washington/03-11-02-0149.

53. "General Orders, 12 September 1777," in *The Papers of George Washington*, 204–205, http://founders.archives.gov/documents/Washington/03-11-02-0192.

54. Seven Stars Tavern. "History," retrieved October 12, 2015, from http://www.sevenstarsinn.com/history/.

55. General Warren Tavern, "History," retrieved October 12, 2015, from http://www.generalwarren.com/b-and-b-malvern-pa-history.php.

56. "From George Washington to John Hancock, 5 October 1777," in *The Papers of George Washington*, vol. 11, 393–401. http://founders.archives.gov/documents/Washington/03-11-02-0419.

57. Sir George Otto Trevelyan, *The American Revolution*, vol. 4 (New York: Longmans, Green, 1922), 249.

58. "Inns of Bethlehem Pike," pamphlet (n.d.). Springfield Township Historical Society. Flourtown, PA.

59. Benson J. Lossing, *The Two Spies: Nathan Hale and John André* (New York: Appleton, 1909), 95–105.

60. John C. Fredriksen, *Revolutionary War Almanac* (New York: Facts on File, 2006), 237.

61. Tom Fleming, "Why Washington Wept, " *New York Sun*, December 4, 2007, http://www.nysun.com/opinion/why-washington-wept/67471/.

62. Richard F. Welch, *Washington's Commando: Benjamin Tallmadge in the Revolutionary War* (Jefferson, NC: McFarland, 2014), 137.

63. "54 Pearl Street History." Fraunces Tavern Museum, http://frauncestavernmuseum.org/history-and-education/history-of-fraunces-tavern/.

CHAPTER 4

1. "To James Madison from George Washington, 5 November 1786," in *The Papers of James Madison*, vol. 9: *9 April 1786–24 May 1787 and supplement 1781–1784*, ed. Robert A. Rutland and William M. E. Rachal (Chicago: University of Chicago Press, 1975), 161–62, http://founders.archives.gov/documents/Madison/01-09-02-0070.

2. Sismondo, *America Walks into a Bar*, 80.

3. "To James Madison from Henry Lee, 19 October 1786," in *The Papers of James Madison*, vol. 9, 143–45, http://founders.archives.gov/documents/Madison/01-09-02-0056.

4. Leonard Richards, *Shays's Rebellion: The American Revolution's Final Battle* (Philadelphia: University of Pennsylvania Press, 2002), 29–30.

5. "7 September 1786," in *The Adams Papers: Diary of John Quincy Adams*, vol. 2: *March 1786–December 1788*, ed. Robert Taylor J and Marc Friedlaender (Cambridge, MA: Harvard University Press, 1981), 88–105, http://founders.archives.gov/documents/Ad.

6. "From Thomas Jefferson to James Madison, 30 January 1787," *The Papers of Thomas Jefferson*, vol. 11, *1 January–6 August 1787*, ed. Julian P. Boyd. (Princeton: Princeton University Press, 1955), 92–97.

7. "Letter to Henry Lee," TeachingAmericanHistory.org, http://teachingamericanhistory.org/library/document/letter-to-henry-lee-3/.

8. "To James Madison from George Washington, 5 November 1786," in *The Papers of James Madison*, vol. 9: *9 April 1786–24 May 1787 and Supplement 1781–1784*, ed. Robert A. Rutland and William M. E. Rachal (Chicago: University of Chicago Press, 1975), 161–62, http://founders.archives.gov/documents/Madison/01-09-02-0070.

9. "To James Madison from George Washington, 5 November 1786," in *The Papers of James Madison*, vol. 9, 161–62.

10. Richards, *Shays's Rebellion*, 16–38.

11. "Annapolis Convention. Address of the Annapolis Convention, [14 September 1786]," in *The Papers of Alexander Hamilton*, vol. 3, *1782–1786*, ed. Harold C. Syrett (New York: Columbia University Press, 1962), 686–90, http://founders.archives.gov/documents/Hamilton/01-03-02-0556.

12. "Samuel Osgood to John Adams, 14 Nov. 1786," Founders Online, National Archives, http://founders.archives.gov/documents/Adams/99-01-02-0806. This is an Early Access document from *The Adams Papers*. It is not an authoritative final version.

13. Alexander Hamilton or James Madison (attributed to "Publius") "Federalist no. 63," in *The Federalist Papers*, March 1788. http://thomas.loc.gov/home/histdox/fed_63.html.

14. "To James Madison from George Washington, 31 March 1787": in *The Papers of James Madison*, vol. 9, 342–45, http://founders.archives.gov/documents/Madison/01-09-02-0186.

15. "To James Madison from George Washington, 31 March 1787," in *The Papers of James Madison*, vol. 9, 342–45.

16. Gordon Lloyd, "Entertainment of George Washington at City Tavern, Philadelphia, September 1787, *Teaching American History*, retrieved from http://teachingamericanhistory.org/convention/citytavern/#part1b.

17. George Washington, *Diary of George Washington: From 1789 to 1791*, ed. Benson Lossing (New York: Charles B. Richardson & Co., 1860), 19, 20, 24, 25, 28, 30, 47, 49, 50, 52. https://archive.org/stream/diaryofgeorgewas01wash#page/n7/mode/2up pg.

18. Williams, *Rum*, 64.

19. Smith, *Tavern Signs of America*, 48.

20. Sismondo, *America Walks into a Bar*, 91.

21. Smith, *Tavern Signs of America*, 56.

22. "From Thomas Jefferson to Brissot de Warville, 16 August 1786," in *The Papers of Thomas Jefferson*, vol. 10: *22 June–31 December 1786*, ed. Julian P. Boyd (Princeton: Princeton University Press, 1954), 261–63, http://founders.archives.gov/documents/Jefferson/01-10-02-0180.

23. Rice, *Early American Taverns*.

24. Benjamin Rush, *An Inquiry into the Effects of Ardent Spirits upon the Human Body and Mind; with, An Account of the Means of Preventing, and of the Remedies for Curing Them* (1805; reprint ed. HighGravity Free Press, 2013), 15.

25. Centers for Disease Control. http://www.cdc.gov/mmwr/preview/mmwrhtml/mm6353a2.htm.

26. Rush, *An Inquiry*, 18.

27. Ibid., 15.

28. Dennis Pogue and Esther White, *George Washington's Gristmill at Mount Vernon* (Mount Vernon: George Washington's Mount Vernon Estate & Gardens, 2005).

29. "From John Adams to William Willis, 21 February 1819," Founders Online, National Archives (http://founders.archives.gov/documents/Adams/99-02-02-7083 [last update: 2015-09-29]). Source: this is an Early Access document from *The Adams Papers*. It is not an authoritative final version.

30. O'Brien, Jane. "The time when America drank all day long." *BBC News Magazine*. March 9, 2015. http://data.un.org/Data.aspx?d=WHO&f=MEASURE_CODE%3AWHOSIS_000011.

31. Smith, *Tavern Signs of America*, 2.

RECOMMENDED READINGS

Conroy, David. *In Public Houses: Drink and the Revolution of Authority in Colonial Massachusetts* (Chapel Hill: University of North Carolina Press, 1995)

Hitchens, Christopher. *Thomas Jefferson: Author of America* (New York: Atlas Books/HarperCollins, 2005).

Lathrop, Elise. *Early American Inns and Taverns* (New York: Arno Press, 1977).

Rice, Kym. *Early American Taverns: For the Entertainment of Friends and Strangers* (Chicago: Regnery Gateway, 1983).

Salinger, Sharon V. *Taverns and Drinking in Early America* (Baltimore: John Hopkins University Press, 2004).

Sismondo, Christine. *America Walks into a Bar* (New York: Oxford University Press, 2006).

Smith, Helene. *Tavern Signs of America* (Greenburg, PA: MacDonald/Swärd Publishing Company, 1989).

Williams, Ian. *Rum: A Social and Sociable History of the Real Spirit of 1776* (New York: Nation Books, 2006).

INSIGHT EDITIONS
PO Box 3088
San Rafael, CA 94912
www.insighteditions.com

Find us on Facebook: www.facebook.com/InsightEditions
Follow us on Twitter: @insighteditions

Text copyright © 2016 Adrian Covert

All rights reserved.

Published by Insight Editions, San Rafael, California, in 2016.
No part of this book may be reproduced in any form without written permission from the publisher.

Library of Congress Cataloging-in-Publication Data available.

ISBN: 978-1-60887-785-0

Publisher: Raoul Goff
Co-publisher: Michael Madden
Art Director: Chrissy Kwasnik
Designer: Jon Glick
Executive Editor: Vanessa Lopez
Project Editor: Dustin Jones
Production Editor: Rachel Anderson
Production Manager: Blake Mitchum
Editorial Assistant: Katherine Desandro

ROOTS of PEACE REPLANTED PAPER

Insight Editions, in association with Roots of Peace, will plant two trees for each tree used in the manufacturing of this book. Roots of Peace is an internationally renowned humanitarian organization dedicated to eradicating land mines worldwide and converting war-torn lands into productive farms and wildlife habitats. Roots of Peace will plant two million fruit and nut trees in Afghanistan and provide farmers there with the skills and support necessary for sustainable land use.

Manufactured in China by Insight Editions

10 9 8 7 6 5 4 3 2 1

PHOTO © BLAIR MARDIAN

ADRIAN COVERT is a San Francisco–based author, artist, and expert on California water policy for the Bay Area Council, a nonprofit public policy organization. Covert studied political science at San Francisco State University and enjoys old bars and playing baseball for the Sunset Nobles. He lives in the Mission District with his wife, Rachel.

IMAGE CREDITS

Photographs © 2016 Adrian Covert, unless otherwise noted below

Courtesy, American Antiquarian Society: Pages 1 and 68

Courtesy, the Colonial Williamsburg Foundation: Pages 24, 25, 31, 49, 50, and 65

Courtesy, Fraunces Tavern® Museum, New York City: Pages 90 and 93

The Connecticut Historical Society: Page 45 (top left and right)

Courtesy of the Lewis Walpole Library, Yale University: Page 27

Courtesy, Library of Congress: Pages 3, 18, 32, 33 (detail of engraving by H.S. Sadd after painting by Gilbert Stewart), 41, 53, 62, 75, 78 (top), 80, 84, 86, 87, 88, 89, 95, 98, 101, 109 (Marian S. Carson Collection), 112, 113, 115, 118, 119, 120,121, 128, 130, 131, 133(top right), 134 (detail of engraving by H.S. Sadd after painting by Gilbert Stewart), 135, 137, 138–139, 140, 142, 144, 153, 154, 164, and 169

The Library Company of Philadelphia: Page 56

Courtesy, New York Public Library (digitalcollections.nypl.org): Pages 19, 104, and 125

Courtesy, Old Sturbridge Village: Page 2

Courtesy, Wikimedia Commons (commons.wikimedia.org): Pages 8, 16, 22–23, 54, 71, 149, 151, 159, and 163

Courtesy, Winterthur Museum: Page 48 (Ink Drawing, Peter Manmigault and His Friends by George Roupell, 1757–1760, Charleston, SC, Ink, Graphite, Wash, Laid paper, Winterthur Museum, Museum Purchase, 1963.73)

Shutterstock, © Everett Historical: Pages 57, 63 (top left), and 110

Toledo Museum of Art: Page 171 (John Lewis Krimmel [American, 1786–1821] Village Tavern, 1813–14, oil on canvas, 16 7/8 x 22 inches, Toledo Museum of Art [Toledo, Ohio], Purchased with funds from the Florence Scott Libbey Bequest in Memory of her Father, Maurice A. Scott, 1954.13. Photo Credit: Richard Goodbody, New York.)

After Rain

Weekly Devotions for Comfort and Peace

Cindy L. Freeman

Copyright ©Cindy L. Freeman, December 2020
All Rights Reserved

ISBN: **978-1-945990-44-1**

Thank you for purchasing an authorized edition of *After Rain*.

High Tide's mission is to find, encourage, promote, and publish the work of authors. We are a small, woman-owned enterprise. When you buy an authorized copy, you help us to bring their work to you. When you honor copyright law by not reproducing or scanning any part (in any form) without our written permission, you enable us to support authors, publish their work, and bring it to you to enjoy. We thank you for supporting our authors.

High Tide Publications, Inc.
Deltaville, Virginia 23043
www.HighTidePublications.com
Edited by Cindy L. Freeman

Printed in the United States of America
First Edition

Note: The author and publisher are donating all proceeds for the sale of this book to:

Hospice House & Support Care of

Williamsburg, Virginia,

the most uplifting haven of comfort and peace this side of heaven.

"Hospice House & Support Care of Williamsburg is a social-model hospice that provides physical, emotional, social and spiritual support to enhance the quality of living for individuals facing the last phases of life and the people who love them. The Hospice House itself is a spacious residence that is a home away from home for our guests and their families. Support care services range from companionship in families' homes to extensive bereavement programs provided to families throughout the community. Hospice House & Support Care of Williamsburg is a 501(c)(3) organization that is entirely funded by contributions. No family or individual ever receives a bill for our services and support; nor do we accept Medicare, Medicaid or other reimbursements."*

*williamsburghospice.org

Preface

For some time God has been whispering to me to write a book of devotions, and I have resisted the whispers, thinking surely not I, Lord. I'm not a divinity graduate, preacher, theologian, or prophet. I'm not qualified to interpret scripture or offer words of wisdom or guidance to others. I mess up all the time and find myself in need of forgiveness every day, both from God and other people. How can I write a devotion book?

Lately, the whispers have been accompanied by nudges, and I am compelled to listen and obey, trusting that whatever I write is not from my limited wisdom, but from a limitless God. So, like King David, another flawed human, I pray, "May the words of my [pen] and the meditation of my heart be acceptable in your sight, O Lord, my rock and my Redeemer (Psalm 19:14)."

The year is 2020, the year of the COVID-19 worldwide pandemic. As citizens of the world shelter in place, we don't know what the future holds. Schools are closed, travel is restricted, and businesses are failing. My family and community are okay, but throughout the world, thousands are not. We are still able to see humor in the midst of this rapidly spreading virus. On social media sites, we share jokes about toilet-paper hoarding and pictures of each other working from home in our pajamas. But thousands have lost loved ones to the disease and can't even hold funerals or memorial services because of mandatory physical distancing. Healthcare workers and first responders are placed in danger every day as hospital ICUs overflow with COVID patients.

It is a time of worry, fear and uncertainty. I'm in my seventies, and nothing like this pandemic has occurred in my lifetime. During such a profound crisis, there's a steep learning curve for governments, medical personnel and individuals regarding how to handle it. We have no precedent upon which to base our procedures. The Spanish Flu of 1918 is not even a memory for people living today.

What I know for sure is that we can count on our living, loving God to see us through. Believers in the risen Christ are never alone in any circumstance. It is Jesus Christ who brings us the comfort and peace that transcend earthly circumstances, even a pandemic.

My fervent prayer for this book is that, in these pages, readers will find comfort amid chaos and hope for an uncertain future.

All biblical references are from the NASB edition of the Ryrie Study Bible, copyright 1995. Specific quoted verses are indicated in quotation marks with the chapter and verse noted. Italics indicate paraphrased references or inspired messages to the author.

Invitation

On the lined pages at the end of each month's devotions, I invite you to sit in stillness and allow God to enter the silence. Use the space to explore your responses to the meditation and to record any Spirit-inspired thoughts:

Week One: New Year; Renewed Spirit

____

____

____

____

____

____

January

Week One: New Year; Renewed Spirit

Living on Planet Earth can be chaotic and confusing. We become overwhelmed by media messages, responsibilities, and concern for ourselves and loved ones. We may let our days control us instead of the other way around. Our culture teaches us to value busyness, professional accomplishment, accumulation of wealth, and physical strength and beauty. These aspirations, in themselves, are not bad or wrong. But the Bible tells us that when we place them above God, they become idols. Then, we are in danger of provoking God to take action. "You shall have no other gods before me (Exodus 20:3)" is a pretty clear commandment.

R.A. Salvatore, author of *The Stowaway,* wrote, "Every day is an opportunity to start over." While it is not a quote from scripture, it sounds scriptural. It reminds me of the petition attributed to Jeremiah in Lamentations 5:21, "Restore us to you, O Lord, that we may be restored; Renew our days as of old." Jeremiah had warned the Israelites to turn from their idol worship, but they didn't listen. After the Babylonian army destroyed Jerusalem in 586 BC, Jeremiah lamented the physical destruction of the city and the temple, but also the spiritual desolation of its citizens.

Time after time, God had tried to get the Israelites' attention, so he could lead them, his chosen people, to the promised land, but they were determined to rebel. Aren't we just as stubborn sometimes? I know I am. I start to worry and fret. I try to manipulate my surroundings and control people and situations. That's when God must get my attention, sometimes even allowing me to experience failure, illness, or tragedy. I struggle in my humanness to restore order and balance to my life, my surroundings and my relationships. Finally, with no recourse, I acknowledge God as Sovereign and fall on my knees in desperate prayer, crying, "Help me!" But what would happen if, instead of saving prayer for moments of desperation, I made prayer a daily habit, like brushing my teeth or eating vegetables?

I've learned that, through practice, it's possible to develop the habit of communing with God daily. Even when I don't *feel* grateful, I can start with a simple "thank you" then listen in stillness for God's direction. Just as daily brushing prevents tooth decay, daily prayer prevents soul decay. My spiritual health is nurtured by embracing holy silence and feeding on God's Word.

There are no shortcuts when it comes to developing a new habit or restoring one we have let slip. Yet the process of connecting with God is as simple as stopping, sitting or kneeling, and waiting in expectation. Thankfully, God stands ready to listen and respond every time, even after a long period of neglect on our part.

"Every day is an opportunity to start over." What better time than the first day of a new year to seek restoration with our loving Creator, inviting God to renew our spirits one day at a time? Besides, what do we have to lose by eating more vegetables, brushing our teeth, and praying daily?

Prayer: God of the universe, renew our spirits and restore us to you this year. We thank you for the gift of life and all its blessings. Help us develop the habit of communing with you daily that we might experience your presence and discern your will.

Meditation: As I begin a new year, what practices will help me establish or reestablish a connection with my Creator? How will these habits change my life for the better? Am I willing to take a chance on getting to know God better?

Week Two: Soul-Searching

New Year's resolutions tend to focus on improving physical fitness, losing weight, or adopting habits to increase success in our work lives and home lives. All are worthy goals, but with each passing year, I realize how important it is to nurture my soul as well as my body. As I count the new gray hairs on my head and wrinkles on my skin, as I feel little twinges that accompany aging, I'm aware that my body will eventually fail me. There's no escaping it. I can exercise, eat right, get plenty of rest, and maybe even indulge in some plastic surgery, but I can't prevent the inevitable destiny of my earthly body.

In our Western culture, we are uncomfortable talking about death, especially our own. It makes us feel powerless. That's because we *are* powerless to prevent it.

Have you ever wondered where the human soul resides? Have you thought about where it goes after the body dies? In preparation for eternity, is it possible to nurture the soul, to make it healthier through exercise?

Most of the world's religions include a tenet about that intangible, mysterious entity known as the soul. Movie-producers and psychics earn billions from peoples' natural curiosity about the paranormal. Despite our limited capacity, we are determined to understand the supernatural world. We are attracted to speculating about other-worldly presences like ghosts. But are ghosts the same as souls?

The Hebrew word, "nephesh" translated by most biblical scholars as "soul" literally means "living being." If the soul is a living being, it stands to reason we can strengthen it through exercise.

I'm convinced the soul shows up wherever we decide to encounter The Divine. For some people, being in nature by walking in the woods or digging in the garden are where they encounter The Divine. For others, this soul-searching happens through meditation, prayer or corporate worship. Whether we recognize it or not, seeking God is as natural to humans—and as essential—as breathing. It is as if God created a soul-shaped hole in each of us. Only God can fill the void...not personal accomplishment, material possessions, or even loving family and cherished friends.

Soul-searching is not complicated. Communicating with The Divine is as simple as showing up, embracing silence, and listening for the still, small voice.

Prayer: Creator God, remind us this week to make a conscious effort to encounter you every day. Help us exercise and strengthen our souls through scripture reading, meditation, and prayer. In the silence, as we listen for your still small voice, we ask you to fill the soul-shaped hole in each of our hearts.

Meditation: What do I need to do to encounter The Divine today, tomorrow, and every day after that? Do I need to choose a quiet space in my home, take a walk, attend a Bible study, go to church, write in a journal...?

Week Three: Hymns of the Ages

I love hymns, especially old hymns with their poetic language. "Amazing grace! How sweet the sound that saved a wretch like me! I once was lost but now am found; was blind but now I see." Such words ascend from the depths of my heart today as fervently as they flowed from John Newton's pen three centuries ago. I wonder if Newton sensed that his intimate poem would one day be set to music and sung in multi-denominational churches throughout the world.

When I am overcome with joy at God's generous gifts, there are no adequate words to express my gratitude. That's when Charles Wesley's hymn, "Rejoice, the Lord is King" resonates with me. His simple refrain, "Lift up your heart, lift up your voice; rejoice; again I say, rejoice" conveys what I am too overwhelmed to speak.

"It is Well with My Soul" is a hymn I turn to in times of sadness or disappointment. "When peace like a river attendeth my way; when sorrows like sea billows roll; whatever my lot, thou hast taught me to say it is well, it is well with my soul." In 1873, these words were written aboard a ship by Horatio Spafford, a man who knew the deepest sorrow—the death of not one, but all of his children.* How is it possible to lose your whole family, yet declare, "It is well with my soul?" Truthfully, it is *not* possible in our human strength amid profound sorrow to experience "peace like a river." But Spafford discovered that in our weakness, God's strength is made perfect. Only through trusting God, was a grieving father able to declare, "...though trials shall come, let this blest assurance control, that Christ has regarded my helpless estate, and has shed his own blood for my soul."

Hymn writing goes back even further than three centuries. While the book of Psalms is filled with hymns of praise, its authors also express longing and desperation. Psalm 3 is a Lament Psalm where the author cries for help, "Oh Lord, how my adversaries have increased! Many are rising up against me. Many are saying of my soul, 'There is no deliverance for him in God.'" There are times, even now, centuries later, when we feel God has deserted us. Someone we love has cancer or COVID-19; we fail to accomplish what we set out to do at work, school or home; our spouse, parent or child dies. We feel alone, confused and desperate to restore peace to our aching hearts.

There was a period in my life when I cried out to God for healing of a physical ailment. My condition was painful and relentless. It was destroying my life and relationships. I felt that God had deserted me. For fifteen long years, I prayed, but healing didn't come. God had much to teach me, lessons I could learn only through suffering. Instead of submitting and trusting, I railed against God, allowing anger and frustration to turn me bitter.

The day I decided to stop struggling and trust God again, something inside shifted. Like the psalmist, I had been lamenting, wallowing in self-pity, and begging for deliverance. But unlike him, I was so caught up in my pain and misery that I failed to praise and thank God for his myriad blessings.

In Psalm 5, besieged by enemies, the psalmist cries out, "Give ear to my words, O Lord. Consider my groaning. Heed the sound of my cry for help, my King and my God." These words of desperate supplication also assert the author's trust in the sovereign God's power to deliver him. In his next breath, he proclaims, "In the morning, O Lord, you will hear my voice. In the morning I will order my prayer to you and eagerly watch."

When I finally let go of stubborn willfulness and began to express undeniable confidence in God; when I changed my prayers to "not my will, but thine be done," the healing began. Physical healing wasn't instant, but God in his mercy replaced my despondency with hope. All these years later, whatever befalls me, like Horatio Spafford, I declare, "It is well with my soul."

Prayer: Loving God, open our hearts and minds to recognize your blessings even when we're grieving. May your peace flow through us like a river, bringing healing to our raw wounds so that we might find joy in living. Grant us the compassion and energy to minister to others who are hurting.

Meditation: Who in my life needs compassion and care? How can I minister to someone who is hurting?

* *Then Sings My Soul*, Robert J. Morgan, 2011, W Publishing Group, p. 185

Week Four: Perfect Peace

I'm convinced that what every person, regardless of race, gender, religion, or sexual orientation seeks, above all, is perfect peace. Whether through overt or subconscious effort, we want to know that we are loved, that we have worth, and that our lives have purpose.

The God of the universe is generous and delights in showering us with abundance. God's desire is for his children to prosper, to be content, to find meaningful work and relationships, and to abide in perfect peace. It is not God who stands in the way of our peace. The book of Genesis illustrates how original sin entered God's perfect creation, resulting in a fallen world and flawed humans.

In Luke 12, Jesus is speaking to a crowd of people when a frustrated individual calls out, "Teacher, tell my brother to divide the family inheritance with me." Jesus refuses to intercede in this family feud, but instead grasps the opportunity to teach about covetousness. "Beware and be on your guard against every form of greed," he warns. "For not even when one has abundance does his life consist of possessions." Jesus is saying that peace is not found in the riches of this world. Fleeting happiness perhaps, but not lasting peace.

In his letter to the Galatians, Chapter 5, Verse 22, Paul spells out the true gifts—Fruit of the Spirit—

with which God desires to lavish us: love, joy, peace, patience, kindness, goodness, faithfulness, gentleness, and self-control. Paul says this fruit can be found only in a relationship with Jesus Christ. When we abide in Jesus and invite Jesus to abide in us, we begin to produce fruit, sweet, ripe and abundant.

Only when we walk with Jesus daily, rest in his presence, and seek his will in all decisions, can he produce fruit in us. Our reward is perfect peace that transcends every earthly circumstance, even "though [we] walk through the valley of the shadow of death (Psalm 23:4a)."

Prayer: Heavenly Father, may we seek your presence every day, recognizing your hand in all of creation and responding in gratitude. We hunger to produce Fruit of the Spirit. May love, joy, peace, patience, kindness, goodness, faithfulness, gentleness and self-control ripen in us as we allow you to prune away the decaying branches of greed, envy, and selfishness.

Meditation: How can I use God's spiritual gifts this week to ease someone's suffering? Who needs to receive God's Fruit of the Spirit through my loving attention?

Week One: New Year; Renewed Spirit

Week Two: Soul-Searching

Week Three: Hymns of the Ages

Week Four: Perfect Peace

February

Week One: Washed Clean

As I stepped out of the shower, I noticed how good it felt to be clean. I dried my dripping hair and squeaky-clean body with a freshly laundered towel; I dressed in clean clothes. Then, standing in front of the mirror, I tried to imagine what it would feel like to be homeless or living in poverty, perhaps with no place to shower and wash my hair. I imagined the odor of a perpetually dirty body dressed in soiled clothes and crowned with stringy, greasy hair.

What a blessing it is to be clean, to smell of lemon or lavender, to feel light and fresh, not having to wonder when or where we might shower again! It is easy to take for granted the abundant blessings that most of us enjoy daily: the morning's first cup of steaming coffee; a thermostat that does our bidding according to the weather; so much food that we must exercise self-control to keep from overindulging and over-exercise to counteract our gluttony; a safe place to sleep where we need not worry about being violated; a warm winter coat; and clean water.

Water, whether for bathing or drinking, is life giving. In the Bible, the image of water is used repeatedly. In Genesis, flood waters covered the earth for forty days and nights to cleanse it from sin; in Exodus, Moses stretched his hand over the Red Sea and, through God's power, parted the waters so the Israelites could escape to freedom. In the New Testament, Jesus turned water into wine for wedding guests; and water became the symbol of baptism that we still employ today, whether by sprinkling, pouring, or immersion. Water symbolizes new life in Jesus who holds the power to wash us clean of sin and guilt.

Like air, water is a universal need. While not everyone has access to clean water, the water that quenches spiritual thirst is a free gift available to all. It is neither the sprinkling nor the pouring nor the immersion that washes us clean. Rather it is the act of accepting Jesus Christ as Lord and Savior. Jesus is the living water that quenches spiritual thirst.

Prayer: Father, we thank you for the blessing of life-giving water. Hear our prayer for those who lack clean water. We thank you for offering us the same living water that you provided the Samaritan woman, promising that "...whoever drinks of the water that I will give shall never thirst…(John 4:14)."

Meditation: Are there tangible ways I can provide for communities or individuals without access to clean water? Who in my life is thirsting for the living water of Jesus Christ?

Week Two: Never Alone

Have you ever felt alone even in a crowd of people? Do you sometimes feel that God has abandoned you? Are you overwhelmed by your present circumstances and the condition of the world? "Do not let your heart be troubled; believe in God, believe also in me (John 14:1)." The truth is God has not left you. "I will never desert you, nor will I ever forsake you (Hebrews 13:5)." Is it possible that, instead, you have moved away from God?

The times I've felt separated from God's presence were when I neglected or even rejected God's companionship. Like Jesus' disciples who deserted him in the Garden of Gethsemane, I have sometimes turned away from God, thinking I could handle life on my own. But whenever I attempt to "do" life without God, when my ego convinces me I am strong and independent, I become like seaweed tossed to and fro by waves of worry.

Only one relationship is steadfast, unwavering and unchanging. That is my relationship with the resurrected Son of God. When I remember to let go of self-serving pride and stubborn independence, turning instead to my Heavenly Father in humble petition, coming into his presence with expectation, he welcomes me every time. It is then I wonder why I left in the first place. I hear him saying, *My child, I love you. When will you finally accept my promises and welcome my fellowship?*

To experience the privilege of communing with the Creator is to experience heaven on earth. When we enter into the presence of Agape (unconditional love and acceptance), when we confess our sins with sincere repentance and experience forgiveness, when we seek divine direction for our lives and decisions—only then can we truly be at peace. "I will never desert you, nor will I ever forsake you (Hebrews 13:5)."

Prayer: Holy Lord, we thank you for standing ready to receive us into your presence. When we stray from you, tempted to think we can handle life on our own, remind us to whisper your name then wait in stillness and trust. May we remember to speak, in expectation, the powerful words, "Come, Lord Jesus."

Meditation: Did I remember to commune with God yesterday? Have I come into The Presence today? Is anything standing in the way of my connection with God?

Week Three: Messenger of Forgiveness

History abounds with people who have risen above bleak circumstances, remaining steadfast in faith. When I think of true heroes of faith, Corrie ten Boom comes to mind. She and her father were Dutch watchmakers and devout Christians who hid Jews during the Nazi occupation of Holland. Eventually, their risky actions were discovered, and they were sent to concentration camps where both Corrie's father and sister, Betsie, died.

After the war, Corrie wrote about her experiences and traveled the world, speaking about God's grace and forgiveness. As a teenager, I read her books, *Tramp for the Lord* and *The Hiding Place.* They influenced my life's direction. I never imagined I would hear her speak in person.

When the Billy Graham Crusade came to the coliseum my town in the 1970s, the church choir I directed was invited to sing in Graham's crusade choir. Corrie ten Boom was the guest speaker at that crusade. I will never forget her accounts of unwavering faith amid one of history's most horrific events. She recounted instances where only God's hand could have turned an impossible situation into a blessing. For example, at the first concentration camp, a miraculous distraction during the body searches caused her to be passed over, allowing her to smuggle in her Bible.

I'll never forget ten Boom's powerful story of an incident that happened after the war. She was speaking to a church group in Munich. She had gone to post-war Germany for the purpose of telling the German people about God's forgiveness. In her message, she mentioned that she had been a prisoner at Ravensbruck Concentration Camp. As she was leaving, a man approached her with his hand outstretched. She recognized him as the cruel Nazi guard who had processed her and Betsie at Ravensbruck, the camp where Betsie later died. He didn't remember her, although she and Betsie had been forced to file naked past him. Immediately Corrie's heart filled with hatred toward the former soldier who now claimed to be a converted follower of Jesus Christ. He averred that God had forgiven him for his terrible actions. When he held out his hand, requesting her forgiveness, Corrie stood frozen as horrific memories flooded her mind.

All these years since that night in the coliseum, I still have a clear vision of Corrie ten Boom's crystal eyes and outstretched hand as she relived the most difficult decision of her life, a decision that no act of human will could have accomplished. She knew God was calling her to forgive this man who had once been an agent of evil. She said when she uttered the simple prayer, "Help me, Jesus!" a warm surge of love flowed through her into her stiff, reluctant arm as she grasped the man's hand. In a heavy Dutch accent she proclaimed that she had never felt the love of God so powerfully as she did the moment she was able to say to her former captor, "I forgive you, my brother."

Jesus' followers are called to forgive others as he has forgiven us. It can be a tall order to forgive those who have gossiped about us, said hurtful words, made false accusations, or betrayed our trust. Yet, we know that God stands ready to forgive *our* sins when we confess them in sincere repentance. How, then, can we refuse to forgive those who have wronged us? Like Corrie ten Boom, we must cry, "Help me, Jesus!" and then allow God's unfailing love to flow through us.

Prayer: God, grant us your power to forgive those who have harmed us by word or deed. Forgive us for the harm we have caused and show us where we need to make amends. Only as we pray for your supernatural courage, can we move forward in expectation of miraculous healing.

Meditation: Who do I need to forgive? From whom do I need to seek forgiveness? Am I ready to take responsibility for my injurious words or actions?

Week Four: The Helper

Our house stayed on the market for two-and-a-half years after we bought and moved into a condo. We had retired, confident that our assets would be enough to support us. But our assets were tied up in the house, and the market had stalled. What if one of us got sick and needed long-term care? What if one of us passed away, leaving the other with monumental debt? It was a time of uncertainty, and while I wanted to trust in God's timing, I confess that sometimes I worried.

Often I don't know how to pray. Something stands in the way of communing with God. I may be overcome with worry, doubt or fatigue; perhaps there is conflict in my thinking that I can't seem to resolve. The enemy thrives on my confusion, tempting me to distrust God. It is those days when I can only call out the name "Jesus," the name above all names. I sit and wait, resting in the presence of the Most High. For I know that the Holy Spirit, the third person of the Godhead, will intercede for me when words stick in my throat.

In John 14:16, Jesus says, "I will ask the Father and he will give you another Helper, that he [the Holy Spirit] may be with you forever." Jesus is addressing his disciples who are deeply concerned about how they will continue their ministry after he departs. They don't understand where their Teacher is going and why he must leave them. Can you imagine how frightened and confused they must have felt? They gave up everything to follow their *Raboni*, and now he's going to leave them.

I'm reminded of an old Gaither hymn that proclaims, "Jesus, Jesus, Jesus, there's just something about that name!" In the Hebrew language, the name, Jesus, means, "The Lord is salvation." Mary and Joseph did not choose his name. Rather, an angel of God instructed them to name him Jesus because he would bring salvation to the world.

For believers in the Triune God, there is power in invoking the name of Jesus! For we are calling out to the Son of the Most High. Instantly, God sends a Helper (the Holy Spirit) to intercede for us, to utter the prayers that are in our hearts, but not yet on our lips.

Listening and waiting become acts of trust. Answers may not come immediately; problems may not disappear instantly, but if we trust in the Holy Spirit, The Helper, we find that perfect peace replaces worry, and we are able to wait.

We are assured that answers will come in time—in God's time, which is always perfect.

Prayer: We have no words today, Lord; Something is blocking our prayers. We call upon the Holy Spirit to pray for us. Send The Helper to intercede for us. Thank you.

Meditation: I am invited to call upon the third person of the Trinity to intercede for me until my mouth is able to form the words that lie buried in a wounded heart. When I'm too worried, upset or grieved to pray, do I remember that the Holy Spirit dwells within me and stands ready to intercede?

Week One: Washed Clean

Week Two: Never Alone

Week Three: Messenger of Forgiveness

Week Four: The Helper

March

Week One: After Rain

Often during my daily walks, my brain bursts forth with a scripture passage. Usually, it is scripture that has been set to music in a choral work I performed or conducted sometime during my music career. Music, it seems, provides powerful memory triggers. In fact, music is used to help Alzheimer's patients access their long-term memories. I can only identify these unexpected mental explosions as divine gifts. Why? Because as I begin my walks, I pray for God to instill in me awareness of his presence and his direction.

As I struggled with the decision to write this book, the words "after rain" came to me. It was a glorious sunny day, unseasonably warm for February, too early for the crocuses and daffodils to poke their heads through the soil, but there they were lining my path in anticipation of spring. That's when I heard the words "after rain" repeated three times to the tune of Randall Thompson's exquisite choral piece, "The Last Words of David." I hadn't sung it since college, nearly fifty years earlier, but now, like a clear bell, the musical passage rang in my head. I was able to recall a few other snippets but couldn't quite piece together all of the lyrics.

I rushed home to look up the text for "The Last Words of David." I needed to know why God was using this text to speak to me:

> *He that ruleth over men must be just, ruling in the fear of God.*
> *And he shall be as the light of the morning, when the sun riseth, even a morning without clouds; as the tender grass springing out of the earth by clear shining after rain.*
> *Alleluia. Amen.*

It turns out the paraphrased scripture is from II Samuel 23:1 - 4, understood to be the last public words spoken by King David. Thompson's musical setting is so stunning that, for me, the music has always overshadowed the words. But, clearly, this time God wanted me to focus on the words.

David knew God had chosen him, a lowly shepherd, to one day rule over Israel. In fact, God anointed him three times. Perhaps the first line of the song is David's reminder to himself to rule justly and in the fear (loving -kindness) of God. But then, I'm convinced David is no longer referring to himself. Rather, "He who shall be as light of the morning" is a reference to another ruler, The Messiah. Through his earthly father, Joseph, Jesus was a descendant of the house of David. Here, David is referring to the words of the prophets Isaiah and Zechariah. Much time will pass—much rain will fall—but "after rain" The Messiah will spring forth "as the tender grass." Throughout the Old Testament Jesus was prophesied to return after chaos, unrest, and disaster. After rain.

David was a strong ruler, but he was far from perfect. He acted immorally, not only committing adultery, but then attempting to cover up his indiscretion with Bathsheba by killing her husband—an honorable soldier in his army. Again and again, in his human weakness, David broke his promises to God and had to confess his sins and plead for forgiveness. But even after David's darkest sins, God never reneged on his part of the covenant. He sent his son, Jesus, The Messiah, to save all who would believe in him and follow his teachings.

God's covenant will be fulfilled "after rain," after we humans have exhausted every form of rebellion against God's sovereignty, after God has given us more chances to repent than we deserve, God will fulfill the final phase that began with David. "Christ will come again." Alleluia, Amen.

Prayer: Lord, we thank you for your patience with us, your rebellious children. We thank you for your love, the same love that surrounded David both as a shepherd boy and a King. Thank you for your promise that Jesus will return "after rain" when your Kingdom will be established on Earth, when your Son, The Messiah, will rule justly and "in the fear of God."

Meditation: If Jesus returned tomorrow, would I be ready? Would I recognize Him? What parts of my life do I still need to relinquish to God's control? What keeps me from taking those final steps of surrender, allowing God to rule justly over every facet of my life?

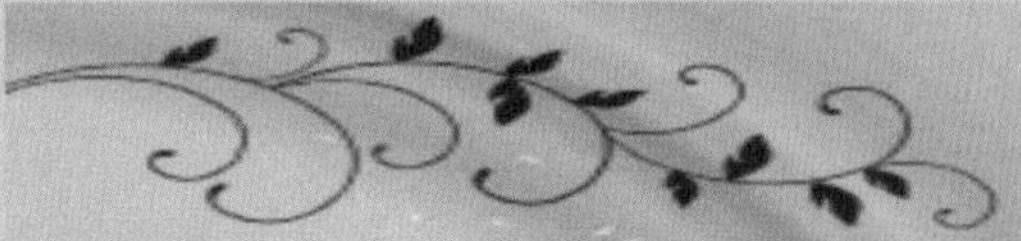

Week Two: Remembering the Cross

Every Ash Wednesday, I look forward to frequenting public places because on that one day of the year, I can identify fellow Christians by the ashes on their foreheads in the shape of a cross. I smile and nod in recognition because I know I have met, however fleetingly, a brother or sister in Christ. That gray smudge reminds me that even in this bustling, secular world, I am not alone on my faith journey.

The season of Lent, leading up to Easter, begins on Ash Wednesday and lasts forty days to represent the time Jesus spent in the desert preparing for his earthly ministry. He used his self-imposed isolation to fast and commune with his Father in preparation for a mere three years in which he changed the world.

For Christians, Lent is a time to reflect on the cross. Perhaps we give up something like chocolate or going to the movies as a sacrifice representing Jesus' ultimate sacrifice for us. It is an important time for believers to prepare for Easter through prayer, penitence, charitable giving, and self-denial.

Unlike Easter, Lent is not a celebration. Rather, it's a time to remember the cross. The cross reminds us of how God overcame the worst possible circumstance: the shameful dishonor and brutal murder of his innocent Son.

Roman citizens were accustomed to seeing criminals and slaves killed by this cruel, humiliating and painful method. Reported in the June 04, 2018 edition of *Life Science* magazine, "Roman crucifixions were designed to cause maximum pain for a prolonged period — victims' feet and wrists were usually nailed [or tied] to a wooden cross, which would hold them upright while they suffered a slow and agonizing death, often taking several days … the bodies were often left on the cross to rot or to be eaten by animals, but in some cases, they were removed and buried."

Although God the Son suffered the most extreme, unjustified abuse and death possible, God the Father walked with him through his suffering and death bringing him, at last, to triumphant glory… all for the love of you and me. "All have sinned and fall short of the glory of God (Romans 3:23)." That means not one of us can be good enough to earn God's forgiveness. No one deserves to inherit eternal life. That's why we need the cross. On the cross, Jesus took our punishment for us. We cannot save ourselves by being good people, donating to charities, helping neighbors, or becoming church and community leaders. Salvation cannot be earned. That's why we remember the cross.

"For by grace you have been saved through faith; and that not of yourselves; it is the gift of God (Ephesians 2:8)."

Prayer: Father, we thank you for providing a solution to our lostness. We thank you for the cross that reminds us of your ultimate sacrifice in sending your Son to take our place. "For the wages of sin is death, but the free gift of God is eternal life in Christ Jesus our Lord (Romans 6:23)." Salvation is a precious gift!

Meditation: As I consider that Christ entered Jerusalem with full knowledge of his impending suffering and death, I think about how much Jesus must love me to have taken my sins upon himself and carried them to the cross, that I might have eternal life with him.

Week Three: The Battle Within

For most of my life I have been addicted to food. Food has been my comfort. I have turned to food to ease anxiety and deny negative emotions like anger, frustration, fear, shame and guilt. The problem with turning to addictive substances instead of dealing with emotions is that the resulting state of euphoria is only temporary. The problem with a *food* addiction is that the addict can't go cold-turkey in attempting to conquer it.

During all those years of addiction, I suffered guilt and shame for abusing God's abundant gift of food.

Yet, I couldn't stop overeating.

Food is intended to strengthen the body, satisfy hunger, and promote good health. Its purpose is to be used as fuel, to nourish the physical body, not as a substitute for dealing with uncomfortable emotions. My mind understood this principle, but my addictive personality could not stop the destructive behavior of binge eating.

An obvious issue with food addiction is that it can't be hidden even under loose clothing. The body can take only so much overeating before its effects become apparent to everyone. That's when the abuser might begin to adopt other destructive behaviors like purging or hyper-exercising to counteract the effects of too many calories. Like all addictions, it becomes a vicious cycle of gaining and losing control.

It took decades of denial, failed diets, and struggle—both mental and physical—for me to recognize my binge triggers as any feelings too uncomfortable to deal with. I hadn't yet identified the dietary culprit as sugar. But once I made this discovery, I launched into a three-year period of losing, winning, and losing battles to purge sugar from my system. It was only by God's grace and strength that I finally won the war.

In his letter to the Romans, Paul describes the struggle with his "old" self even after experiencing new life in Christ. He notes that the temptation to sin does not disappear when we receive salvation. He uses the metaphor of slavery to describe what humans experience in trying to resist evil. In Romans 6:14, Paul proclaims the good news of salvation in Christ Jesus: "For sin shall not be master over you, for you are not under the law, but under grace." When I was a slave to my food addiction, reading that verse caused deep guilt. I knew I had been saved by God's grace, but I continued to allow my addiction to own me.

Like Paul, once I recognized that salvation is not only the end of one's old life but the beginning of a new life in Christ, I was able to address my addiction for what it was: a means of escape, escape which is ever only temporary. Recovering alcoholics and drug abusers refer to their addictions in the present tense. "I *am* an addict" not "I *was* an addict." There is no cure for addiction. Rather, it is managed one day at a time. This management is possible only after we admit our powerlessness and address the underlying issues.

Prayer: Lord, help those of us who are addicted to mind-numbing substances face our demons honestly without shame or guilt. Give us courage to reach out for help, recognizing addiction as a disease that cannot be cured but can be managed.

Meditation: Am I addicted to anything? Does any substance or habit control me? Do I feel powerless to stop? Am I, at last, ready to abandon control to God's grace, seek help, and experience freedom?

Week Four: The Color of Life

"It's not easy bein' green," sings Kermit the Frog. "Having to spend each day the color of the leaves…" In stanza two, he explains why being green is difficult. "It seems you blend in with so many ordinary things. And people tend to pass you over cause you're not standing out like sparkles in the water or stars in the sky."

For me, green represents the color of life. I am the most creative and productive in my sunroom, surrounded by the variety of lush, green plants I've placed there. The expanse of windows before me reveals additional layers of green beyond the glass where sun-kissed leaves pirouette in the breeze. It is a feast for the eyes.

I've wondered what it is about the color green that is so life-giving. Is there science behind this phenomenon? According to the Farlex Dictionary, the color green is "...evoked in the human observer by radiant energy." So it's not just me. The color green produces physiological responses in *most* people. It's no wonder, then, that people with color-blindness exhibit extreme emotional responses to those new-fangled glasses for restoring color perception. It must be mind blowing to see green leaves and grass for the first time after years of viewing the world in shades of gray.

In the color green, we see evidence of God's perfect plan for creation. We know that trees and other plants are life giving. Through photosynthesis, they emit oxygen and consume carbon dioxide, important functions for sustaining human and animal life. Green plants produce essential vitamins for the nutrition of humans and herbivores. Likewise, green algae form the base for the aquatic food chain as they, too, produce oxygen and consume carbon dioxide, removing pollutants from freshwater environments.

When God's plan is interrupted by human greed, we see the gradual disappearance of green. Trees are stripped from the earth to build structures, roads, and parking lots; the rainforest burns, causing deforestation and invasion of lands that once supported indigenous species.

What does the Bible say about the color green? According to the website, womanofnoblecharacter.com, "Most biblical scholars agree that one of the primary meanings behind green in the Bible is immortality."

Jeremiah 17:7 - 8 states: "Blessed [how happy] is the man who trusts in the Lord and whose trust *is* the Lord. For he will be like a tree planted by the water, that extends its roots by a stream and will not fear when the heat comes; but its leaves will be green, and it will not be anxious in a year of drought nor cease to yield fruit." Here, the prophet Jeremiah is paraphrasing Psalm 1:1 - 3 where the psalmist compares a God-fearing, God-trusting person to a tree that yields healthy green leaves.

It seems the most important function of green in the environment is to serve as the visible reminder of the greatness of God, its life-giving Creator.

By the end of his song, even Kermit the Frog has a change of heart about "bein' green."

But green's the color of spring
And green can be cool and friendly like
And green can be big like a mountain
Or important like a river or tall like a tree
When green is all there is to be
It could make you wonder why
But why wonder?
I'm green and it'll do fine.
*It's beautiful. And I think it's what I want to be.**

*https://genius.com/The-muppets-its-not-easy-bein-green-lyrics

---

Prayer: We thank you, Lord, for eyes to see every color of the rainbow, especially green, the vibrant color of life. Hear our prayer for those who cannot see and those who are colorblind. Grant them the ability to see green in their minds' eyes by miraculous means that only you can provide.

Meditation: When is the last time I thanked God for the beauty of the earth and the ability to see all the colors of life? What if my neighbor or co-worker were black...or brown...or even green? Could I see the worth of that person through God's eyes?

Week One: After Rain

Week Two: Remembering the Cross

Week Three: The Battle Within

Week Four: The Color of Life

April

Week One: The Mystery of Faith

Not one person deserves God's grace (unmerited favor) and it cannot be earned through good works. "Christ has died; Christ is risen; Christ will come again."* The mystery of faith. Accepting the mystery of faith is the path to salvation and lasting peace.

Whenever I take communion, I am overcome with gratitude for Jesus' sacrifice in giving his life for me. Whenever I read the Passion story, recounting Jesus' pain and suffering as he carried that heavy wooden cross uphill to Calvary with full knowledge of the fate awaiting him, my heart feels like it will burst with both sorrow and gratitude.

By the time Jesus hauled his instrument of death to Calvary, he had already experienced false accusations, betrayal, taunts, physical lashings, and a crown of thorns digging into his scalp. Is it any wonder that, in his humanness, Jesus pleaded with his Father to "remove this cup from me (Luke 22:42)?" At the same time, his acceptance of his divine destiny manifested in such love that he willingly carried our sins to the cross and bore the ultimate sacrifice so we might have eternal life.

"Greater love has no one than this, that one lay down his life for his friends (John 15:13)." I love my husband, but could I die to spare his life? I love my children and grandchildren, but could I give my life if I knew my death would save them? If someone held a gun to my head, promising to let my family live, could I take that bullet? Honestly, I don't know. What I *do* know is that Jesus took my bullet; Jesus carried my sins to the cross. Because of his ultimate sacrifice, I am granted unmerited favor both in this life and throughout eternity. Thanks be to God!

Prayer: Father, Son and Holy Spirit, we are sinners who do not deserve your favor. We can do nothing to earn your grace. Yet, in your perfect Agape, you give it freely to those who accept it. In gratitude, for this great gift, the mystery of faith, may we serve you all the days of our lives.

Meditation: Who within my scope of influence needs to hear the message of the Gospels? Who needs to experience the lasting peace that passes all understanding? How can I use whatever time I have left in this life to ease suffering, alleviate poverty, minister to the elderly and infirm, and support the faith journeys of the young?

*From The Great Thanksgiving, Communion Service I, *United Methodist Book of Worship*

Week Two: Embracing Peace

I've spent much of my adult life striving, planning, and reaching for self-imposed goals. For many years, I sought my worth through my career and achievements. I was lured by the false premise that the so-called American dream must be attained in one's lifetime for that life to be worthwhile. A schedule filled with frenzy shows that life is full and rewarding. Right?

I've come to realize there's a difference between an accomplished life and a significant life. I'm not saying that accomplishment is a negative goal, but that a life of significance first strives to glorify God. When our accomplishments honor God they are significant.

Does our striving for significance mean we're seeking perfection? Only Jesus lived a perfect earthly life because, while Jesus was fully human, he was also fully divine. Jesus wasn't just a good person who did good deeds and cared about others. Jesus was God in the flesh.

In our humanness, we are incapable of achieving perfection in this life. But peace results when we strive to obey and glorify God through our accomplishments. While achieving perfection is not possible, peace is an achievable goal.

The formula for peace is simple in theory but difficult in practice: seek God's will in all things; confess to those we have harmed, asking for their forgiveness; and confess our sins to God, seeking reconciliation. There's one more part to the formula, and I'm convinced it is the most challenging: forgive ourselves.

Both my sister and I harbor regrets regarding our deceased parents. I don't think we're alone in this feeling. The problem with regret is that it holds the power to block peace. Regret is possibly the most difficult emotion to resolve. Often, the people we harmed—or think we harmed—are gone from this earthly life, and we are left with if-onlys. If only I had said or done this or that. If only I *hadn't* said or done this or that.

I've learned that, although it may be too late to resolve our if-onlys with the people we've harmed, it's never too late to seek God's forgiveness. Believers are promised that nothing can separate us from God's love, not even regret. When we harbor regret, it's difficult to accept that God's forgiveness is both free and final. We keep taking back the regret and carrying it around like a teenager's backpack filled with heavy books. Regret weighs us down, causing us to drag through our days, maybe even keeping us awake at night, until finally after the tenth time or hundredth time of shaming ourselves, we accept God's forgiveness, forgive ourselves, and embrace the peace that God has been offering all along.

Prayer: Father, help us remember that once we confess our sins in true repentance and make amends where we can, you grant us forgiveness. We need not carry the heavy burdens of guilt and regret anymore. Help us to forgive ourselves and move on to the fullness of life.

Meditation: Am I ready to let go of my regrets about the past and accept God's forgiveness once and for all? Am I ready to experience the peace that comes from forgiving others and finally forgiving myself?

Week Three: Hidden Stories

Suffering is hard to understand and even harder to experience. When it's our own pain, we question God's purpose. We might even question God's existence. It's natural to cry out, "Why?" or "Why me?"

We don't always know what other people are going through. When we ask, "How are you?" we expect an answer of "Fine, thanks." We're asking to be polite, not to hear a tale of woe. Often, people truly are fine. But everyone has hidden stories. Everyone experiences suffering at one time or another. Illness, grief and loss are part of the human experience.

For fifteen years, I suffered from chronic, debilitating pain. Living was nothing more than a heavy burden to be endured, day in and day out. The pain had a negative effect on my marriage, my parenting, my career, my weight, my friendships, and my self-esteem. Because of strong medication and ever-weakening resolve, I walked through most days like a zombie. I began to convince myself that my family would be better off without me. I even entertained the idea of taking my own life. It was only God's generous grace and mercy that saved me.

Now my life is so rich and full, I shudder to think of the abundance I would have missed and the grief I would have caused if I had acted on my selfish impulse to end it all. It's difficult to recount those horrific years. I don't want to remember the pain, and truthfully, I can't recall much detail about the 1980s. Many events during those years are a blur. Yet, it's important to revisit my suffering because it reminds me that, when I encounter people at the supermarket or at church or book signings or walking their dogs, they may have hidden stories of pain like I did. One of them might even be entertaining thoughts of suicide.

We don't know the stories that others are hiding. We can't imagine the emotional or physical weights they might be carrying. At one time or another, we all find ourselves on the brink of exhaustion, perhaps even riding waves of depression and hopelessness. It's called "life" and life can be tough.

I learned so many lessons from my pain. One lesson was to be on the lookout for the hidden stories in others. Only then can I minister to them as God leads me. The most important lesson was this: Jesus stands ready to calm the storm and lift us above our earthly circumstances, but first we must allow him to calm *us*. There was much work to be done in my spirit before I was ready to accept God's lifeline.

Prayer: Sometimes this earthly life is hard, Lord; you never promised it would be easy. But you did promise to be with us always. Come now, Lord, and walk with us through this valley. We're tired and discouraged. Grant us your strength as we place our trust in you.

Meditation: Who needs a kind word, a smile or a note of encouragement? Where can I be God's hands and feet today and lighten someone's burden?

Week Four: Infinite Love; Finite Patience

In Isaiah Chapter 64, Verse 8, Isaiah prays for God's divine intervention in response to the Israelites' rebellion. The Israelites are the chosen people, whom God has brought out of captivity, whom God desires to shower with blessings, yet they think they know better than God. In their arrogance and willfulness they turn away from God's purposes, leaving them vulnerable to enemy attack. Again and again, God saves them, but instead of gratitude and trust, they respond with defiance, grieving his Spirit and finally provoking his wrath.

Isaiah was a prophet who knew The Messiah (the chosen One) would be coming not once, but twice. The first coming has been fulfilled in Jesus, the pre-existent Christ who became the visible manifestation of God. The second coming is yet to occur. Here Isaiah reminds the Israelites that God is not only benevolent and loving but also a God of wrath against evil and selfish purposes. Just as benevolence is the Creator's exclusive privilege, righteous anger is also God's prerogative.

If Isaiah were living among us today, I believe he would pray the same prayer, in essence, saying, *You have been patient, Lord, but your patience with your disobedient children is wearing thin. Who will repent and turn back to you?* Isaiah was convinced there was a Godly remnant in Israel, that repentance and revival were possible, even among people who worshiped false idols and rebelled against the Laws given to Moses. But the faithful remnant had no time to waste. The period of grace would not last much longer.

In Verse 6, Isaiah affirms, "O Lord, you are our Father, we are the clay and you our potter, and all of us are the work of your hand." Our unchanging Father God desires to shower us with his presence, provision, and love. But if we are to find peace in this life and presence with God in the next life, we must accept God as our Master who requires obedience to his will.

Once I was like a sapling in a hurricane, tossed about by the winds of circumstances and emotions. I have learned that when I swim against the current of God's purposes, life is a meaningless journey, but when I seek God's will in every decision, the future falls into place.

Prayer: Lord, help us recognize that "...we are the clay and you our Potter, and all of us are the work of your hand." May we repent and return to you before it's too late. Thank you for the peace that comes with submission to your perfect plan.

Meditation: Am I part of Earth's Godly remnant or am I afraid of what God will require of me if I commit my life and my will to him? Am I contributing to the righteous war against evil and oppression?

Week One: The Mystery of Faith

Week Two: Embracing Peace

Week Three: Hidden Stories

Week Four: Infinite Love; Finite Patience

May

Week One: Mother's Day

I've often wondered who invented Mother's Day—other than Hallmark. Someone told me it was a woman named Anna Jarvis in the early 1900s, so I did a Google search. Sure enough, according to Wikipedia, Anna Maria Jarvis was responsible for founding the holiday in memory of her own mother for the work she did during the American Civil War to promote unity.

As a mother, I must admit I enjoy being showered with cards, flowers, phone calls and pampering. In fact, I wouldn't mind celebrating three or four Mother's Days a year. While my mother was living, Mother's Day was especially significant for us because I was born on Mother's Day. But there are women for whom Mother's Day brings only painful memories and sorrow.

A friend of mine wasn't able to bear children. She and her husband wanted children, but their lost dream of having a family left them disappointed and heartbroken. Another friend suffered multiple miscarriages before finally having a healthy child. I know a young woman who carried her first baby to term, only to experience the unimaginable anguish of stillbirth. Others who have lost a beloved child or a cherished mother dread the day that many of us find so special. They wish they could stay in bed with the covers pulled over their heads until the day passes. They long for tomorrow when they will no longer have to smile and respond with an empty "thank you" as their fellow worshiper or restaurant server wishes them a Happy Mother's Day. For them, Mother's Day is anything but happy.

I am so grateful for the gifts of my children and grandchildren. My world lights up when I see them or talk to them, especially on Mother's Day. On Mother's Day we moms forget the labor pains, sleepless nights, dirty diapers, toddler tantrums, fevers, sprains, stains, and teenage angst. We recall only the good times with our children.

My heart aches for the women who would give anything to share in—or relive—every experience of motherhood, diapers, tantrums and all.

Prayer: Thank you, God, for the gift of motherhood. Grant your abiding peace to those women who find Mother's Day a painful reminder of their loss. Replace their emptiness with blessings beyond their imaginations. Turn their sorrow to joy.

Meditation: How can I ease the pain of a woman for whom Mother's Day is a heart-wrenching reminder of loss? How can I honor the women in my life who have mothered me with love and care?

Week Two: God is Not the Author of Confusion

My spirit is troubled; I wrestle with God; I struggle within myself; My mind is a web of confusion. Have you ever felt like this? What do you do? How do you resolve spiritual confusion?

As I write this, the United Methodist Church anticipates a schism because of differing beliefs. As a member of a United Methodist congregation, my heart is grieved by this controversy. At the same time, my head feels confused, torn, at sea. My spirit is troubled. The political and racial scenes of 2020 are also battlegrounds, and the world is ravaged by an invisible, powerful virus.

Again, my grief and confusion are heightened by the fact that my fellow Christians—followers of Christ—are divided in their opinions and loyalties. I want to understand. Most of all, I desire to know God's mind and heart in these matters.

You and I are not the first people to feel confused about major issues in our churches, our personal lives, and our government. Throughout the Bible we find God's people struggling in confusion to understand God's will. Sometimes it's referred to as spiritual warfare. Indeed, it feels like we're fighting battles.

In his agony, Job cried, "My spirit is broken, my days are extinguished (Job 17:1)." Job had lost everything that was possible to lose: his family, his wealth, and his health, and now his so-called friends are telling him it's his fault, that God is punishing him. He despairs of ever finding contentment again. What he doesn't understand is that God in his wisdom is allowing Job's suffering to fulfill *God's* purpose in a battle against evil. In the end, God restores Job's health and bestows on him blessings he never could have imagined.

When we are suffering like Job or drowning in confusion, we must first recognize that God is not the author of confusion. Therefore, God wants us to have spiritual clarity. We may need to struggle for a while; we definitely need to go to God in prayer and search the scriptures. Even so, we might never understand God's purposes completely during this earthly life. "For my thoughts are not your thoughts, neither are your ways, my ways, declares the Lord (Isaiah 55:8 & 9)."

When we accept that God's plan is infinitely superior to anything we humans could devise, only then can we begin to experience the answers we desperately seek. The most important part of God's plan is crystal clear. God sent his Son, Jesus, to bring a new commandment that supersedes (or more precisely) *summarizes* the old commandments: "A new commandment I give to you that you love one another, even as I have loved you (John 13:34)." In Verse 35, Jesus adds, "By this all men will know that you are my disciples, if you have love for one another." How's that for dispelling his disciples' confusion? For believers, the answer to every quandary and every conflict is simple. We are to love God and love one another.

Prayer: Dear Father, help us approach every quandary and every conflict in love. It's hard to love those who treat us badly or disagree with us on issues of eternal importance. But love is what Christ's commandment requires. Help us remember that it's more important to be loving than to be right.

Meditation: Why me? This is a natural response to suffering, but asking this question accomplishes nothing more than self-pity. The sooner I acknowledge that confusion is not of God, the sooner I can move on from pain and grief. When I accept my Creator's wisdom and authority, my confusion disappears. Am I ready to accept that God's ways are not my ways, that God's thoughts are higher than my thoughts? Am I ready to commit myself to the simple Commandment of Christ?

Week Three: Never Say Never

The words, "never" and "always," hold the power to destroy relationships. "You never listen to me; you always embarrass me in public; you never pick up your dirty clothes; you always need to be right." Not only is it impossible for such statements to be true 100% of the time, but they create further conflict and distance by attacking the listener and putting him/her on the defensive.

Marriage therapists teach couples the art of "fighting fair" and discourage the use of the words "never" and "always" in communicating with a spouse or significant other. When inevitable conflicts arise, instead of spouting venom borne of resentment, partners in therapy are encouraged to use active listening techniques, like mirroring (reflecting back) or paraphrasing what the speaker has just said. "I hear you saying that you don't feel respected by me" is an example of reflecting back. This technique, while unnatural to most of us, demonstrates that we truly heard what the other person was trying to convey.

Being heard is a universal need in relationships. Being able to trust that the other person desires to understand our point of view (empathy) is the foundation of respect in any relationship whether romantic, professional, or parental.

There is only one relationship in which the words "always" and "never" build up rather than tear down. That is our relationship with the Almighty, the giver of life, the One who loves us without condition. When Jesus said to his disciples, "I am with you *always*, even to the end of the age," they knew he meant it, and we can trust that this promise is 100% true for us today.

When the author of Hebrews quoted Moses in

Deuteronomy 31:6, he recalled God's promise, "I will *never* desert you, nor will I ever forsake you." This writer post-dated Moses by nearly 1500 years, yet the truth of God's words remained unchanged. Now, 3,000 years later, the believer can still rest assured these promises of God are true for us.

"Rejoice in the Lord *always*; again I will say rejoice! (Philippians 4:4)" The apostle Paul was in prison when he wrote these words in his letter to the Christians at Philippi. He was imprisoned for his belief in the risen Christ, who, after his resurrection from the dead and before his ascension to heaven, appeared in the flesh to Cleopus and a companion. He also appeared to the disciples and even ate with them! The promise of God was made manifest through Christ's incarnation; the prophecy was accomplished through Christ's crucifixion. Eyewitnesses verified it. We can believe it. Thanks be to God!

Prayer: God of the ages, we thank you that your promises proclaimed in both the Old and New Testaments are 100% true. Help us remember that you are with us *always*; You will *never* leave or forsake your followers.

Meditation: When I disagree with someone, do I fight fair? Do I listen in love, attempting to understand the other person's point of view? Do I believe the promise that God the Spirit will never desert me?

Week Four: Rainy Days

I'm old enough to remember the song, "Rainy Days and Mondays" by that brother-sister duo, The Carpenters. Before I retired, I often dreaded rainy days, especially Mondays. Like The Carpenters' song expresses, "they always [got] me down."

When I was teaching full-time, rainy days meant that my classroom looked dreary and my students arrived dripping, droopy and lethargic. I understood because I, too, lacked energy. On rainy days, I had to work twice as hard to infuse vitality into my teaching and engage my students' interest and enthusiasm.

Now that I work from home, all that has changed. I look forward to rainy days. The sunroom where I write is cheerful, rain or shine. On sunny days, the teasing sunlight beckons me outside to play, but on rainy days, a hypnotic pitter patter against the window panes relaxes me and bids me to recline with my laptop and enter the worlds of my imagination.

I gaze upward through the arch of a high Palladian window and watch clouds rushing by. Even gray clouds remind me that all of life is movement, forward movement of mind, body and soul. I think about the blessings that rain brings to the earth, providing life-sustaining hydration for plants, animals and humans.

Tree branches catch the wind and dance freely, reaching outward and upward. They appear to swirl in space, unattached. I stop and watch God's ballet recital, no ticket required.

I offer a silent prayer of thanks for life and sustenance, for meaningful work both present and past, for whatever the future holds. When a stray sunbeam peeks through the grayness, ephemeral, yet piercing, I'm reminded of how God's love can penetrate even my darkest days…if I'm ready to receive it.

Prayer: Father, we thank you for rainy days and sunny days, alike. Remind us that each day is what we make of it; each is a gift in its own way.

Meditation: When dark clouds descend, do I remember to say "thank you" or do I praise God for only the sunny days?

Week One: Mother's Day

Week Two: God is Not the Author of Confusion

Week Three: Never Say Never

Week Four: Rainy Days

June

Week One: Heavy Burdens

Today my discouragement with the world's situation is too heavy to bear. I'm disillusioned with our country's leadership. I am distressed by the inequality of justice for my black and brown neighbors. The news is bleak; the future seems hopeless. I feel anxious and confused.

As I seek God's wisdom and understanding, God invites me to bring every burden to him. God reminds me that even now there is good news. Jesus Christ is with me and his followers of all races and colors, regardless of the challenges this life presents.

Even if the earth should pass away, Jesus remains. One day, he will take us with him to glory. He does not change; his love is not shifting sand. He holds us by the hand and walks us through this earthly life into the Father's eternal presence. When Jesus commanded the wind, "Hush, be still (Mark 4:39)" the wind obeyed. Likewise, God commands us to "cease striving and know that I am God, (Psalm 46:10)," to remember who he is and Whose we are.

When I feel confused and torn, it is because I have forgotten to acknowledge my Master and Savior. He has granted me free will to heed or ignore the message. I choose to listen. May the Holy Spirit control my mind and my direction. When I choose trust and obedience, I step into the light of love and my heavy burden is lifted.

Prayer: Lord Jesus, you command the wind and it obeys. All of creation is under your throne of glory. May we obey your commands and trust your purposes. Calm our fearful thoughts that we may discern your will; still our racing hearts that we may know your peace. Show us where we need to speak up or take action, knowing that you walk with us through every trial.

Meditation: When my heart is burdened by sorrow or fear for myself or a loved one or for the whole of creation in all its chaos, do I become anxious and fearful or do I remember to rest in stillness and trust God's love and care?

Week Two: Finding Purpose

I think every human wants to know that his or her life has a purpose and that s/he is fulfilling that purpose. A life lived in vain is a life lived in pain. We wake up. We go to work or school. We come home. We go to bed. Within that twenty-four hour period we eat meals, pay bills and rush to appointments, games, meetings, and the grocery store. On a good day, we find time to interact with family members or connect with a friend, but after we accomplish all of the mundane tasks, what is the ultimate purpose of a life lived on Earth?

I spent much of my adult life in relentless physical pain, all while trying to raise a family and sustain a career. Feeling useless and hopeless, I reached a point of desperation. Life was not worth living, not like that. I wondered how my existence could have any purpose. I held so many unfulfilled dreams, yet I could barely get out of bed each morning and put one foot in front of the other. But most of those unfulfilled dreams were *my* dreams, not necessarily God's plans for me.

After many years of struggling to merely exist, I surrendered everything—all the pain and all the aspirations—to God. I surrendered my will to God's will for me. Ultimately, I asked God to grant me just five worthwhile, pain-free years. Lo and behold! Since I uttered that desperate prayer, God has given me twenty-five amazing, fulfilling years.

What is life's purpose? Each person must seek the answer for himself or herself. As for me, I've discovered that my life's purpose is to serve and glorify God. Since accepting that purpose, my life has become worth living. That's not to say it is easy or pain-free or without mistakes. There are challenges, sorrows and frustrations. As my body ages, there will be more physical pain. There will be loss and grief. But I can face it all with courage because I know God is leading me and walking with me through it all. I am not alone. In seeking God's purpose, I have received life's most precious gift: Peace.

Prayer: Heavenly Father, thank you for your healing love. Thank you for showing us that when we align our dreams with your dreams for us, we experience perfect peace. In all words and deeds for the remainder of our earthly lives, may we seek to serve and glorify you.

Meditation: What is God's purpose for my life? What would happen if I surrendered my dreams to God's plan for me today and the next day and the next?

Week Three: Betrayal

My new colleague was a classic narcissist and a bully. I had already held my position for ten years when he arrived on the scene. I knew what I was doing and had built a successful program. But in his insecurity, he engaged in nit-picking, criticizing and micromanaging.

Like many abusers, he was charming at first, treating me like a valued confidant. We became "friends," and I went out of my way to help him adjust to his new position. But as the "honeymoon phase" of our relationship waned, I began to notice subtle patterns emerging: manipulation of the system, always for his benefit; flagrant lying which he then denied; power plays; and tantrums. For a while, I refused to listen to the complaints of others about him. I would remain neutral, I decided. I would do my job to the best of my ability and ignore the ever-increasing signs that something wasn't right. I would pray for him. In confidence, I would listen to and comfort the dedicated volunteers whom he alienated one-by-one with angry outbursts he could no longer control.

When he unleashed his jealous anger on me directly, the evidence of his erratic, abusive behavior was no longer hearsay. I began to document each instance of abuse. Finally, I could no longer remain silent. I approached our supervisor. Although he knew and respected me and trusted my word, he reacted with utter shock. He too had been manipulated and deceived by this deranged person. He conducted his own investigation and verified the facts for himself.

Life is full of difficult people with whom we must interact, but psychologists recognize that the narcissist is the most difficult of the deviant personalities to treat. By definition, narcissism is a personality disorder characterized by an exaggerated sense of self-importance, a constant need for admiration, and a lack of empathy for others.

King David and his friend had enjoyed close fellowship, but his trusted companion betrayed him. In Psalm 55, David expresses the pain of this betrayal. "For it is not an enemy who reproaches me, then I could bear it…but it is you, my equal, my companion and my familiar friend; we who had sweet fellowship together…" David is so distraught that he implores God to inflict vengeance on this enemy who had once been his closest friend. I remember feeling like that toward my colleague.

Like David, I had been deceived by a duplicitous traitor. I was angry and hurt! Like David, I cried out to God. I told God exactly how I felt, holding back nothing. I wanted my abuser to suffer like he had made me and many others suffer. But after some healthy venting to my husband, a few trusted friends and God, I remembered my salvation, and I was able to change my prayer from "Punish him" to "Strengthen me."

In Psalm 56:3 & 4, David prays, "When I am afraid, I will put my trust in you. In God whose word I praise, in God I have put my trust. I shall not be afraid. What can mere man do to me?"

God already had my back; I was sheltered under his wings of protection. Yes, my feelings had been hurt, but I didn't need to worry about the outcome. God took care of the situation.

Prayer: Lord, help us remember that you have our backs. When we trust in you, we need not worry about outcomes, even in dealing with narcissistic personalities. If we take the high road, refusing to engage, and pray for strength and guidance, you will take care of the rest. Use these opportunities to help us grow in patience, self-control and trust.

Meditation: In what areas of my life do I need to trust that God has my back?

Week Four: Emancipated Living

Nearly every day presents problems, most small and easily managed, but some monumental. The very nature of living in a fallen world dictates that problems will arise. There are decisions to make and people to deal with; and there is ever-evolving technology that threatens to leave me in the dust.

I grow impatient, wanting things to happen according to *my* timetable, forgetting that God's plan is perfect and God's timing is exact. I need to slow down and rest in the presence of the Most High. *Be present with me,* God invites. *Make me your focus; still your racing mind; breathe in my Spirit; release your problems to the One who loves you now and always.*

"And we know that God causes all things to work together for good [conforming to his perfect will] to those who love God, to those who are called according to *his* purposes (Romans 8: 28)." This is God's faithful promise to those who love and follow him.

I have learned that when I accept God's sovereignty, trusting God's unconditional, sacrificial love for me, he takes my problems and my mistakes and turns them into blessings; he carries my sorrow and strengthens my weakness. But I must allow God to trim my ego so that his loving presence can shine forth, leading me ever closer to righteousness. Until I humble myself before the throne of the Most High, God cannot lift me closer to him where he desires to bless me more abundantly than I could imagine.

Whatever each new day brings, I have a choice. I can choose to worry, fret and agonize or I can respond to life's challenges with trust. The first choice results in unhealthy stress; the second promises emancipated living.

Prayer: We are impatient, Lord. We want immediate answers to our prayers. But sometimes you require us to wait because you have more to teach us. We try to pray according to your will, but our egos get in the way. Give us the strength and confidence, in all matters, to pray, "Thy will be done."

Meditation: What is God trying to teach me during this time of waiting?

Week One: Heavy Burdens

Week Two: Finding Purpose

Week Three: Betrayal

Week Four: Emancipated Living

July

Week One: Dark Days

We can expect to encounter dark days on this journey called life. We go along, living out our days, when suddenly someone we love dies; our marriage starts to fall apart; a child becomes ill; our job is in jeopardy; our best friend moves away. Without warning, even on a bright sunny day, darkness descends and we aren't prepared to deal with it. We are plunged into a blue funk, perhaps even deep depression.

"This is the day which the Lord has made; let us rejoice and be glad in it (Psalm 118:24)." When I was depressed, I mocked this scripture. How could I rejoice in a beautiful day when I could barely get out of bed? How could I thank God for a day I knew I could only drag through, struggling to survive?

Sometimes depression requires medical intervention such as medication or counseling or both. There is no shame in needing and seeking treatment. Depression is a disease. The good news is that depression is treatable!

There's more good news. When we choose to trust God in all circumstances, even through physical pain and depression, we begin to see the light of his love sustaining and guiding us to keep us from stumbling in the dark. Trusting God one-day-at-a-time, especially through the dark days, doesn't come naturally even to the most seasoned, mature Christian. It's something we must work at every day because the enemy continually tries to steal our joy. God calls us to develop the habit of thanking him in all circumstances, even in our bleakest hours. But it's hard!

When I invite God to walk with me through the gray clouds of despair, he holds my hand and pulls me forward gently, aiming me toward the sunshine of his love. I may not feel better instantly, but with patient trust, healing comes in God's time. I've learned to choose trust. When I cling to my Maker, rest in the light of his presence, and wait or act according to his prompting, I receive assurance that I am loved and cared for.

Prayer: Father, we cry out to you in the darkness, seeking relief for the aching emptiness in our souls. Lead us in the direction of healing. Remind us that prolonged depression is a treatable disease requiring medical intervention. Move us beyond the feelings of shame and embarrassment to seek treatment and embrace hope.

Meditation: Do I recognize signs and symptoms of depression in others? Where can I offer a glimmer of hope or provide a listening ear? What if I reached out and shared my own happy-ending story?

Week Two: Take Courage

When my routines are interrupted, when life throws me a curve ball, my first instinct is to react with anxious thoughts. Then I find myself tempted to cave in to addictive behaviors. I want the negative feelings to go away. Momentarily, I forget that my Lord is waiting for me to bring all my concerns to him. The One True God is prepared to be my refuge and strength, to carry my burdens until, together, we can discern the next step.

I think we all want to plan our futures, to control outcomes. And some planning is essential, of course. Examples include health insurance and a retirement fund, but we tend to expect guarantees. We want to know what awaits us around the next corner, to be in control of our lives and our futures. God knows that sometimes knowledge of the future is too heavy a burden for us to carry. I think that's why he calls us to depend on him one day at a time. God's perfect plan is to bless us with life that is full, good and satisfying, but we have lessons to learn along the way. Sometimes we cannot learn those lessons without experiencing conflict or hardship.

The scriptures tell us that God created us to need him. He created us for communion with him. When we pull away, we experience emptiness, loneliness and confusion. "Trust in the Lord with all your heart and do not lean on your own understanding (Proverbs 3:5)." Why? Because our loving Father sees the mess that lies ahead, and knows exactly how to organize it in our best interest. But there is a caveat. Verse 6 continues, "In all your ways acknowledge him, and he will make your paths straight."

So, I don't need to let stress and worry dominate my thoughts? And if I give in to that temptation, I can start over? How freeing! When I remember to acknowledge God as Lord of my life, trusting him for my future and the future of my loved ones, balance is restored, allowing me to feel peaceful amid the most uncertain circumstances.

John 16:33b records these words of Jesus, "In the world you have tribulation, but take courage; I have overcome the world." Every problem, every broken relationship, every difficulty and disappointment pales in comparison to God's promise of companionship both in this life and the next.

Prayer: Gracious Heavenly Father, not until we relinquish our future to your hands will we experience lasting peace. Help us to cease striving and struggling in our stubborn willfulness. Help us to view this life, not only from our limited vista but from your eternal perspective.

Meditation: Experiencing stress is normal. Worrying is a natural response to stress. But what would happen if, instead of engaging in non-productive worry, I reached out in courage and turned to God immediately, seeking guidance, and trusting God for tomorrow and every day after that?

Week Three: Science or Faith?

In the movie, *The Crown*, Prince Phillip is depicted as a doubter, lacking faith in God. As he reaches middle age, he questions everything he has ever known about faith and the church. In his frustration, he ridicules a group of priests whom he has permitted to meet in an unused building on the palace premises. These religious leaders are tired, burned out, and in need of rest, retreat and reflection. Phillip criticizes them for turning to prayer and reflection for answers to the mysteries of life and faith rather than trusting science with its absolute laws and tangible results.

According to the movie, Phillip had just witnessed man's first landing on the moon. Like all of us who were around in 1969, he was glued to his television set watching this momentous scientific achievement. It was a human attainment of the highest order, a technological, mathematical, scientific victory for humankind.

During what he later recognized as a mid-life crisis, Phillip had been questioning his purpose and worth in the grand scheme of life. Overwhelmed with wonder at what these American astronauts surely must have learned about the universe and God, he invited them to the palace. He prepared questions that he was sure they could finally answer. What he discovered was that the astronauts, having achieved an extraordinary feat, were not the superhuman gods he had put on a pedestal, but rather ordinary humans. As he questioned them, they offered no spiritual insight or wisdom. They viewed their trip to the moon as merely a job, one that kept them so busy throughout the flight that they had no time to reflect on the enormity of their mission.

Phillip had expected the astronauts' findings to prove the existence of God. Surely they would provide him with the secrets of the universe he so fervently sought. Instead, he discovered that science is no more the gospel than the gospel is science. Phillip was looking in the wrong place for answers to his questions about faith. He came to understand why the priests were focusing inward through philosophical and theological inquiry and prayer. His spiritual awakening was so overwhelming that he returned to the group and apologized for his previous insults. They became lifelong friends.

I think it may be difficult for scientists to believe in God. Scientists work with visible, provable data. The scientific method seems to leave no room for faith. But science may be closer to faith than many people think.

Sir Francis Bacon was the founder of the scientific method of research, but he was foremost a theist who believed science and theology were interconnected. Sir Isaac Newton was a genius in the fields of physics, mechanics, and mathematics. He was also deeply religious, viewing physics as God's system of order for the universe. Albert Einstein's most famous saying was, "Science without religion is lame; religion without science is blind (*Out of My Later Years*, Albert Einstein: Citadel Press 1956 p. 26)."

If *The Crown* is accurate in its depiction, Prince Phillip, like Bacon, Newton and Einstein, discovered that faith in science and faith in God are not mutually exclusive. Do you believe in the resurrection of Jesus Christ and eternal life or do you believe that science can't possibly support this premise? Perhaps you're looking in the wrong places for evidence.

Romans 10:9 says, "If you declare with your mouth, 'Jesus is Lord' and believe in your heart that God raised him from the dead, you will be saved." How does Paul know this? Paul (then Saul, a brutal persecutor of Christians) was an eyewitness. After Jesus' crucifixion, burial, and resurrection, Paul met the living, breathing Jesus on the road to Damascus, an experience that forever changed him. From then on, Paul became a fervent follower of The Way and spent his life proclaiming to Gentiles that the Jesus who died on the cross was, indeed, resurrected from the dead. He knew with certainty because he had seen and heard Jesus after his resurrection.

That same Jesus offers us new life in him and the promise of eternal life in heaven. Does this truth negate science? On the contrary. The New Testament records eyewitness evidence convincing the apostles, even doubting Thomas, that the resurrected Son of God is raised from the dead.

No one makes it out of this existence alive, but the believer in Jesus Christ is assured of life after death. In 2 Corinthians 5:1, Paul wrote, "For we know that if the earthly tent we live in is destroyed, we have a building from God, an eternal house in heaven, not built by human hands." Science serves important functions, but it can never replace faith in Jesus Christ, the Savior of the world.

Prayer: Thank you, God, for your gifts of science and grace. Thank you for revealing the truth of Jesus' death, resurrection, and ascension and for the eyewitness reports that support this truth. Thank you for the scientific discoveries that you have allowed humankind to uncover through our God-given intelligence. May we exercise that intelligence with integrity.

Meditation: Where do I turn for answers to the questions about science and theology? Are they mutually exclusive disciplines or is God the Creator of both?

Week Four: Clearing Clutter

As a teenager and young adult, I moved through many days with my head so filled with unresolved stuff from the past that often I couldn't focus on the here-and-now. I was a thought-hoarder. Incessantly swirling, buzzing, random thoughts distracted me from important tasks.

Journaling helped me organize the clutter in my mind, one thought at a time, one day at a time. While I once poured memories, longings and musings onto the pages of a notebook, now I write on virtual paper, using a keyboard. The process, while different in execution, remains effective in helping me to be present in the Presence, to prepare me for communing with God.

It's like removing clutter from a room. Once the extraneous stuff is cleared away, it ceases to distract the eye, leaving the space, itself, visible. Not until I purge the clutter of my random thoughts, can God begin to replace chaos and confusion with calm.

Psalm 46:10 says, "Be still and know that I am God." Ironically, learning to be still is hard work. To be still in God's presence, I must quiet not only my physical surroundings and body, but also my swirling brain. Transferring thoughts to a journal allows me to let go of the tension and worry that can easily fill a racing mind. Along with deep breathing, this process that I call "calming the crazies" creates a God-space in my head. Then and only then can I be receptive to the holy messages God desires to share.

For me, journaling is a form of meditation. I write whatever thoughts come without regard to structure, spelling, grammar or punctuation. I don't attempt to edit or rewrite until I've finished an entry. This allows my thoughts to flow freely before I forget them and before I have the chance to evaluate their literary worth. Then I am free to meditate and pray.

It's hard to imagine that the Creator of the universe cares about the clutter inside my head, but Jesus assures me in Matthew 10:30 that the very hairs on [my] head are numbered. That's how important I am to God. In I Peter 5:7, I am encouraged to cast all [my] anxiety on him because he cares for [me].

Prayer: Calm the crazies, Lord. Clear the mental clutter, so we can concentrate on communing with you, and so we can discern your voice from all the others that try to crowd in and clutter our minds.

Meditation: Have I been still in the Presence today? Have I found a way to silence the noise and clear the mental clutter, giving the Holy Spirit an opportunity to speak?

Week One: Dark Days

Week Two: Take Courage

Week Three: Science or Faith?

Week Four: Clearing Clutter

August

Week One: Prayer

What have you come to expect from prayer? Do you pray expecting answers or do you go through the motions, hoping for the best? Do you pray regularly or only when you need something from God?

Sometimes the old, familiar rituals become stale. As we recite the communion liturgy, renew our baptismal vows, or say the Lord's Prayer, often we simply parrot those memorized phrases. They can become overworked and ineffective in changing our hearts and nurturing our faith.

Several years ago, Catherine Marshall wrote a small but mighty book entitled *Adventures in Prayer*. First published by Ballantine Books in 1975, a copy has rested on my bookshelf for many years, and I've read it more than once. In her book, Marshall identifies seven types of prayer, devoting a chapter to each:

The Prayer of Helplessness
The Prayer that Helps Your Dreams Come True
The Waiting Prayer
The Prayer of Relinquishment
The Prayer in Secret
The Prayer of Joyous Blessing
The Claiming Prayer

For Marshall, each of these prayer attitudes emerged out of a particular stage of need in her life. She describes them as "mountain peaks" rather than valleys because each need, each resulting petition, and each answer provided a significant learning experience for her.

Throughout the book, she emphasizes three important aspects of an effective prayer life: the simplicity of our requests, admitting helplessness, and expectation.

Matthew 18:3 & 4 records Jesus' answer to his disciples who wanted to know who would be greatest in the kingdom of heaven. Jesus said, "Truly I say to you, unless you are converted and become like children, you will not enter the kingdom of heaven." He added, "Whoever then humbles himself as this child, he is the greatest in the kingdom of heaven." I think those statements apply to how Jesus wants us to approach our prayer lives. It seems he's cautioning against the need to be eloquent and articulate in prayer because it can become a stumbling block to a sincere request. Rather, Jesus wants us to come to him with the trust, simplicity and openness of a child.

We value our strength and independence. Admitting helplessness is difficult, but this act of confessing to powerlessness is one of the most important tools for recovery in Alcoholics Anonymous, Alanon, and Drug Addicts Anonymous. Step One of the twelve-step program on which AA is based states, "We admitted that we had become powerless over [addictive substance] and that our lives had become unmanageable."*

When we pray, admitting our helplessness, we acknowledge God's power and accept God's authority over our circumstances.

When, at last, we pray expecting God to answer, we show that we trust God's promises. Romans 8:24 reminds believers, "For in hope we have been saved, but hope that is seen is not hope; for who hopes for what he already sees?" This statement is, for me, the best definition of faith.

Catherine Marshall's book on prayer convinces me that Jesus wants us to pray simply and expectantly, believing for the answer, as he assured his disciples, "And all things you ask in prayer, believing, you will receive (Matthew 21:22)." Does that mean if I ask God for a million dollars to buy a yacht, the Publishers Clearinghouse will show up at my door with balloons and a giant check?

In Chapter 8 of her book, Marshall points out that there are conditions to our expectation of answered prayer. She refers to Jesus' words in Matthew 6:33: "But seek first his kingdom and his righteousness, and all these things will be added to you." From the perspective of Jesus' words, I don't think "all these things" refer to personal riches and expensive boats. However, I did once pray specifically for the money needed to sustain a ministry that depended entirely on grants and donations. That year, during an economic recession, I anticipated a $5,000 shortfall. I prayed for God to provide the means, and a week later a check arrived from a generous donor. The amount written on the check was exactly $5,000.

Prayer: Dear God, help us approach our prayer requests like children, with simplicity, humility and trust. We thank you for your faithfulness in answering every prayer according to your wisdom and authority.

Meditation: What changes do I need to make in my prayer life? Do I pray with simplicity, humility and trust? Do I pray expecting God to answer or do I just hope for the best?

* *Twelve Steps and Twelve Traditions,* Bill W, 1981, AA Grapevine, Inc.

Week Two: I Choose Foolishness

If you're a frequent movie-goer, you may have noticed that Christian characters in movies are often depicted as either naive and foolish or arrogant and judgmental. For years, Hollywood has openly shown disrespect toward God and promoted anti-Christian messages. This is nothing new. I remember watching *Steel Magnolias* with a group of friends when it first came to theaters. While I loved that movie starring many of my favorite actresses, I noticed that Annelle, the Christian character played by Daryl Hannah, was portrayed as unsophisticated in manner and appearance, even unintelligent.

In the movie, *Edward Scissorhands*, the town's so-called Christian character is portrayed as mentally deranged and judgmental, lacking any love or acceptance. Interestingly, she is also physically ugly, wearing no makeup, and never associating with the townspeople. Instead she isolates inside her house, playing the organ.

Aside from the blatantly false doctrine of stories like *The DaVinci Code* and *The Last Temptation of Christ*, many movie references are subtle in their disparagement of biblical principles and in their negative portrayals of so-called followers of Christ.

While in some cases, there may be a purposeful effort by screenwriters and movie producers to denigrate followers of Christ and belittle Christian beliefs, I see these phenomena as both more and less than intentional. More intentional in that there are very real forces of evil at work in our fallen world, many of them swirling on movie sets in Hollywood, and less intentional in that there is pervasive ignorance among movie producers regarding the Christian faith. Since it appears as folly to them, they portray it as foolishness to the public.

The Bible says that God's wisdom appears as folly to the unsaved. "Woe to those who are wise in their own eyes and clever in their own sight (Isaiah 5:21)." In verses 24d-25a, Isaiah talks about what will happen to those who mock God's Word as foolishness: "For they have rejected the law of the Lord of hosts and despised the word of the Holy One of Israel. On this account the anger of the Lord has burned against his people, and he has stretched out his hand against them and struck them down." In essence, Isaiah is saying that the Israelites have taunted God, and forced his hand to discipline them.

Like the Israelites, we Americans taunt God with our idol worship, greed, dishonesty, bigotry and nationalism. I wonder how long God will have patience with his disobedient, mocking children. If following Jesus Christ is folly, sign me up. I choose foolishness.

Prayer: Father God, when our faith is challenged by the media's inaccurate depiction of Christianity, fill us with your conviction. When we are called foolish for following you, grant us your strength and courage to stay the journey, assured that you are with us.

Meditation: Do I allow my faith to be challenged by mockery or do I stay the course as a follower of Christ?

Week Three: Finding God in Chaos

Children, jobs, spouses, to-do lists, housework, yard work, hobbies, volunteering... Life is one big distraction after another, pulling our attention away from our Creator who desires daily communion with each of us. How do we discipline our minds to focus during our daily prayer time when there are so many distractions? When we can't seem to concentrate, when decisions and duties loom, when we feel confused about the next step, is it possible we've forgotten to lay our problems at the foot of the cross? "Blessed be the Lord, who daily bears our burden, the God who is our salvation (Psalm 68:19)."

Free will is a gift accepted with risks. Along with exercising free will, comes the responsibility to align our purposes with God's purposes. How much fuller and richer is our earthly existence when we relinquish control, let go of our obsessive planning and useless worrying, and open our minds to *God's* perfect plan for us, a plan which includes spiritual abundance!

I know that in order to discern *God's* will, I must spend time with him daily. But how do I commune with a Spirit? Do I pick up the phone and dial 1-800-G-O-D? Do I send an email or text message to heaven? In the silence that I set apart for him, God whispers: *Seek me in stillness and you will find me. Meditate on my word and you will learn of me. Replace the burdens of this life with my easy yoke and allow me to carry your heavy loads.*

Throughout the day, I can watch for miracles, big and small, and shoot those quick arrow prayers to my waiting Father: "Thank you for the glorious sunshine; Help me find my keys, Lord, so I won't be late for work; give me patience with this person who always seems to push my buttons; be with that store clerk who is obviously having a bad day."

"Therefore humble yourselves under the mighty hand of God, that he may exalt you at the proper time, casting all your anxiety on him because he cares for you. (1 Peter 5:7 & 8)."

Prayer: Life can be chaotic, Lord. We seem to be pulled in every direction. There is so much to do at work, at home, and at church. Sometimes life presents us with too much of a good thing or…is it *we* who manufacture this busyness? Do we equate busyness with importance? Show us where we need to slow down. Reveal to us the activities that you have *not* chosen for us and give us the courage to drop them from our to-do lists. Prune our egos so that your plan is evident. Let your light shine in the darkness of our self-importance.

Meditation: What activities do I need to cross off my to-do list? Is it possible that I even need to say "no" to some of my church responsibilities in order to spend time with God?

Week Four: Taming Ego

Sigmund Freud defined the three aspects of the human psyche as id, ego and superego. According to his theory of psychoanalysis, the ego (sense of self) serves as a mediator between the id (natural instinct) and the superego (moral judge). It is our ego that makes conscious decisions after weighing evidence presented by the id and the superego. So, Freud defined ego as a neutral entity. But, a more common understanding of ego is that of self-promotion or self-importance. To say someone has a big ego, infers that the person is arrogant or pompous.

What does the Bible say about ego? The word ego is not used in the Bible, but there are many references to pride. Micah, one of the Old Testament prophets, reminds the Israelites of all the things God has done for them, God's chosen people, including rescuing them from Egypt and bringing them into the Promised Land, despite their haughty disobedience. Now, they are proposing to make up for their sins by offering sacrifices of calves and rams and oil. But in Micah 6:8, he reminds them of what God has always required of them. "He has told you, O man, what is good; And what does the Lord require of you but to do justice, to love kindness, and to walk humbly with your God?"

The New Testament has even more to say about pride. In 1 Peter 5:5b-6, we read "...and all of you, clothe yourselves with humility toward one another, for God is opposed to the proud, but gives grace to the humble. Therefore, humble yourselves under the mighty hand of God, that he may exalt you at the proper time."

In Christ's teachings, we find that the ego (pride) can be a great deceiver. When ego or self-pride is overindulged, it becomes a destructive force. But when we allow God's Holy Spirit to fill the empty, insecure spaces of our psyches, there is no place for pride to take hold.

The earthly Jesus was the personification of humility. As royalty, Jesus was entitled to a palace, a gilt throne, and a jeweled crown. Instead, he was born in a lowly cave, laid in a cow's feed trough and surrounded by smelly animals. Raised by a simple carpenter in the unremarkable town of Nazareth, his childhood was unpretentious. Yet this Jesus was the Son of God, the promised Messiah. He was entitled to the biggest ego ever. But he chose humility. Why?

Christ came in lowliness to show us how to approach God, the Father, in humble repentance. In Matthew 23:12, Jesus admonished the egotistical Pharisees with these words, "Whoever exalts himself shall be humbled; and whoever humbles himself shall be exalted."

Throughout his adulthood, at any point, Jesus could have said, "Enough!" He could have summoned an army of angels to destroy his accusers, but instead, he chose to complete his Father's plan to save sinners from death. Because of Jesus' willingness to humble himself and die an excruciating, shameful death for our sakes, he was raised to the highest honor, and sits at the right hand of the Father.

"Since Christ...committed no sin, nor was any deceit found in his mouth; and while being reviled, he did not revile in return; while suffering he uttered no threats, but kept entrusting himself to him who judges righteously; and he himself bore our sins in his body on the cross, so that we might die to sin and live to righteousness; for by his wounds, you were healed (1 Peter 21b -24)."

Prayer: Heavenly Father, we can never repay you. Thank you for giving us the right to become your sons and daughters, not because we are worthy, but because we accept your free gift. "By his wounds we are healed."

Meditation: Where is my ego standing in the way of closer relationships with God and fellow humans? In what areas do I need to humble myself and model the lowliness that Christ assumed in coming to Earth, living simply, and sacrificing his life for me?

Week One: Prayer

Week Two: I Choose Foolishness

Week Three: Finding God in Chaos

Week Four: Taming Ego

September

Week One: The Good Shepherd

In the Bible, numerous names are used to describe Jesus: Son of God, Redeemer, Savior, Christ, Lord, Messiah, Holy One, to name a few. But my favorite is Good Shepherd. Why? When Jesus came to Earth, the job of shepherding a flock of sheep was considered lowly, at the bottom of the social strata. A shepherd's life was one of poverty and hardship, especially a good shepherd who truly cared about his sheep.

In biblical times, a shepherd had to be on the job day and night, protecting the herd from predators, rustlers, and poisonous plants. He made sure his flock always had access to adequate food and water, which meant moving constantly to new pastures. Often he had to search for strays and usher them back to the fold. According to Wikipedia, he groomed and sheared the coats, helped deliver lambs, and, in ancient times, even milked the ewes and made cheese. The work was solitary and lonely as he lived out in the open with no shelter from the weather. The shepherd's rod was used to both guide and discipline the sheep, and a staff aided him in walking over rough terrain and defending against predators.

When Jesus referred to himself as The Good Shepherd, he was using imagery to which the rural people of the time could relate. They understood that a good shepherd loved his sheep and cared for them. He provided everything they needed, even placing his own life in peril for their benefit. He disciplined gently, but with authority, and the sheep followed him because he proved trustworthy. They knew he would protect them from danger, leading them to "green pastures" and "still waters." He was their beloved master.

From what I've read about the nature of sheep, it seems that human nature is similar. We humans are willful, often fearful, and easily led astray by herd mentality. Often, we become rebellious, refusing to acknowledge The Good Shepherd as Master. We tend to equate "master" with "tyrant." What right does a tyrant have to rule my life?

When I gave my life to Jesus, I acknowledged his singular claim on me. All of me. I accepted him, not only as my Savior and Master, but as my Good Shepherd. Whenever I stray, I trust him to find me and bring me back to the fold. When I am greedy, self-centered or dishonest, I expect him to discipline me. When I am tempted by evil forces, I must turn to my Good Shepherd to protect me. Rather than a tyrant who seeks to overpower, The Good Shepherd is a Master who loves his sheep so much that he has already laid down his life for them.

Prayer: Thank you, Good Shepherd, for your loving care and gentle admonition. When we stray from you, may your staff reach out and bring us back into the fold.

Meditation: Am I willing to allow The Good Shepherd to lead me or do I stray whenever life is tough and temptations arise? Do I remember to respond in gratitude for my Master's protection, sustenance, guidance, and authority or do I insist on going my own way in stubborn willfulness?

Week Two: Perspective

In my high school art course, I learned that a painting or drawing needs a focal point from which perspective emerges. Without that point of origin, the viewer's eye wanders, looking for a place to land. It was Oscar Wilde who first said, "Life imitates art far more than art imitates life." I think what he meant was that all of life seeks expression, and life is best expressed through the Arts. Wilde's philosophy is opposite Aristotle's mimesis theory that art imitates life.

In Wilde's essay, "The Decay of Lying," he claims

that the energy of the art form, whether painting, drawing, music, dance or any artistic expression is not fully realized until it is imitated by life. At least I think that's what he meant. What I know for sure is that all of art requires a creator and all of life is art. Without the Creator there is no focal point to center the work and provide perspective.

The concept of perspective in art reminds me that, when God becomes my focal point, my life is in perspective. Just as the morning fog lifts when exposed to warm sunlight, problems, worries and temptations fade in the glorious light of God's presence and power. God, the Creator of all lifeforms and all art forms, desires goodness *for* me, but he requires devotion *from* me.

Problems can be expected in this life. Troubles occur as a natural part of living in a fallen world. Sometimes God allows affliction as a tool to help us grow in perspective and faith. How we choose to respond is what matters.

In John 16:33, Jesus encourages his disciples, "These things I have spoken to you that in me you may have peace. In the world you have tribulation, but take courage; I have overcome the world."

When we encounter problems, it's important to remember that God, in his infinite wisdom, created everything for good. When paint is slapped on a canvas without perspective, the painting is chaotic. When we seek to solve problems without God's eternal perspective, our lives become a chaotic mess. "Do not let your heart be troubled; believe in God. Believe also in me. In my Father's house are many dwelling places; if it were not so, I would have told you; for I go to prepare a place for you. If I go and prepare a place for you, I will come again and receive you to myself, that where I am, there you may be also (John 14:1 - 3)." When I remember this promise, my earthly problems fall into perspective.

Prayer: We thank you, Lord, for overcoming a world filled with tribulation. Help us to see trials from your Holy perspective, and give us the courage to trust you in good times and bad. May our lives imitate the artistry of your wondrous creation.

Meditation: As I begin each new day, do I remember to commit it to God and give thanks? When is the last time I observed a miracle because I was tuned in to God's Holy perspective?

Week Three: Identity

I have always identified as a singer. My first public performance was at the age of three when I stood on a chair at the front of my church sanctuary and sang "Silent Night." I don't remember it, but my mother described it as "perfect in pitch and diction." In school, I was the one chosen to sing solos. I was the singer accepted to represent my school at All-District and All-State Chorus festivals. In college, I majored in voice, and after college, my career of nearly fifty years focused on singing and conducting choral groups. For my entire life, "singer" has been my primary identity.

So, with the onset of asthma and the vocal changes of advancing age, I felt betrayed by my voice which no longer responded as it once did. Not only was I losing confidence in my voice, but I was losing my identity. At first, I was devastated to give up such an important activity as singing, but despite all the vocal skills I had studied and practiced, I could no longer make my singing mechanism cooperate. I stopped performing because I didn't want to expose those limitations and be accused of not knowing when to let it go. Singing for weddings, church services, funerals and concerts was no longer my thing, my identity. I turned down invitations, not willing to risk embarrassment. For a while, I grieved the loss of my identity.

But God in his wisdom had begun planting a new—or perhaps dormant—desire in my heart. I had always loved writing nearly as much as singing: letters, stories, journal entries, poems and plays. Writing was a means of expression as ingrained as singing. But a busy music/teaching career hadn't allowed me the time necessary to pursue a writing career.

After retirement, I began to write blog posts and decided to tackle a novel. Now, I cringe at those first awkward efforts...but I had to start somewhere. I began to read and study the writing craft. I attended workshops and webinars, read books on writing, and joined writers' organizations and critique groups. As I continued to learn and grow, I authored three novels and numerous award-winning essays. I was fortunate to find a publisher whose mission was to promote "literary late-bloomers" like me.

The most important thing I've learned through this metamorphosis from singer to author is that earthly identities are fleeting. I've learned that whatever vocation or avocation I assume in this life pales in comparison to my *true* identity. I am first and foremost a precious, beloved child of God. That is an identity I can count on now and forever. Nothing, not age nor asthma nor arthritis nor even death can separate me from my true identity, which is in Christ Jesus.

Prayer: Thank you, God, for the gifts and talents you give us at just the right times in our lives. But remind us that our identities are not defined by those fleeting labels and pursuits. We rejoice in our true identities as your beloved children and ask you to show us how best to use our God-given talents to serve you.

Meditation: How am I using my God-given abilities to serve the One who formed them in me? Do I associate my identity with the labels I've given myself or do I recognize that my most important label is "child of God?"

Week Four: The Struggle Within

When I was a child, I remember my mother saying, "You dwell on things too much." Another of her admonitions was "Everything will look better in the morning." I resented both statements because they indicated to me that she didn't understand my anxiety and worry. Instead, it seemed as if she dismissed my feelings.

In truth, despite her seeming lack of empathy for her anxious child, my mother was correct. I was a worrier who tended to imagine the worst possible scenarios unfolding. And even the most negative situations didn't seem quite as dire when exposed to the light of day. Undoubtedly, my mother grew weary of my complaining. She didn't recognize these behaviors as symptoms of depression because, let's face it, depression looks and sounds a lot like whining.

Many years later, in my forties, a doctor finally identified my depression and began treating it. For the first time in my life, I learned that depression is a disease, not a character flaw. As a Christian, I had carried enormous guilt and shame over not being able to control the negativity associated with this disease. I had perfected the art of greeting the world with a fake smile. In order to survive, I became an actor on the stage of life. Every day, feeling like an imposter, I pretended to be okay. It took all my energy to maintain this ruse, energy that I needed for my family and my job.

Much of my guilt resulted from the fact that I knew I was a saved follower of Christ. Long before, I had accepted Jesus as my Savior, but I wasn't thinking or behaving like someone who had been set free through grace. No amount of self will or self control could change my worrying or destructive complaining. Like Paul in Romans 7:15 & 16, I lamented, "For what I am doing, I do not understand: for I am not practicing what I would like to do, but I am doing the very thing I hate." Paul recognized that he was attempting the impossible. He was trying to overpower the urge to sin in his own strength, through sheer will.

Paul shared this personal shortcoming with the Roman Christians because he knew they were fighting the same battles, the same wars we continue to wage against our sinful natures today. Thankfully, Paul didn't leave his teaching there. In Chapter 8, Verses 2 and 3, he proclaimed with confidence, "For the law of the Spirit of life in Christ Jesus has set you free from the law of sin and death. For what the law could not do, weak as it was through the flesh [sinful nature], God did…so that the requirement of the Law might be fulfilled in us."

I still worry and I still experience anxiety, but now instead of "dwelling" on unproductive thoughts and allowing anxious feelings to overwhelm me and keep me awake at night, I turn them over to the Holy Spirit who supplies all my needs. "Be anxious for nothing, but in everything by prayer and supplication with thanksgiving let your requests be made known to God. And the peace of God, which surpasses all comprehension, will guard your hearts and your minds in Christ Jesus (Philippians 4:6 & 7)."

Prayer: Lord, when we are tempted to worry and complain, when we feel anxious and out of control, remind us to let you guard our hearts and minds. Help us to recognize true depression in ourselves or our loved ones, and grant us the courage to seek help.

Meditation: Do I know someone who is depressed? Do I know what behaviors point to possible depression and reach out in love and compassion or do I dismiss others as cynical, critical and complaining and keep my distance?

Week One: The Good Shepherd

Week Two: Perspective

Week Three: Identity

Week Four: The Struggle Within

October

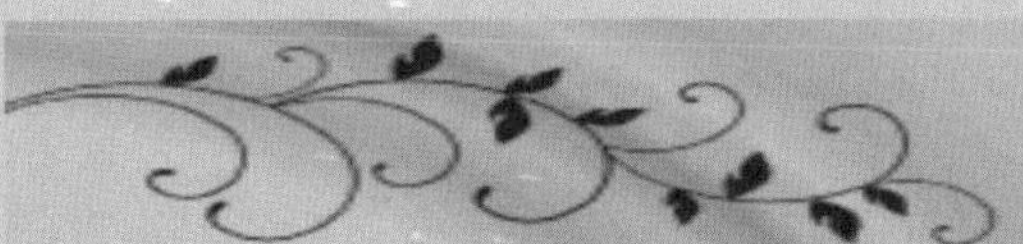

Week One: Seek First the Kingdom of God

The Gospels record some of the most familiar words from Jesus' earthly ministry, such as "The Beatitudes" and "The Lord's Prayer." Jesus addressed human issues like physical problems, marriage, wealth, and taxes. He also preached about hypocrisy, repentance, faithfulness, and forgiveness. Much of his teaching was a radical departure from that of the Pharisees and scribes who thought they needed no repentance.

Imagine sitting on a hillside listening to such revolutionary preaching from a humble carpenter raised in Nazareth. In the presence of the Pharisees, who considered themselves superior in holiness and knowledge of religious law and tradition, this man spoke with authority and even claimed to be the Son of God. For this reason, they accused him of blasphemy and attributed his healing miracles to sorcery.

Jesus turned the world upside down when he fulfilled the ancient prophecies of Isaiah and Jeremiah. The Jewish people were expecting an earthly king who would sit on a throne and be their political and military leader. But this man was claiming to be the long-awaited Messiah and saying crazy things like, "Love your enemies and pray for those who persecute you... (Matthew 5:44)" and "Many who are first will be last [in the Kingdom]; and the last, first (Matthew 19:30)."

Would you have believed such a radical teacher to be God in the flesh? Would you have trusted him, accepted his Lordship, and followed him?

With authority, Jesus preached to the Jews what they needed to hear, and he told the Gentiles what they needed to hear. When the Jewish leaders prayed and fasted and gave alms, they did it publicly to be viewed as pious. Jesus called them hypocrites and warned them that their public displays of piety would not be rewarded. The Gentiles worried about what they would eat and what they would wear. Like the rich young ruler, they had made wealth their god. Jesus told them, "Do not store up for yourselves treasures on earth...but store up for yourselves treasures in heaven...for where your treasure is, there your heart will be also (Matthew 6:19 - 21)."

So, when Jesus said, "But seek first his kingdom and his righteousness, and all these things will be added to you (Matthew 6:33)," he was talking about surrendering to his Lordship in every area of our lives. It was a call to examine priorities. When we give anything—wealth, position, property, hobbies, even loved ones—more importance in our lives than we give God, we fail to place God on the rightful throne of our lives.

Salvation is only the beginning of a relationship with Jesus Christ. Growing in our Christianity means surrendering every aspect of our lives to the Lordship of our Savior, Jesus Christ. It may sound like a sacrifice, but it is just the opposite. When we "seek first the kingdom of God" in all our decisions and actions, not only do we receive everything we need for our physical existence and the promise of the Holy Spirit's presence in our daily lives (in the present kingdom), but we have the promise of eternal life (in the future kingdom). That doesn't sound like a sacrifice to me.

Prayer: Thank you, Lord, for providing everything we need. Teach us to share our abundance during this time when others are experiencing economic hardship. Help us to seek first your kingdom "on earth as it is heaven."

Meditation: Where is my treasure? What are my priorities? Do I "seek first the kingdom of God" or do I seek first the kingdom of self?

Week Two: Sowing Seeds

The Creator of the universe and all of its galaxies desires abundant life for me, a tiny speck in the cosmos, a barely negligible figure in human history. Wow! When I consider this truth, my mind is overwhelmed with wonder and my heart bursts with gratitude. I want every living creature to experience the joy of God's life-giving presence. I want to shout from the rooftops with a giant megaphone that God desires abundance for them, too. Accepting Jesus as my Savior was the most important decision of my life. I want every person to share the intimate relationship I have experienced with my Savior, not because I am worthy of His love, but because I said "yes" to his invitation.

But then I remember the Parable of the Sower that Jesus used to teach his disciples about how the soil of salvation must be prepared before the seed can germinate and grow. In this story, some seeds fell beside the road and the birds (evil forces) ate them; other seeds fell on the rocks (shallow hearts) and were scorched by the sun; some were choked among the thorny bushes (worldly temptations); but the seeds that fell on fertile soil grew and produced fruit (Matthew 13:3 - 9). This parable illustrates the free will that God gives each of us. We have a choice about whether to receive him, whether to accept abundant life or reject it.

Jesus instructed in parables (analogies drawn from everyday life) because he knew that only those who were ready to hear the truth would understand their lessons. He didn't force himself on anyone; he didn't shout from rooftops with a megaphone; he didn't say, "You must follow me or burn in hell forever." Rather, he sat among the people on a grassy hill, picnicking on fish and bread or he climbed into a boat so they could hear him as they gathered on the shore or he joined them in the synagogue and told them about his Heavenly Father. His approach was gentle, welcoming and loving. Resisting the urge to force himself on his listeners must have taken tremendous self-control, knowing that his time on Earth was limited.

As much as I want everyone, especially my beloved family and cherished friends, to know Jesus as I am blessed to know Jesus, I am reminded that it is up to God to prepare the soil of their hearts to receive him. I can sow seeds all day long, but only God knows which soil is ready to receive them, which seeds will germinate, grow and produce fruit.

Prayer: Give us patience, Lord, with those we care about. We want them to know you as we know you, but we need to trust your timing as you prepare the soil of their hearts. Help us to respect the pace of each person's spiritual journey.

Meditation: Am I living a life that would cause another person to be curious about my faith in God? Do I demonstrate love, joy, peace, patience, steadfastness, goodness and self-control in my daily interactions?

Week Three: Releasing Pride

God is showing me that pride is a form of idol worship. Pride is a destructive force that convinces me I must be perfect, that my mistakes are failures, and that I should be able to solve problems on my own.

When a problem arises, I agonize, turning it over and over in my mind. When the answer doesn't come immediately, I think I have failed. That's when God reminds me that I'm being prideful; I'm worshiping the idol of self-sufficiency. I'm wasting time and energy on the future that I could be spending on the present.

What if I viewed problems as opportunities to grow in faith and wisdom, trusting God to provide the answers in his perfect time? What if, instead of fretting and worrying and agonizing, I thanked God for problems as lessons and trusted God to reveal the next step and the next?

It seems counter-intuitive to be thankful for problems. But when we look at challenges as opportunities and approach them in gratitude, we release their negativity, allowing God to turn them into blessings. "Come to me all who are weary and heavy-laden, and I will give you rest. Take my yoke upon you and learn from me, for I am gentle and humble in heart, and you will find rest for your souls. For my yoke is easy and my burden is light (Matthew 11:28 - 30)." In these verses, Jesus contrasts salvation in him with trying to follow the inflexible laws of the scribes and Pharisees, which could end only in failure because of human imperfection.

Jesus came to free his followers from trying to follow stringent rules and regulations that set people up for failure. Rather than being restrictive, his yoke (discipline through instruction) is easy compared to trying to adhere to the religious laws of the time.

You have only today, God is reminding me. *Release your selfish pride, thinking you should have all the answers. Humble yourself and trust me with tomorrow. Rest in the confidence of my holy purpose for you. Thank me for this opportunity to pave your way today and prepare you for tomorrow. Come to me and find rest for your soul.*

Prayer: Forgive us, Lord, when we are prideful, thinking we have all the answers. Help us to accept life's inevitable problems with humility and gratitude as opportunities to learn important lessons that help us grow in our faith.

Meditation: When problems arise, as they will inevitably, how will I handle them? Will I berate myself for not having all the answers; will I consider myself a failure when I make a mistake; or will I trust God to lead me to solutions that honor him?

Week Four: Fear or Peace?

The world is a frightening place. I wonder how anyone can face a new dawn on this planet without acknowledging God's presence and trusting God's promises. God is the only constant in an ever-changing world. He is the same "yesterday, today and tomorrow (Hebrews 13:8)," and when we accept the gift of salvation in Christ, the Holy Spirit is as near as our own breath.

God created a perfect world for his children to enjoy, and God created each human perfectly, yet uniquely, in his image. Often our ego (the great deceiver) convinces us we are too sophisticated, logical, scientific, or intelligent to believe such seemingly foolish concepts.

I'm convinced that in each person God placed a hunger that can be satisfied only through companionship with him. But there are other forces making us fearful and trying to steal our joy. Sin and evil have wounded our hearts and our world. All of creation is now flawed, uncertain and in disarray. It would be easy to throw up our collective hands and say, "It's no use! We give up!"

Why do we insist upon struggling through life on our own? Why do we see dependence upon our loving Creator as weakness? Why do we feel helpless and hopeless in the face of life's challenges? When living presents us with its inevitable change and loss, why do we blame God?

Even in a frightening, uncertain world there is good news. The good news is that we don't need to be bound by the constraints of earthly life or threatened by the evil that surrounds us. Jesus assured his disciples, "These things I have spoken to you, so that in me you may have peace. In the world you have tribulation, but take courage; I have overcome the world (John 16:13)."

Prayer: Father, we thank you for the magnificent universe you created for us to explore. We thank you for the beautiful earth you created to provide sustenance for us and all of your creatures. We thank you for the hunger you placed in our hearts, a hunger for your companionship.

Meditation: When I witness the forces of evil and selfishness that have already destroyed much of God's creation, I sometimes feel like giving up, like what I do about conservation makes no difference. What steps can I take to ensure that the earth will be preserved for future generations? How can I be a good steward of God's generous resources?

Week One: Seek First the Kingdom of God

Week Two: Sowing Seeds

Week Three: Releasing Pride

Week Four: Fear or Peace?

November

Week One: "They Get on the Walls."

As a writer, I believe that words are living, breathing entities. Words hold the power to heal or destroy, to build up or tear down. For this reason, I try to choose my words with care. When I was sick and depressed, often my words were sarcastic and cynical. I was hurting so much, both physically and emotionally, that no matter how hard I tried to control my words, they shot out of my mouth like poison porcupine quills. Again and again, I would have to apologize to the people I had harmed or offended with my words.

Dr. Maya Angelou, who I believe was one of the greatest people of our century—of any century—believed that words, once spoken "get on the walls." I remember the first time I heard her say this. It had such an impact on my thinking that I recorded her complete quote in my journal:

"Words are things. You must be careful, careful about calling people out of their names, using racial pejoratives and sexual pejoratives and all that ignorance. Don't do that. Someday we'll be able to measure the power of words. I think they are things. They get on the walls. They get in your wallpaper. They get in your rugs, in your upholstery, and your clothes, and finally into you."

Every human has said or written words they wish they could retract. Harsh words spoken in the heat of the moment: a patronizing compliment uttered out of manipulation rather than sincerity, a complaint or criticism arising from one's own insecurity. Such words do not make the world a better place. They tear down rather than edify.

As a writer, I must remember to choose my words carefully, for my words will outlive me. Whether spoken or written, "They get on the walls." Now if I could just learn to control my tongue!

Prayer: Lord, help us to speak and write the truth in love. When we offend or hurt someone with our words, show us so we can confess our wrongdoing, apologize, and experience forgiveness. Speak through us, Lord, that our words may build up rather than tear down. With our words, make us instruments of your peace and love.

Meditation: Who needs to hear an apology from me for words spoken in carelessness, haste or anger?

Week Two: Always Near

How quickly I forget that God stands ready to help me in times of need! The world crashes in. My heart begins to race and my mind churns with details. I allow worries to creep in. For me, it happens most often with technology. I lose a document or file that I was just working on yesterday; after an update, the screen looks different and throws me off kilter; or I forget a password and then forget how to access my password file. Panic grips me.

But, wait! That's the old me, the anxious me that taunts, "You should be able to figure this out; you aren't capable of solving problems; you aren't good enough; don't ask for help; accepting help confirms your incompetence."

Fortunately, I'm married to a computer wizard. When he hears my cries of frustration, his transmission shifts into fix-it gear. "Why didn't you call me earlier?" he asks. He encourages me to stop and breathe then walks me through to the solution. I always learn something new about technology—whether I want to or not. Best of all, I am reminded that I'm not alone, that I don't have to handle computer issues by myself. If I were not married to a geek, there would be someone else to call on, but first I must admit I need help.

There's another One who stands ready to walk me through life's problems, to release me from the anxiety that is inevitable in an ever-changing world. God, too, reminds me to stop and breathe. God stands ready to supply all my needs, but I must remember to call on him. God reminds me that there are people and resources to help in times of need. I can draw on the strength of others when I am weak. When I ask for and accept help, it doesn't mean I'm a failure.

Like me, many of God's children carry in their heads mental recordings from the past that taunt, "You are not good enough; you are alone in the world; you don't have enough courage or wisdom to take care of yourself or handle responsibilities." Perhaps they grew up in a home where love was withheld, where they felt abandoned emotionally. Perhaps they had a learning disability that caused them to feel insecure about their abilities. Perhaps they were bullied in school.

The good news is that we don't need to carry the burdens of our past. Not any more. With God's help, we have the power to stop the audio-tapes in our heads. We can even record over them, replacing negative messages with positive affirmations. We can learn something new every day. With God's help, we can use problems to help us grow stronger in ourselves and closer to the One who loves us and desires to walk with us through this life, during good times and bad.

Even Jesus was tempted in the wilderness to believe he was alone and abandoned by his Father. So you see, it is the evil one who tempts us to think we are walking through this life alone. It is a lie. Humans will be tempted to believe this lie until Christ returns.

Prayer: Forgive us, Lord, when we are tempted to believe the evil one instead of standing firm in you. Remind us to call out for help. Show us how to erase the audio-tapes in our heads that try to convince us we are incompetent and alone.

Meditation: What are the messages in my head saying about me? What are the past lies that I've come to believe about myself? What positive affirmations can I record over them?

Week Three: The Key to Abundance

When is the last time you reflected on the blessings that God has showered upon you? When you awaken each morning, do you remember to say, "Thank you, Lord, for sleep?" While staying awake all night may seem like the perfect opportunity to get things done, insomniac friends tell me it is anything but productive. To be productive, the body requires rest and rejuvenation. Wakeful hours while everyone else is sleeping are wasted and lonely.

Do you thank God for your meals? Most of us are so well fed that it's hard to imagine going hungry. Yet, according to a 2018 Economic Research Service report by the United States Department of Agriculture, even in the US, 88.9% of households were food insecure at some time during that year. The USDA defines food insecurity as "uncertain of having, or unable to acquire, enough food to meet the needs of all their members because they had insufficient money or other resources for food." This is an appalling statistic, especially when the other 10% of us eat so well we must restrict our diets to maintain a healthy weight.

When we witness poverty, starvation, and homelessness, we ask why. We wonder why a loving, generous God allows such suffering. But it was never God's intention for his children to suffer. Referred to as original sin, disobedience to God's will is what created suffering, as illustrated in the book of Genesis. Even natural disasters are related to humans' interference with the physical world. Yet, we blame God.

What is the answer to why God allows suffering? Undoubtedly, there is more than one answer. But perhaps we are asking the wrong question. The more important questions are: what can I do to help alleviate suffering in the world; if I have more than enough to eat, can I share donations of food or money with those who are hungry; if a friend is hurting, can I minister to that friend with a card, call or visit; if someone has lost a loved one, can I sit in silent support or listen with an open heart? Gratitude for God's abundance seems to call us forth with the desire to help. Perhaps our own suffering serves to encourage empathy for others.

Billy Graham once said, "There's a mystery to tragedies…. We don't know the answer. We may never know until God explains it all to us." What we do know is God's promise through the Person of his Son, Jesus Christ, that whatever happens in this earthly life, God will go through it with us if we turn to him and turn it over to him. The moment we believe in the resurrection of Jesus, we receive the Holy Spirit, The Helper.

"When you pass through the waters, I will be with

you; and through the rivers, they will not overflow you. When you walk through the fire, you will not be scorched, nor will the flame burn you (Isaiah 43:2)."

The fact remains that all of us will die. But there are two kinds of death. Physical death of the body is final, but the spirit lives on. The question we should be asking is not, "Why does God allow suffering," but "Will I say 'yes' to Jesus Christ who suffered, died, and rose again so that my spirit might live on in oneness with him?" As we thank God daily for our blessings, God showers us with spiritual abundance from his limitless storehouse and provides comfort in our suffering.

Prayer: Teach us, Lord, to recognize the parts we play in the suffering of others and to seek forgiveness—theirs and yours. Show us how to recognize suffering in others. Thank you for the spiritual growth that occurs through life's inevitable hardships.

Meditation: How can I be God's agent of comfort, one who identifies and relieves the suffering of others? For whom do I need to pray and to whom can I minister this week?

Week Four: Why I Love Advent

The weeks leading up to Christmas bring thoughts of celebrations with all the trimmings we associate with the holidays. We think of adding festive decorations to our homes, feasting at large tables shared with loved ones, and buying just the right gift for each one. We plan parties, attend concerts, and embark on trips that take us "over the river and through the woods." Familiar carols, sparkling lights, and Hallmark Christmas specials lift our moods. It's a season that most of us anticipate with delight, even though we know it will involve a measure of harried rushing.

But that's not why I love Advent. Rather than encouraging us to surrender to all the busyness we've come to associate with Christmas, Advent invites us to slow our pace and focus on our spiritual preparation. From the Latin word *adventus,* advent means "coming." In the church calendar, Advent marks the beginning of a new liturgical year. For Christians, the season, starting twenty-four days before Christmas, bids us to prepare our minds for the coming of Christ, the promised Messiah. It opens our hearts to receive the hope, peace, joy and love that are symbolized by the candles on an Advent wreath.

Since we live in a fallen world, filled with imperfect people, including ourselves, it's challenging to place our hope in the future. Every day brings news of yet another terrible event somewhere in the world. With media sources clamoring to report negative news, each in the most sensational way, we begin to lose hope that God is still in charge and will ultimately triumph. Sometimes it seems that evil is winning. And what about peace? Is peace on Earth even possible? Our joy diminishes as hate seems stronger than love. But that's exactly why God sent Jesus: to replace hate with love. Ours is not the first generation to feel hopeless, joyless, devoid of peace and longing to know God's love.

"O Come, O Come Emmanuel" is one of the best-known Advent carols. The text, originating in the 9th century, speaks to the Israelites' longing for a political savior to release them from captivity. They "mourn in lonely exile" feeling hopeless and without joy. They plead with God to send a Messiah who will "bind all peoples in one heart and mind."

The Israelites were expecting an earthly king who would deliver them from captivity. But God had a mightier plan. He sent his Son, Jesus, to offer deliverance from sin and death to *all* people, Jews and Gentiles, alike.

It's fundamentally impossible to commercialize the season of Advent. But leave it to retail corporations to give it their best shot with the likes of "Elf on a Shelf" and Advent calendars that hide a piece of chocolate behind each day leading up to Christmas. Not that there's anything wrong with helping children count down the days. It's just that the twenty-four days of Advent are about so much more than moving an elf or finding a piece of candy. During the days of Advent we are encouraged to connect or reconnect with God in a personal and powerful way through meditation, study, prayer, and music. That's why I love Advent.

Prayer: Slow our pace, Lord, that we might have time to immerse ourselves and our families in spiritual preparation for your coming.

Meditation: Which Christmas preparations are stealing my Advent joy? What can I eliminate?

Week One: "They Get on the Walls."

Week Two: Always Near

Week Three: The Key to Abundance

Week Four: Why I Love Advent

December

Week One: Perfect Love

I'm convinced we learn to love others the way we have been loved. If we were smothered by an emotionally needy parent, we become clingy and needy. If we were raised by an emotionally distant, unresponsive parent, we may find it difficult to express love. If children are told "I love you," but are treated with harsh words or even physical abuse, they may grow into adults who equate those negative behaviors with love.

Sometime during my religious education, I remember learning that the Greek language contains six words meaning "love." What a practical, specific language! Two of these terms are used in the New Testament. *Philia* is the love of deep friendship or brotherly love. *Agape* is the Greek term meaning perfect love, the kind of love God has for us. It occurs to me that whatever the type of love, if behavior doesn't match the word, the word becomes meaningless. If I say, "I love you" to a friend, but never call, write or visit, I may be perfectly sincere in my feeling of philia, but how can my friend trust this declaration of love without actions to back it up? If a parent says, "I love you" to a child but constantly berates or even hits him or her, how can that child grow up with a healthy sense of what agape (unconditional love) entails? Chances are the child will, instead, become an adult who has difficulty trusting, expressing or even understanding true love.

Agape is the one love we can always trust because agape is of God. It is the perfect, unconditional love from a perfect, loving higher power. Agape love never fails and it never ends. It is unmerited and eternal. We cannot earn it and we cannot be separated from it. Agape is a free gift to be received, cherished and reciprocated.

It is easier to trust God's agape once we have broken the cycle of our past experiences with so-called love that did not match in word and deed. Not until we can practice genuine philia, can we insist that others treat us with love that matches their words and actions. Then and only then will our hearts be open to giving and receiving God's agape.

Prayer: Thank you, Father, for showering us with your agape. Help us learn to embrace others with agape—sincere love that matches in word and deed.

Meditation: How can I make sure my deeds match my words? When I say "I love you," do my actions reinforce it? Do I place conditions on my love or, like God, do I offer it freely?

Week Two: Facing Life's Storms

Imagine you are out to sea on a cruise ship. Only minutes earlier, you were lounging in your stateroom, making plans for tomorrow's on-shore adventure. Earlier, the captain warned of an impending storm and advised all passengers to shelter in their cabins. He assured you that you could trust your well-being to the crew.

As a nearly imperceptible movement of the ship shifts to a more noticeable rocking motion, you sense a significant change in the weather. You climb the steps to the deck, determined to experience all that this cruise has to offer. The wind whips your hair and tries to push you backward down the steps. Amid the captain's urgent warning from a loudspeaker, you pass other passengers heading inside, but you will not be swayed from your purpose. You're used to tackling every challenge that life has thrown at you. You pride yourself in being strong, and you thrive on excitement, even the risky behavior of walking blindly, boldly through a storm at sea, ignoring your captain's warnings.

Just as you reach the rail, a sudden squall rocks the vessel violently from port to starboard. You grab the railing and hold tight, afraid to let go. It's too late to return to the safety of your quarters. The wind picks up speed, and a sheet of rain mixed with powerful ocean waves soaks you top-to-bottom, shoving you to the deck floor. Determined to pull yourself upright, you fight against the force of nature's fury.

With the next storm surge, you lose your grip and fall overboard into the black abyss that only hours earlier had invited your languid gaze. At first, you panic and flail about, trying to keep your head above the mountainous waves. The more you fight, the more salty water you swallow. In this moment, you know you are going to die, all because of your foolish pride. Someone on the deck is trying to throw you a life preserver, but you're too focused on saving yourself to notice. You could have been saved, but now it's too late.

This story illustrates how God's human creatures ignore his warnings again and again, thinking we know best, planning our days and our futures from our comfortable staterooms. Our Captain has warned us multiple times and even sent Jesus, our life preserver, to save us. But, first we must cease struggling in our own strength and surrender to the One who has already conquered the raging sea. *Relax and focus on me,* Jesus invites. *Then swim toward me. I will lift you above Earth's dimension and give you glimpses of eternity even as you struggle against this temporary storm.*

Sin and evil have seriously wounded God's children and scarred the beautiful Earth he created. All of creation is flawed and in disarray. But we need not lose hope. When we choose to walk through life with God as our Captain we need not fear the storms. He created each of us with a hunger that can be satisfied only through companionship with him. He sent his Son, Jesus, to be our life preserver, but if we are focused on saving ourselves instead of reaching toward his outstretched hand, he cannot save us.

Prayer: Forgive us, Lord, when we turn away from you, plunging into life's storms alone. Humble us to reach out and accept your lifeline, allowing you to lift us above Earth's finite dimension. May we respond in trust before it's too late.

Meditation: What steps do I need to take now to prepare for future storms? In what ways can I provide a lifeline to others who are facing life's storms?

Week Three: Holiday Perfection

During this season, many people suffer from the contagious disease known as *holiday perfection*. Much like the flu, this dreaded infection returns year after year to ruin our celebrations.

Holiday perfection is pervasive, starting with general malaise. We feel it coming as soon as retail merchants display their Christmas decorations in October. Suddenly, our mystique-radar springs into action, telling us—especially women—that it is up to us to create the perfect holiday for our loved ones.

We choose the perfect gift for each person, wrap it with glittering paper, and add a perfectly formed bow. We place it under the perfectly decorated, perfectly shaped tree in our perfectly adorned (and scented) home that rivals any house in the *Better Homes and Gardens* Christmas edition. Oh, and we mustn't forget to select the perfect Pandora station to pipe beautiful Christmas music throughout our perfectly decorated rooms.

Our children must each have a new, festive outfit in which to visit Santa, so we can take that perfect holiday photograph. We must prepare and execute a perfect dinner, using the good china that must be washed by hand because of the platinum trim we thought was "just perfect" when we registered for our wedding pattern. Fortunately, the table and the mantle are still decorated from that perfect Christmas party we hosted for our colleagues two days after Thanksgiving.

We must not forget to bake perfect Christmas cookies to share with friends and neighbors, who, of course, are accomplishing all of these tasks more perfectly than we are, while working full-time, raising children, taking care of pets, keeping a spotless house, volunteering, and taking extra Yoga and Pilates classes to counteract the extra calories from their perfect holiday feasts.

Is it any wonder we wear out our imperfect selves before December 25th and collapse into a coma on December 26th? I blame the retail industry for fueling this vile contagion that strikes many of us every winter, usually starting the day after Halloween.

So, what can we do to inoculate ourselves against

holiday perfection? I have three words of advice for all of us, myself included, who fall victim to this insidious ailment year after year: get. over. it! The mystique is not real. All those magazine celebrities who promise to help you create the perfect holiday meal/aura/mantle/wreath/outfit/hairdo? They have a staff! They are not one person trying to be all things to all people. Furthermore, they don't care about you and your exhaustion. They care about selling you a magazine, a magical image, and a lot of stuff.

When did we forget that Jesus, the King of Kings, was born in a plain old stable (a cave, actually), surrounded by farm animals? There were no decorations, no sparkling trees, no cookies baking in the oven. And the magis' gifts were for *him*, not for each other. It is *his* birthday we celebrate, not ours. As royalty, Jesus could have chosen a life of ease and comfort. Instead he chose to live in simplicity.

Only Christ's incarnation can fill the emptiness of our imperfect hearts and heal the disease of *holiday perfection*. We need not over-achieve to receive his salvation. It is a free gift to all who accept it.

Prayer: Slow us down, Lord. Remind us that our desire for the perfect holiday celebration is not from you. Forgive our pride that insists everything must be perfect, and that we must do it all ourselves.

Meditation: What holiday preparation can I simplify or eliminate next year so that I have time for what's really important, celebrating Jesus' birthday by spending time with him?

Week Four: Christmas Carol Snob

Some people, even loving members of my own family, have called me a Christmas carol snob, and I cannot deny the accusation. I can't help myself. When I enter a store, expecting to be filled with the Christmas spirit but, instead, I'm greeted with, "Grandma Got Run Over by a Reindeer" piping loudly throughout the store, I start to feel nauseous.

Last week, I finally got around to doing some Christmas shopping. Okay, maybe I've been called a procrastinator on occasion, too. As I entered the first store, my ears were accosted by strains of the ever-reverent "Santa Baby" followed by another sacred classic, "Rockin' Around the Christmas Tree." I could scarcely keep the bile from rising in my throat. I'm not above a sentimental rendition of "White Christmas" or "I'll Be Home for Christmas," but when you interrupt my holy Advent season with tripe like "Run Rudolph Run" and "Gee Whiz it's Christmas," I get offended.

Don't get me wrong. I adore Christmas music and anticipate it eagerly all year long. Handel's *Messiah* still gives me chills. Britten's *A Ceremony of Carols*, Bach's *Christmas Oratorio*, and Respighi's *Laud to the Nativity* are a few of the exquisite musical settings that capture the true spirit of Christmas for me.

There are arrangements of traditional carols that, when performed by groups like The King's Singers, Chanticleer, The Mormon Tabernacle Choir or the Choir of King's College, Cambridge, leave me awestruck. "Mary Did You Know?" makes me weep whenever I hear it sung well.

Since retiring, I've participated in a program through my church that ministers to shut-ins. Until the pandemic necessitated social distancing, I would visit two elderly women at a local senior living facility. Being with them was a blessing beyond words, and I looked forward to our precious moments together.

One ninety-six-year-old woman was confined to her bed day and night. Although her mind was sharp, macular degeneration caused blindness, and her hearing was greatly impaired. She spent most of her time sleeping or listening to audio books. She often told me she felt useless and wished the Lord would take her home.

Last year, two weeks before Christmas, my elderly friend asked if I'd help her sing Christmas carols. I pulled out my phone to Google the words in case some of them had slipped my memory. She requested song after song: "O, Little Town of Bethlehem," "Silent Night," "Joy to the World," and my favorite, "What Child is This." Despite the oxygen tube in her nose and a thin, croaky voice, she joined in with gusto, loud, strong and in no way pleasing to the ear. If she forgot a strain, she asked me to repeat it, helping her commit it to memory. "Let's do this again next week," she said. "I just love those carols, and I want to remember every word."

We prayed together, and I left her room with tears flooding my cheeks. Though I was hoarse and exhausted from the effort, my heart and eyes overflowed with Christmas joy. This self-professed

Christmas carol snob had been blessed by the rawest, ugliest, most atonal rendition of carols ever—"singing" that came from the heart and reached God's waiting ears. Surely the Lord Jesus was in that room!

Prayer: Holy Lord, we thank you for loving us so completely that you sent your Son, Jesus, to fulfill the Old Testament prophecies and bring A New Commandment, one that encompassed the other Ten Commandments, but took them a step further: "You shall love the Lord your God with all your heart, mind and soul and your neighbor as yourself."

Meditation: Where does God want me to serve? Where can I love my neighbor by offering comfort and mercy in the name of Jesus Christ?

Week One: Perfect Love

Week Two: Facing Life's Storms

Week Three: Holiday Perfection

Week Four: Christmas Carol Snob

Looking Back; Striving Forward

Now I understand why God called me to write this book. It was God's plan for my personal revelation and renewal. The task with which God commissioned me—during the year of a worldwide pandemic, escalating racial unrest, and political chaos in the United States—has caused a paradigm shift in my faith.

I have known God my whole life. At an early age, I accepted Jesus as my Savior. I was baptized as an infant and confirmed into the church at age twelve. I have worked in churches, directing choirs, for forty-five years. I have experienced God's healing and God's miracles throughout my life. But during this period of social distancing, while physically isolated from friends and family members, I have been blessed to experience an even closer, more conscious relationship with Jesus Christ. The scripture research that this project required has provided new and deeper insights and precipitated an even more conscious connection with the Holy Spirit within me, for which I am abundantly grateful.

If, through these pages, a reader should find comfort or peace or renewed faith, I would consider it a remarkable blessing. This is my prayer for you: May you find strength for living in an ever-changing, ever-challenging world; may your spiritual blessings abound; and may you look forward with hope to a new year in renewed relationship with our Triune God—Father, Son and Holy Spirit. Amen.

About the Author

Cindy L. Freeman began writing after retiring from a forty-five-year career in music education and music ministry. A published author of novels, blogs, and award-winning essays, she also edits for High Tide Publications. In her novels, she enjoys tackling sensitive subjects where her protagonists are strong women who find the courage to overcome challenging circumstances. Cindy lives in James City County, Virginia with her husband, Carl. They have 2 amazing children, 5 favorite grandchildren, and numerous granddogs.

Cindy L. Freeman's novels, *Unrevealed*, *The Dark Room* and *I Want to Go Home* are available from Amazon or High Tide Publications.

To learn more, visit her:
Website
http://www.cindylfreeman.com,
Facebook
https://www.facebook.com/cindy.l.freeman.9,
or
Blog site:
www.cindylfreeman.blogspot.com

Dedication

I dedicate this book to my loving husband, Carl and my favorite children Tracey Freeman Tunstall and Brian Freeman.

Made in the USA
Middletown, DE
06 March 2021

34609544R00040